Southampton forte
L

Devonsh... Redoute

A Scale of 8 Miles
| 1 | 2 | 3 | 4 | 5 | 6 | 7 | 8 |

...by these Figurs.
5. Pembrok — 7. Smith
6. Cauendish — 8. Hambleton
...er Hs.

B C P D E F G
H
B
I
K
L
Q N M

Vincere est Viuere
32 Deg: 25 M.

The 3 Bridges
A.B.C.

P

Riches Mount

Pagets forte
H

Penistons Redoute
G

Charles forte
N

Printed by Iames Reeve

Conyers Dill & Pearman:
A History

Conyers Dill & Pearman:
A History

Roger Crombie

The Walsingham Press

THE WALSINGHAM PRESS
P.O. Box 324, St. George's GE BX, Bermuda

ISBN 962-7762-35-0

Designed by Matcham & Matcham, Pembroke, Bermuda
Printed in The United States of America

for Charles T.M. Collis

Contents

List of Plates

x.   His Excellency Governor Lt. Gen. Sir Thomas Astley-Cubitt at the Bridge Hill station of the Bermuda Railway, 31 October 1931. The railway had been opened earlier in the day in Hamilton; dignitaries and officials rode the train to Somerset, where His Excellency opened the line across the bridge to the west. Standing immediately behind him, to his right, is Reginald Conyers, Vice President of the company. To the left in dark suits are General Manager Ronald Stemp and Chief Engineer Harold Kitchen. *From the Photographic Collection, courtesy of the Bermuda Archives*

xi.   Trestles carry the railway line over the Flatts, May 1941. *Courtesy of The Bermudian*

xii.   Sir Reginald Conyers. A portrait painted from this photograph hangs in the reception area of the Clarendon House headquarters of Conyers Dill & Pearman. *Courtesy of the estate of Charles T.M. Collis*

xiii.   Reginald and May Appleby with their grandchildren. *From left:* Josephine Firth, James Pearman *fils*, Richard Pearman, Maj. Reginald Woodifield Appleby, William James Howard Trott III, Christine Trott, May Appleby *née* Gosling, Angela Firth, *circa* 1937. *Courtesy of the estate of Sir James Pearman*

xiv.   Col. Thomas Melville Dill. Colonel Tom Dill, as he was known, was Bermuda's Attorney General for 25 years. Photograph taken by W.G. Parker in London on 28 December, 1934. *Courtesy of the estate of Sir Bayard Dill*

xv.   Nicholas Bayard Dill upon graduating from Trinity College, Cambridge, summer of 1927. *Courtesy of N.B. Dill*

xvi.   James Eugene Pearman, *circa* 1925. Contact sheets delivered to clients by a photographer in this manner enabled them to order their favourites. *Courtesy of the estate of Sir James Pearman*

xvii.   James Eugene Pearman, *second right*, on his marriage to Prudence Appleby, supported by best man Bayard Dill and Clare Watlington, whom Dill would marry within two years, 15 April 1929. *Courtesy of the estate of Sir James Pearman*

xviii.   Photograph taken on the steps of the Royal Bermuda Yacht Club, *circa* 1930. *Left to right, front row:* James Pearman, Henry Butterfield, Kenneth Trimingham, Walter Wadson, Owen Darrell; *second row:* E.G. Gosling, Bayard Dill, Eldon Trimingham; *third row:* Lloyd Jones, Alfred Darrell, A.E. Darrell. Eight of the 11 men pictured would become Commodore of the Club. *Courtesy of the estate of Sir James Pearman*

xix.   The Executive Council of the Governor, His Excellency Lt. Gen. Sir Alexander Hood, in the Senate Building on Front Street in the City of Hamilton, 1955. *From left:* James Pearman, Henry Vesey, W.W. Davidson, Colonial Secretary A.G.T. Chaplin, Governor Hood, David Huxley, Hal Butterfield, Hereward T. Watlington and Assistant Colonial Secretary Edward Smith. The photograph is signed by each. *Courtesy of the estate of Sir James Pearman*

xx.   Governor Maj. Gen. Sir Julian Gascoigne invests the Hon. James E. Pearman, M.C.P. as a Commander of the British Empire at Government House, Pembroke, Bermuda on 7 October 1960. *Courtesy of the estate of Sir James Pearman*

xxxiv. Over the course of a 27-year relationship, management consultant Michael Esmond James Woods, later Partnership Secretary of Conyers Dill & Pearman, stamped his mark on the firm and its development. © *Justin Leighton.*

xxxv. Alan Brown, *left,* head of the Duke of Edinburgh Awards Committee in Bermuda, himself receives an award from His Excellency Governor Viscount Dunrossil. *Courtesy of the estate of Alan Brown*

xxxvi. Riders in the second international Conyers Dill & Pearman Classic, in May 1997, reach the foot of Burnaby Hill in Hamilton. The Classic is a criterium held at the climax of the annual four-day Conyers Dill & Pearman Grand Prix of Cycling.

xxxvii. The support of Conyers Dill & Pearman for cycling in Bermuda has been extended to include the sponsorship of Bermudian cyclist Elliott Hubbard, now with Team Navigators.

xxxviii. Looking west along Front Street, the original Bank of Bermuda Building at Albuoy's Point is seen here in the mid-1950s. The building stood until 1965, when it was razed to make way for its successor. The original building and its replacement were the home of the partnership of Conyers Dill & Pearman for more than 40 years. *Courtesy of The Bank of Bermuda Ltd.*

xxxix. Clarendon House, *right foreground,* stands on the south side of Church Street in the City of Hamilton. The usually busy street is named for the Cathedral seen at the centre of the photograph.

Partners and staff of Conyers Dill & Pearman, 1998:

xl. Nicholas Bayard Dill, J.P. at Fort St. Catherine, St. George's

xli. Richard Shafto Love Pearman at Fort Hamilton, Pembroke

xlii. Charles Forster Alexander Cooper at Fort St. Catherine, St.George's

xliii. *From left:* Graham Brenton Ross Collis, Charles Grant Ross Collis and John Charles Ross Collis at the gate of Fort Hamilton, Pembroke

xliv. Narinder Kumar Hargun, *left,* and Robin Joan Mayor at Fort Scaur, Sandys Parish

xlv. Alec Ross Anderson, *left,* and Nicolas George Trollope at Fort Hamilton, Pembroke

xlvi. *From left:* David William Peter Cooke, Anthony Devon Whaley and Lisa Joanne Marshall in the Keep at the Bermuda Dockyard

xlvii. James Morrison Macdonald, *left,* and Nicholas Paul Johnson at Fort Scaur, Sandys Parish

xlviii. Donald Harrigan Malcolm, *left,* and Michael James McCabe at Fort St. Catherine, St. George's

xlix. *From left:* Stephen De Silva, Roger Younie and John Buckley in the Keep at the Bermuda Dockyard

Gangaramani, Bernadette Chen, Christopher W.H. Bickley, Kemmy Cheng, Rowan Wu; *second row:* Mina Jinn, Jennifer Wan, Lun Ping Yeung, Reena Khua. © *Graham Uden*

lxxi.   Beef Island, British Virgin Islands. *From left:* Roselyn Francis, Malcolm Becker, Enid Gordon, A. Guy Eldridge, Shaunda Scatliffe.

lxxii.   Grand Cayman Island, the Cayman Islands. *From left:* Keisha Powery, Neil Cox, Theresa Pearson

lxxiii. The Royal Exchange, London. John Anthony Ellison, *left,* and Martin S. Lane. © *Justin Leighton*

lxxiv.   *From left:* Beverley Minors, Darlene Tavares, Vicki Johnston, Darlene McGinnis, Che Burgess and Robin Tucker in the Law Library at Clarendon House

lxxv.   *Clockwise, from bottom left:* Denise Whitter, Michele Bisson, Robin Trott, Sylvia Simpson, Marlene Flynn-Simons, Deidre Shakir and Eddrena Zuill at the fourth floor reception area of Clarendon House

lxxvi.   *From left:* Kirsty Johnson, Randell Woolridge, Karen O'Connor, Paul Lambert, Shella Udoh, Debra Lindsey and Sharmaine Butterfield on the third floor of Clarendon House, overlooking the atrium

All photography © Hamish Shorto/Catalyst, except as noted.

Endpapers:

The Summer Ils. by Capt. John Smith, 1624. *From the collection of Conyers Dill & Pearman*

Captain Smith may have obtained this illustration of Bermuda and some of its forts and bridges from Governor Nathaniel Butler.

An earlier Governor, Richard Moore, began to build forts in Bermuda immediately after his arrival in 1612. The Spanish were seen off with shots from King's Castle as early as 1614. Eleven of the forts of Bermuda were completed before 1622 and forts continued to be built in Bermuda until the early 1940s, when the last, the United States Army Base at St. David's, was christened Fort Bell.

King's Castle has become, with time, the oldest standing English masonry fort in the Western hemisphere. It was but one of a total of 90 forts constructed in Bermuda, many of which have survived in varying conditions.

Coin:

1928 George V shilling, *reverse*

The image is taken, with permission, from a coin found among the effects of Sir James Pearman. The shilling was believed to have played a critical role in the development of Dill & Pearman, one of two firms which merged in 1928 to form Conyers Dill & Pearman.

Foreword

Some years ago, it was suggested by Michael Woods that a history of the firm of Conyers Dill & Pearman should be written. After a number of attempts by various authors, Roger Crombie has successfully put pen to paper and produced this formidable work. It cannot have been an easy task, as this is not only a history of the partnership but also a history of Bermuda's astonishing growth from the 1920s to the 1990s.

The purpose of the work was to capture the development of the firm and modern Bermuda while there were those around who could remember the early days. For instance, James and Dick Pearman and I are probably the only people associated with the firm today who remember all of the partners, including Sir Reginald Conyers. I clearly remember him and his direct manner of speaking. I also remember the four-room back office in the Bermuda Fire & Marine Building, now The Bank of Bermuda Building, with its small swinging gate leading to the inner sanctum.

The author has cleverly sought to include a time capsule of Bermuda and the firm's history with each chapter. This gives a clear picture of the scene, both locally and internationally, at the time when those who would become principals first joined the firm.

As one reads the pages of the book it is clear that, from a very slow start in the 1920s and 1930s, Bermuda's momentum has picked up to a pace today which is almost frenetic.

One cannot help but wonder where it will all end. Can we maintain the charm and personal touch for which the Islands are noted and at the same time provide the instantaneous service which is so much in demand today? Would all of our former partners have understood this great requirement for haste? They accomplished a great deal without it and maintained a quality of life second to none.

It is very sad for me that Charles Collis is not the author of this foreword, as he was so intensely proud of the firm and everyone associated with it. He would have loved to see this book brought to publication.

I do hope that you enjoy it as much as I have.

Nicholas B. Dill
20 June 1998

Preface

In December 1995, the partners of Conyers Dill & Pearman agreed to let me profile the firm for a business magazine published with Bermuda's daily newspaper. The article, entitled *The Rainmakers* at the suggestion of Charles Collis, was published in April 1996.

Later that year, Conyers Dill & Pearman commissioned a project which had defeated previous efforts: the preparation of a history of the practice. My friend and colleague Hamish Shorto agreed to supervise the photographic content.

The nature of a publication on a professional practice precludes the disclosure of the identity of clients. Nevertheless, a few of the firm's clients are named within; in every detail, such references have been taken from material in the public realm.

What follows is not the history of Bermuda in the 20th century, which has yet to be written, and might best, in the popular prejudice, be the work of a Bermudian author. Nor should it be considered the all-embracing or definitive history of the development of Bermuda's international business industry, which has also yet to be published.

It is, rather, a selective attempt to trace the metamorphosis of what has been described as a "small country practice" into a disproportionately large legal enterprise, in the context of Bermuda's international financial services industry; and to make of it the engaging and interesting story it is.

It would have been impossible to explore every detail of the firm's seven decades of existence, the life's work of hundreds of people. I have chosen to portray, in a human light, the affairs of the principals and the often far-reaching effects of their activities on others. This approach of necessity sheds little light on the labours of some whose efforts have contributed significantly to the firm's success.

I must record my gratitude to the partners and staff of Conyers Dill & Pearman for their forbearance as I wrestled with the text and with the details of their lives. To John Buckley, whose faith in me was a continuing inspiration, a special vote of thanks.

History is never complete without coincidences. My favourite is that James Adam Conyers, Sir Reginald's father, with whom the story starts, was born 100 years to the day before I was.

Roger Crombie
Smith's Parish, Bermuda

1 June 1998

Conyers Dill & Pearman:
A History

CHAPTER ONE

Conyers

The Conyers family arrived in Bermuda not long after the original colonists and became farmers on Tucker's and Morgan's Islands between 1620 and 1660. By the middle of the 19th century, the family was well-established as merchant farmers and commission agents.

James Adams Conyers joined the business in 1865, just a few weeks after Abraham Lincoln was assassinated. Eight years later, Conyers was made a partner, by which time the company had been renamed J.T. Darrell & Co., after Senior Partner Josiah T. Darrell. When Darrell died in 1884, Conyers continued as sole owner, later adding a shipping company, James A. Conyers & Co., to his fold.

For many years, Conyers was the largest dealer in Bermuda produce in the Colony. He became Manager of both the Bermuda Coal Company Ltd. and the Bermuda Lumber Company Ltd. and was a vice-president of the Bank of N.T. Butterfield & Son Ltd. One of the largest shareholders in the Bermuda Fire & Marine Insurance Company Ltd., he was also a director of the Bermuda Electric Light, Power and Traction Company Ltd. He was Consul for Sweden, Germany and Spain, and passenger agent for all the great transatlantic lines.

Conyers concentrated on his business and family to the exclusion of almost everything else, fending off all attempts to co-opt him into the world of politics. In 1892, the King of Sweden knighted him in recognition of his services to the Swedish man-of-war *Saga*. On a visit to Bermuda, the crew of the vessel, including the ship's surgeon, had fallen victim to influenza, in those days a killer. Conyers' performance "went far beyond that which his official position as Consul demanded; and the results which accrued were evidence of what his good judgement and persistent perseverance produced."

He married Emma Marie Trott, a woman of German extraction who had been adopted by the family of Duncan Trott. James and Emma Conyers had 13 children, of whom seven survived into adulthood. The third oldest of the seven survivors, James Reginald Conyers, was born in Bermuda on 3 September 1879.

Reginald attended Saltus Grammar School and decided at an early age that he wanted to pursue a career in Law. He studied in London and was called to the Bar at the Inner Temple in 1902, at the age of 23. On his return to Bermuda, he was called to the local Bar—for which prior admission to another Bar was adequate qualification—on 8 July 1903. He began at once to practise law under the name of J.R. Conyers & Co.

It is probable that he set up his office in the very same room in which, some 26 years later, he would admit two younger men into partnership. The law office of J.R. Conyers & Co. was in what became the pharmacy of the Conyers Building, today part of the H.A. & E. Smith Building used by Trimingham Brothers.

The life of a lawyer in the Colony of Bermuda at the turn of the century was not overly demanding of a man's time. A fellow might walk to his Chambers in the morning, pop into the Supreme Court for an hour and then head down to the Yacht Club for lunch. If he looked in at the office near the end of the day, it would be to collect the post, sign a few letters or draw ten shillings from Petty Cash to cover an unexpected evening out. Bermuda was a relaxed place, protected by its remoteness.

Conyers put up his shingle in the year that the Wright brothers took to the air for the first time, although commercial flight was decades away. If Bermuda at that time was a more parochial and insulated place than it is today, the issues which dominated the newspaper headlines were not that far removed from current concerns. In its issue of 7 July 1903, *The Royal Gazette, Bermuda Commercial and General Advertiser and Recorder*, in a style as verbose as its name, reported on Legislative Council debates on the rights of foreign wives of Bermudians, changes at the Public Library and improvements to Middle Road in Devonshire.

Conyers' practice would have been founded on the legal interests and responsibilities of his family's business empire. In time, however, he began to develop a clientele on whose behalf he would appear in the courts. The extent to which he had the time and the will to play his part in matters beyond his practice became evident less than a year after J.R. Conyers & Co. was established. In 1904, barely 25 years of age, Conyers was elected in Pembroke Parish to serve in the House of Assembly. Also elected to the House for the first time that year was his close friend and associate, Thomas Dill.

Both were young men—Dill was three years older than Conyers— but the two new Members of the House at its 1904 opening were from the oldest and most respected of Bermudian families. Their lives, and the grand scale of their achievements, would intertwine as the years unfolded.

Conyers was short, with an abrupt nature. Able and straightfor- ward, he was a self-possessed man of the world. He sailed, played a competent round of golf and enjoyed a game of billiards or a hand of poker. He and his younger brother Gerald shared an appetite for cricket, and made names for themselves at the game. Reginald was the batsman and Gerald the bowler. They played for the Serpentine Cricket Club with other famous cricketers of the day, such as the Adderley brothers, A.W. West and Sir Henry Tucker's father, Harry.

The Conyers brothers played for Bermuda against a number of international teams, including Australia, when they visited the Island. Reginald captained a Bermuda team which played several international matches abroad, notably against the Philadelphia Cricket Club, now known as the Merion Cricket Club. That MCC, still active today, hosted a visit from the original, the Marylebone Cricket Club, in the mid-1980s. The Conyers brothers' overseas exploits—the team toured for a total of two or three months over a two-year period at around the time the First World War was starting—were recounted in some detail in a book by Sir Henry Sayen.

Something of Conyers' character can be surmised from an outrageous tale faithfully reported by the Bermuda media of the day. A Bermuda cricket team had travelled to the West Indies for a match against Jamaica. The story has it that Conyers and a number of his fellow players were to be found in a bar at four in the morning on the day of the match. One of the players, well-fortified, made a bet that Conyers would outscore the entire Jamaican team. Just before the match got underway, Conyers reportedly drank three 'black velvets', a mixture of champagne and stout ale. He then strode out to the wicket and started to knock the ball about. By the end of the day, his optimistic team-mate had won the bet by a wide margin. For much of his adult life, Conyers sported a bent finger, believed to have been broken playing cricket and badly set.

Early in 1908, Conyers' father, James, died. One of his last business decisions had been to admit to partnership in the family firm his second surviving son, William Middleton Conyers, together with another young Bermudian, H.W. Watlington. The firm was renamed Watlington and

Conyers. Within a year, James was dead, at 59. "Practically the whole official and mercantile body of the colony were present at his funeral," noted the *Gazette*.

His son Reginald moved ahead in life. Through the First World War and into the 1920s, Conyers' practice continued much as it had since its founding. In a manner almost incomprehensible in the hard-pressed modern world, the learned professions were vocations, rather than, as now, gainful employment. The systems of voluntary social service which mark Bermuda now were even more keenly pronounced when the population was smaller, and therefore the number of financially comfortable individuals was more limited. A man of the right background with drive and commitment might write his name large on the affairs of a small community such as Bermuda in those times. Conyers' practice was sufficient to enable him to keep his household ticking over and left him free to attend to the grander matters in which he chose to play a hand.

The enhancement of Bermuda's tourism industry in the 1920s was fuelled principally by the Furness Withy shipping line, which saw the advantages of carrying passengers to Bermuda from the Eastern Seaboard of the United States, especially the New York City area, who, in wintertime, were hungry for a glimpse of the sun. Furness Withy also recognised the need to provide adequate accommodation in Bermuda for its discerning passengers and proposed developing Bermuda's tourism potential on a more suitable basis.

Accommodation was relatively easy to provide. Transport presented a more difficult problem. The Furness Withy passengers, mostly wealthy Americans, were becoming used to the convenience offered by that new phenomenon, the motor car. They would want to move about the Island on their vacations, which rendered the need for a public transportation policy in Bermuda a matter of urgency.

The narrow, winding dirt roads, made of crushed coral and fringed with oleander, had been adequate for Bermudians for centuries, even if social activity had effectively been limited to the nearby parishes. The roads became sticky with reddish clay when it rained, but the porous soil ensured that they dried quickly. On special occasions, families rode in carriages, but most people simply walked. "Bermuda," Mark Twain wrote, displaying his complete understanding of the ways of the Island, "is a little place of great distances."

A vigorous debate was opened as to the relative merits of public buses, extended ferry services and even a railway. The Motor Car Act of 1908 had banned all but a handful of official vehicles from operation in Bermuda, a policy which maintained the Island's physical integrity and deferred for decades the advent of today's traffic-laden asphalt roads.

With horses, carts and carriages widely used in Hamilton and the countryside, it was argued that a fleet of buses would not prove practical. Ferries, however efficient in delivering passengers and their luggage to waterside landing points, would not solve the problem of their onward transportation on land. Those who believed that Bermuda needed a comprehensive change in its transportation system began to see a railway as the only viable alternative. For others, the very idea of a railway system for so small a group of then mostly unconnected islands was preposterous.

The notion of a railway in Bermuda had been around for 30 years. A number of proposals had been put forward, none gathering wholehearted support. A Bermuda Trolley Company had proposed to supply an electrified tramway grid, and a similar system had been proposed by the Bermuda Electric Light, Power & Traction Company Ltd.

At about the time Conyers was running up his score on a cricket field in Jamaica, a British surveyor and engineer, William T. Foxlee, was completing an analysis the Bermuda Government had commissioned, which led to his issuing *A Report On A Bermuda Light Railway*. Taking account of the Motor Car Act, Foxlee came down in favour of a railway and proposed a narrow gauge system driven by steam tank engines, a choice of locomotive power which sparked a further, lengthy debate.

By 1924, the need for a decision of some kind had become urgent. On 4 August, the Bermuda Railway Company Act 1924 became law. The Act granted the Bermuda Railway Company Ltd. approval to acquire by compulsory order the land needed for the undertaking, as well as exclusive rights of operation. It was the first of a series of Bermuda Railway Company Acts passed into law over the following two decades.

The coming of the railway was eagerly anticipated by its backers and a vociferous section of the general public. The Vice President of the Company, and its legal representative, was the man whose hard work and legal expertise had contributed to making the coming of the railway a possibility, Reginald Conyers.

CHAPTER TWO

Dill & Pearman

James Eugene Pearman was born on 24 November 1904, a little more than a year before Nicholas Bayard Dill. Their age difference did not stop the two becoming fast friends at Saltus Grammar School. They took part in the school's annual Sports Days, which were regularly attended by Old Boy Reginald Conyers. By the time Dill and Pearman were teenagers, Conyers was a Parliamentarian in his cricketing prime.

Pearman spent his final school year at Bromsgrove School in Worcestershire, England. In 1923, he went up to Merton College, Oxford, where he read Law. Dill, likewise, had travelled to England to complete his education at Trinity Hall, Cambridge. He was called to the Bar at the Middle Temple in January 1927 and returned to Bermuda to be called there in March. Pearman was also called at the Middle Temple later in the year and returned to Bermuda in the autumn of 1927.

Having known each other for most of their lives, it must have seemed a logical step for two young lawyers to extend their friendship into a professional arrangement. A decision was made in England and by the end of 1927, both young men had settled back into their island home and were enjoying a busy social scene in the company of the other sons and daughters of Bermudian society.

For both, that scene revolved around the Royal Bermuda Yacht Club. By day it involved outdoor activities, among them yachting, cycling and tennis. Dill had played tennis extensively at Cambridge and Pearman also played a solid game. By night, there were parties, dances and trips to the movies. Pearman pined for his absent sweetheart, Prudence Appleby, while Dill was rarely seen without an eligible companion on his arm.

Both men were scions of long-established Bermuda families. Pearman's Bermudian ancestry can be traced back to 1643. By the end of the 19th century, the Pearman family had established a thriving dry goods business at Shelly Bay. In 1898, Pearman's grandfather, Thomas Joseph Pearman, successfully moved the store to the growing city of Hamilton.

Like most well-placed Bermudians, Thomas Pearman, born in 1848, had a wide range of interests. He was a director of the Bermuda Fire and Marine Insurance Company Ltd., the Bermuda Telephone Company Ltd. and the Bermuda Steam Laundry Company Ltd. He served one term in the House of Assembly, but is best remembered as one of a handful of individuals who, in 1889, founded The Bank of Bermuda. He served as a director from the company's inception. For nine years, he was Vice President and Deputy Chairman of the Board. In 1913, he was appointed President and Chairman of the Board, posts he held until his death three years later.

His son, Eugene Charles Pearman, James Pearman's father, also died holding high office at the bank. Known as a pioneer in the field of bakery, Eugene held a number of local directorships. In 1940, he was appointed to the twin positions his father had held in the bank. On his death in 1946, both The Bank of Bermuda and the Bank of N.T. Butterfield closed at 12.30 p.m. as a mark of respect. The connection between the

Pearman family and The Bank of Bermuda, dating back more than a hundred years, extends to this day.

Dill had equally illustrious forebears, whose arrival in Bermuda Hereward Watlington dates *circa* 1630 in his *Family Narrative*. It has been stated that they were Irish. The Dills became in time substantial landowners, virtually synonymous with Devonshire Parish. Dill's grandfather, Thomas Newbold Dill, followed the family tradition of public service as a Member of the House of Assembly and later of the Executive Council. He was Assistant Justice of the Court of Assize and for five years Mayor of the City of Hamilton.

Thomas Newbold Dill and his wife, Mary Lea, had one child, Thomas Melville Dill. He too pursued the Law and in time became one of Bermuda's most distinguished figures. Attorney General for close to a quarter of a century, Thomas Dill was a man who could lay claim, over a long legal career, to having lost only one case. History remembers him as Colonel Tom Dill, lionised in Lloyd Mayer's biography of the same name as an energetic and untiring lawyer and soldier. Colonel Tom and his wife, Ruth Rapalje Neilson, had six children, of whom the third, Nicholas Bayard Dill, named for his maternal grandfather, was born on 28 December 1905. A distant relative, Nicholas Bayard, had been Mayor of New York in 1685.

On his return to Bermuda, Bayard Dill—he rarely used his given name of Nicholas—took employment in the law office of A.C. Hollis Hallett. Shortly thereafter, Pearman returned to the Island and he and Dill fulfilled the promise they had made to each other in England by forming, in the latter's words, "the famous firm of Dill & Pearman". Having agreed upon a partnership in law, the next matter on the agenda was the name of the firm. Which would it be: Pearman & Dill, or Dill & Pearman? Among gentlemen in their early 20s, there was only one equitable way to decide so important a matter—a coin toss.

"On our return to the Island, and after flipping a coin, we came out with the brand new firm of Dill & Pearman," wrote Dill more than 60 years later. A family member recalls that the coin toss took place at Saltus. Among his photograph collection, Sir James Pearman kept just a handful of mementoes. One, wrapped in cotton wool, was an English George V shilling dated 1928, a coin the size of a modern Bermuda 25-cent piece.

The firm of Dill & Pearman was launched in January 1928 in an office on the second floor of the Miles Building on Front Street, better known these days as the home of the dress shop, Calypso. The two men shared an office and a typewriter, although little typing was called for, since business was not initially plentiful. Shortly thereafter, Dill & Pearman took a three-year lease on offices in Reid Hall, on the corner of Reid Street and Queen Street. Today, the building's ground floor houses clothiers Aston & Gunn.

The moment the firm began to succeed, Pearman planned to ask Major the Honourable Reginald Woodifield Appleby for permission to marry his third oldest daughter, Prudence, then at college in the United States. Pearman chronicled parts of the story of Dill & Pearman in correspondence with Prudence Appleby, excerpted here for the first time.

In an undated letter postmarked 11 May 1928, Pearman wrote: "Bay and I are getting a little work in the office now and I hope by next month that we shall be ahead of the game and shall be able perhaps to cut a melon. That will be a great feeling, to know that we are out of debt." The phrase 'cutting a melon' is a North American colloquialism for declaring an abnormally high dividend to shareholders. In the context of the history of Dill & Pearman to that date, a dividend of any sort would have been abnormally high.

On 25 May, Pearman started his letter on an upbeat note. "What do you think?" he wrote. "We've got some money coming into the office now and next month, maybe, we'll have some that will belong to us instead of to somebody to whom we owe a bill." The frequency of Pearman's letters —two or three missives of ten pages or more every week over a period of six months—shows how much time he must have spent at the office writing letters and, by extension, how little legal work was coming in.

The close quarters at the firm's office affected Pearman when one of Prudence's letters brought especially reassuring news. "I nearly blew all the papers off the desk with my sigh of relief," he wrote in early June. "I caught Bay looking at me when I was partly through the second page and I expect my face must have been a picture." On 11 June 1928, Pearman closed with an upbeat and, as it turned out, accurate prophecy. By the end of the year, he forecast, when Prudence was to return to Bermuda, the firm would be counted a success and the couple would be able to plan their future together.

The extent to which the proposed creation of a railway was on peoples' minds is evidenced by a letter Pearman mailed near the end of June 1928, on the day before the railway's putative sponsors had to post bonds to enable the project to commence. Having outlined the arguments for and against the railway, Pearman expressed his preference for the idea of motor buses. His interest in transport was lifelong and carried him ultimately to a Cabinet position with responsibility for Marine and Aviation Services.

By the middle of July 1928, the volume of business at Dill & Pearman had reached a level which made it necessary to add staff. A stenographer was taken on. In an ebullient and light-hearted mood, Pearman wrote: "It's great to sit off and dictate letters and not feel that you've got to go and pound the typewriter for all the rot you have to write. And you do have to write it, just reams and reams of it." His confidence growing with the practice, he continued: "I think we're beginning to get known around town a bit. There's going to be a lot of work over this railway and perhaps we can get some of it; anyhow I hope so."

A week later the optimism was intact: "We worked so hard last week that we worked ourselves out of a job. That's us, you know, rapid and reliable, speed and efficiency. We've got a seal for fixing our documents now." The letter is sealed with red wax which bears the D&P imprint, in flowery type. Pearman continued: "I understand through very unreliable sources that Bay and I are going to get some of the railway work to do. By George, I hope so. Of course I haven't any idea that it will (come to us), I mean the railway work, but if it should we couldn't turn it down, could we?"

Pearman could have had no inkling at the time of the importance the railway was to play in his life. It was the spark which ignited all that was to follow. The project was touch and go throughout the autumn of 1928 and Dill & Pearman's was by no means the only fate which rested on the outcome. A few days later, again referring to the possibility of work being generated by the railway, Pearman made another forecast. "We heard a rumour around town, I told you, didn't I, that we would get some of the railway work to do? Don't say anything to anyone about it. We feel that should that happen, how we turn the work out might have quite a lot to do with our reputation and future work," he wrote.

In August, Pearman decided to take a short trip to the United States, leaving Dill behind to remain in touch with the railway affair through his father. Pearman expected the work to materialise at any moment, but late that month, out of the blue, matters took a bad turn: "Bay and I have had a most unfortunate time this week," Pearman wrote. "Practically everything has gone wrong. We find we have made two mistakes that may cost us some money and just as we were about to cut our first melon. It's very annoying, but I now see that even the best of us make mistakes." He did not explain what had gone wrong.

The correspondence became cursory thereafter, as Prudence prepared to return to Bermuda and Pearman found his time taken up with the growing demands of his practice. On 28 October 1928, Prudence Appleby fulfilled the first half of Pearman's prophecy on her return to Bermuda. Within three months, the firm of Dill & Pearman was no more, for its principals had joined what would become in time an altogether more famous firm.

CHAPTER THREE

Rattle & Shake

Construction finally began on Bermuda's railway in 1926, with a view to opening the line late in 1928. The work began slowly. Although the Bermuda Railway Company had the right to acquire whatever land it needed, some landowners were not happy with the prices they were offered. As a result, much of the railway would be built on trestles and bridges at the foreshore; the remains of some of this work are still visible today.

The snail's pace at which the land was acquired enabled Conyers to carry out the early run of conveyancing by himself, but it quickly became a burden, taking up time for which he had other uses.

On 19 December 1927, the fourth Bermuda Railway Act extended the period necessary for construction and deferred the opening date until June 1929. In return for this leeway, the railway's backers were to deposit £20,000 in London within six months of the passage of the Act. The necessary bonds were indeed posted late in June 1928, an action which can be seen as the conclusion of the first act in Bermuda's extended railway drama. Following a protracted debate and the emotion which it had stirred, Bermuda was poised to enter the Age of Steam.

The passage of the Act did not create much of a stir. Public attention had moved on to address the potential for change which tourism might visit on the Island. But the green light for the construction of the railway changed forever the face of Bermuda and directly gave rise to the formation of the law firm of Conyers Dill & Pearman. The multi-jurisdictional legal practice the firm has become today can trace its history back to that day in June 1928 when the latest round of railway financing was put in place.

A prospectus issued by the company sought £505,000 in ordinary shares and debenture stock. To attract that amount of capital would have required the promise of a suitable return, say £25,000 a year. It is a measure of the optimism engendered by the idea of a railway in Bermuda in 1928 that the financing was found, although few of the backers were Bermudian. Just two years later, when the financial atmosphere in Bermuda and the world had changed, the Acting Governor of Bermuda advised the Colonial Office in London that "even in favourable conditions, it will be most unlikely that the railway could yield a return on anything like the whole capital now sunk into it."

The plan called for the Bermuda Railway Company to acquire all the land necessary to run the railway from one end of the islands to the other. Hundreds of documents of conveyance would be required. Each would have to be typed individually. A network of more than 40 stations was envisaged, from St. George's Terminus at the east end of the line to Somerset Terminus at the western end. An extension to Dockyard was proposed but never completed. The longest distance between stations was to be 1,470 yards, with most stations and halts separated by distances of no more than 500 yards. In the winter of 1928, Conyers would have faced the imminent responsibility for conveying small parcels of land from any number of owners to his client, the Bermuda Railway Company Ltd.

At the age of 49, he would not have relished the prospect of devoting the balance of his career to conveyancing, which is to law as court reporting is to journalism: hard work through which one gradually learns the ways and meaning of the profession. Conyers' office equipment would have comprised little more than pen and ink and a typewriter. Word processors, scanners and photocopiers would have been the stuff of science fiction in 1928. The railway conveyancing, work measurable in man-years, would involve a large element of copying, by hand, the reams and reams of documents about which Pearman once complained to his sweetheart.

Conyers would not have exercised his mind for long on the problem. He needed help. A quick look at the local legal fraternity would have turned up his friend Tom Dill's son, Bayard, and his partner, Jim Pearman, who were spending much of their time staring out of the office window at their friends courting young women by the entrance to the library.

If Colonel Dill himself did not propose it, Conyers would almost certainly have run the idea by his stalwart friend and colleague, who would have seen the possibilities in the twinkling of an eye. Bayard Dill recalled what followed in a short volume of memoirs, *Reminiscences of an Islander:* "Reggie Conyers, nearer my father's vintage, sent for us and said in his candid Bermuda accent: 'You byes ain't got no business, I'm got too much—come and join me.' " Dill at once raised as a potential problem the fact that he and Pearman had only just signed a three-year lease on their office, but Conyers brushed aside the objection, saying simply: "Get rid of it."

Like many Bermudians, Conyers spoke with two entirely different inflections. The Bermudian accent to which Dill referred has been the subject of several light-hearted dictionaries. Conyers switched happily into more formal English when the moment called for it; on at least one occasion, a relative, listening to broadcasts from the House of Assembly, did not recognise his voice.

The image of the meeting in the autumn of 1928 between Conyers and his protégés is not difficult to conjure. In a small office at the rear of a pharmacy on Front Street sat Conyers, a leading light at the Yacht Club and an increasingly influential member of Parliament. On his desk would have been piled a giant mound of papers; it was always his proud boast that he could find anything in the chaos if he put his mind to it. He had developed with the years a certain gravitas born of supreme self-confidence, which gave him an imposing presence. His business interests were spread throughout the Colony and now Fate, in the shape of one of his clients, had placed him in a position to offer the two young men before him a truly golden opportunity.

Although those two fresh-faced lawyers came from families whose Bermudian origins went back for centuries, neither had much more than a toehold, as yet, in the business life of Bermuda. Dill stuttered, an affliction he would not cure until years later; Pearman was at this stage equally shy and untested.

Conyers, always direct, would have come straight to the point. The evidence suggests that the idea had already been discussed, if not directly, through an intermediary. Each man in the room would have had an idea of what Conyers was about to propose, but the words must still have rung in both young men's ears. The invitation, when it came, would prove the making of Dill and Pearman, who were to spend the balance of their lives in the service of the law firm Conyers now proposed. Pearman, of course, also had a more immediate, extra-legal interest: he could now make wedding plans.

Although no one could have foreseen what the proposed firm would achieve, the stakes as they stood were already high enough for Dill and Pearman. Their practice was not exactly thriving. Partnership with Conyers, a highly respected member of the community, could only mean rapid forward progress for both young men, whatever became of their new partnership.

Little in the way of discussion would have succeeded Conyers' proposal. It was simple and, given the relative status and workload of the elder statesman and the young men before him, eminently fair. Conyers was to have two shares of the firm's profit, and his junior partners one apiece. One doubts that Dill had the temerity to reply to the offer with his trademark phrase, "I'll revolve it around my bean." No, the matter was probably agreed on the spot with a handshake before the three men went their separate ways to make arrangements for the new partnership and, in Pearman's case, a different kind of partnership.

It seems the process of amalgamation took 90 days. Dill took his father's advice and offered Cecil Neave, Secretary of Reid Hall Limited, £100 in cash, if he would tear up the lease. Neave was apparently overwhelmed by the sight of so many banknotes. He urgently telephoned his boss, W.J. Young, and said: "Two young lawyers are here trying to scare the devil out of me!" Since Reid Hall was undergoing extensive renovations at the time, Young promptly accepted the offer.

With their lease rescinded and their few clients suitably advised, Dill and Pearman were free to join Conyers at his office for the formal opening of the law practice of Conyers Dill & Pearman.

CHAPTER FOUR

A Firm Beginning

The partnership of Conyers Dill & Pearman was formally founded on 1 November 1928. It has displayed little sentiment in saving the artefacts of its 70-year history, but the earliest document it has retained paints a vivid picture of the first two years of the firm's existence and, by extension, the 18 years which followed.

Conyers Dill & Pearman's *Professional Account Cash Book Number 1* offers eloquent testimony of a vanished era. "Show me the Cash Book," runs the accountant's boast, "and I will show you the man," or in this case the men and women. In spidery but consistent handwriting, the Cash Book lists on one side the day-to-day legal needs of a cross-section of the Bermuda community. From the other side can be divined the exact details of the financial affairs of a three-man partnership which started its professional life almost exactly a year before the Wall Street Crash, the thunderclap which ushered in the Great Depression.

Dill wrote: "We joined Reggie, the whole firm being then five, namely James Reginald Conyers, Nicholas Bayard Dill, James Eugene

Pearman, Isabelle Lusher (who after married Alfred Darrell) and Adela Churm." Mrs. Churm was Conyers' secretarial assistant. Miss Lusher was probably Dill and Pearman's secretary and Miss Lusher it must have been who maintained *Cash Book Number 1*, since Mrs. Churm took time off in 1929 to have a baby.

The book is burgundy in colour. Covered in the *faux* silk beloved of account book makers, it has fallen victim to termites, their zig-zag trails bringing to mind the child's conundrum about worms eating their way through encyclopædias. The columnar ledger was maintained in blue-black ink, with totals double-underlined in red, in keeping with the best accounting practice of the day. Receipts were entered on the left-hand pages, disbursements on the right. The ledger tracks, in book-keeper's shorthand, deposits to and payments from the firm's account between 1 February 1929 and 31 January 1931 at the West End Branch, now the headquarters, of The Bank of Bermuda at Albuoy's Point.

As much as the Cash Book reveals, it is silent in many respects. The firm has routinely followed the standard Bermudian legal practice of retaining clients' papers for the statutory period of six years after a file is closed, and adds one further year for good measure. Thereafter, documents are destroyed, so we can only wonder at the background and history of the first client to pay a bill to the new firm, which the copperplate handwriting in the Cash Book reveals to have been a fee of £7 in respect of an appearance for the defence by Conyers, in Supreme Court. The balance due of £4 was paid a week later. Neither offence nor verdict can be deduced, but from the 30 or so entries which follow each month, a broader picture emerges.

The initial deposit was succeeded by fees for representation in Supreme Court and, more often, Police Court, consultations on applications for liquor licences, the authentication of documents supporting passport applications, deeds of charge, and the drawing of wills and leases. Occasionally, a small commission appears for the collection by the firm of rent for a client. A significant share of the fee income was earned bi-annually from the Bermuda Railway Company Ltd., whose legal work appears to have run at a fairly constant level during the two years.

After several months, the great majority of entries are listed simply as professional fees, suggesting that Miss Lusher had discovered that no matter how well corporate records may be maintained, hardly anyone, auditors and historians excepted, ever looks at them.

Gross receipts for the first year totalled £8,751 2s. 9d., roughly US$40,000 at then-current exchange rates, and perhaps the equivalent of US$3 million at today's prices, although such comparisons can be notoriously misleading. The figure includes advances from clients, their rental income and recoveries of clients' funds from other sources. Most of the money coming in, therefore, was the property of others.

The balance of fees earned was used to employ six people, including an unnamed office boy, and to manage the day-to-day business of the office. Save for inflation, which was little felt in the Bermudian economy in this period (except during the War years), the firm and its affairs would continue in much the same manner for the next two decades.

The range of clients is much broader than one might have surmised. With few lawyers at work in the Colony, the work was evenly spread among those in practice. Conyers Dill & Pearman provided service to a wide range of clients, including some of the larger non-governmental organisations on the Island and some of its less well-heeled citizens. Many of the client relationships which the three men formed across the spectrum of Bermudian society continue, quietly, to this day. On the local legal front, the firm, now as then, has clients not only on Front Street, but in every quarter of Hamilton and Bermuda. What has changed over the years is the business which the firm derives from overseas.

The majority of fees charged in the fledgling firm's first two years was £3 or less. An occasional client would pay a bill of £50 or £60. Only the Bermuda Railway Company and a couple of others paid larger amounts.

One receipt in September 1929 is worthy of note. A cheque for US$250 was the firm's first international item. It raised £51.1.5. Today it would translate into three times as much Sterling with a paradoxical real value of a tiny fraction of its worth almost 70 years ago.

Within a month of receipt of this first international payment, *The Royal Gazette and Colonist Daily* received reports from New York which it headlined "Panic on Stock Exchange: Losses Run Into Millions". The firm's business continued essentially unaffected by events in the larger world for several months. Although total receipts for the second year were down by more than half, the element which comprised fee income remained consistent.

What is apparent from the receipts side of the Cash Book is the steady way in which the firm first established itself and then went about its business. A law practice does not incur the set-up costs manufacturing companies must expect. Then, too, the new partnership succeeded two existing firms, one of which was doing well. The other, though less active, would have had low overheads, since partners do not take out of a practice money it has not made. The economic activity of the firm's first two years suggests that the merger was a seamless affair.

The credit side of the Cash Book, where expenditure is logged, speaks of the nature of the firm's material requirements and the recompense of its employees and partners. The office boy made six shillings a week in 1929, but his performance must have been satisfactory, because in the next year his salary was raised to seven shillings. The secretarial staff each earned £4 or £5 weekly. The mathematics suggests that in the years since, salaries have evened out somewhat. No deductions were taken out of any of the staff's pay, a situation which continues in Bermuda in only a few cases. Today, a slew of Government deductions and the cost of health

insurance reduce the average Bermudian take-home pay by several percentage points. Others to whom the firm made payments during those two
years include names alive and well-known today, some now operating
under a different corporate style. In the firm's first year, as the staff strug-
gled to get by in the cramped quarters of Conyers' small offices, rent of £30
was payable for six months in advance.

In that it was their capital which owned and supported the business, the partners had an understanding that each might draw out small
amounts of cash as needed. In accounting terms, they represented repay-
ment of monies advanced to the firm by way of the capital necessary to
keep it running. Of the three, Dill used this facility the least often. Conyers
would have the office pay a personal bill from his capital on occasion, and
Pearman withdrew 15 shillings from Petty Cash from time to time. The net
effect on 6 July 1929, when the partners drew their first shares of the profits, was that Dill received the largest cheque, although it amounted to only
a couple of hundred pounds. These were days when a young woman was
advised to marry a man earning a minimum of £1,000 a year.

On 11 April 1929, although he did not yet meet that standard,
Pearman's fondest wish came true when he married Prudence Appleby at
the Cathedral of the Most Holy Trinity, a ceremony attended by everyone
who was anyone in Bermuda. Dill, described in *The Mid-Ocean and
Colonial Government Gazette* of 18 April as "one of Mr. Pearman's partners
in the newly-organized law firm of Conyers Dill & Pearman", was the
groom's best man. Among the bridal party was Lucy Clare Watlington,
whom Dill himself would marry not long afterwards.

A frayed and yellowed copy of *The Mid-Ocean and Colonial
Government Gazette*, the forerunner of the *Mid-Ocean News*, was among
Pearman's personal effects. A report of his wedding appears on the front
page, and by an odd coincidence the last page of the newspaper contains
what must have been one of the very first legal notices placed by Conyers

Dill & Pearman.

In words familiar enough today, the firm gave notice that a petition had been presented to the Legislature by two local entrepreneurs, praying that leave might be given to introduce a Bill for the incorporation of a Company. A lengthy list of corporate objects followed. The final paragraph noted that the petition having been considered by the Honourable House of Assembly, the prayer of the petition was granted and leave given to introduce a Bill to give effect thereto. The advertisement is signed Conyers Dill & Pearman, Attorneys for the Petitioner.

The last of three insertions of the advertisement ran next to an announcement of the sailings of Mail Steamers of the Furness-Bermuda Line, which made the run from New York twice a week bearing mail and passengers to fuel the Island's small but growing tourism industry. The advertisement was placed by Watlington & Conyers, Agents.

CHAPTER FIVE

Establishment

Conyers' office quickly proved unequal to the task of housing the firm's growing practice. Not only was a steady stream of clients coming forward to seek counsel, but the quantity of legal paperwork being generated—including, *inter alia,* copies of all the railway documents—was proving increasingly difficult to manage.

Conyers was devoting the majority of his time in equal measure to the affairs of the Bermuda Railway Company and to those of the Colony. In due course, it was Pearman who took on the lion's share of the court work as the parcels of land needed for the railway were duly processed, which suggests that to Dill must have fallen the bulk of the conveyancing. The broader practices of all three men also continued to build slowly throughout the 1930s. Dill's family connections led to some interesting cases which began to earn him a reputation as an eloquent and impassioned barrister.

Within a few months, the cramped confines of Conyers' office were replaced by slightly larger premises on the second floor of the Somers

Building on Front Street opposite The Bank of Bermuda. The Somers Building had just been completed at the time Conyers Dill & Pearman moved in. Today, the building houses Bermuda Wines & Spirits.

Apart from the move, the firm changed as little as Bermuda did in the 1930s. Conyers Dill & Pearman was, in truth, a relatively small 'country practice' in a largely agrarian community. Easter lilies were an Island specialty. Although there was comparative hustle and bustle in Hamilton, it was by no means the fast-paced international centre we know today. Professionals did not, as a matter of routine, arrive at their offices before eight o'clock every morning, nor did they stay until late in the evening as they do today. Although at least two of the principals of Conyers Dill & Pearman were working a little harder now than had been their previous experience, each of the three men was able to use the firm as a springboard to establish and consolidate his place in Bermudian society.

Conyers continued to forge a civic career which, having already spanned three decades, was on the way to becoming one of the longest and most distinguished in colonial history. In 1933, with the railway company running as smoothly as ever it would and Pearman now handling The Bank of Bermuda's business as part of his varied practice, Conyers was elected Speaker of the House of Assembly, an appointment which followed his election in Southampton Parish, where he finished second to J.E.P. Vesey by a single vote. Conyers had previously represented Pembroke, but in 1933 disqualified himself by forgetting to meet a new legal requirement that each candidate post a £50 deposit to be eligible to stand—the forerunner of today's heftier deposit requirements.

Votes were cast and counted a day or two later in the outlying parishes to allow Returning Officers to complete their work in the central area before setting out to ride to the far ends of the islands. The delay afforded Conyers the opportunity to post his deposit and run in the hinterland of Southampton, thus extending his political service without interruption. His gratitude to the people of Southampton was deeply felt.

In parliaments around the world which have adopted the Westminster model, each Speaker has his or her own way of interpreting the duties and responsibilities of the role. Some act merely as enforcers of parliamentary regulations and protocol, while others view the work as an opportunity to lead. Conyers was of the latter persuasion. He stamped his personality on the job with a vigour few before or since have matched.

It was Conyers who first imported the Speaker's wig and robe to the House of Assembly, adding a degree of dignity which he felt the position deserved. But it was more than a wig which distinguished him. Dill described Conyers' style as "spectacular". Governor Sir Thomas Astley-Cubitt referred to Speaker Conyers as "the Huntsman, with the members of the House as his pack".

Conyers acted in a number of different capacities throughout his career. A Justice of the Peace for more than half his life, he served for years as a Police Magistrate for the central and western districts. From 1925 to 1927, he was Chairman of the Board of Trade. The Board in those days was charged with responsibilities somewhat akin to those of the Department of Tourism today. Such was Bermuda's economy in the early part of the 20th century that the Board of Trade carried an even greater influence, charged as it was with supervision of all aspects of the Island's economic affairs. Dill and Pearman were both later appointed to the Board, following in Conyers' footsteps.

For both Dill and Pearman, the first half of the 1930s was a time to establish the foundations on which their lives would be built. Each transformed himself from the shy young fellow who had returned to Bermuda from England just a few years before. By 1935, each entered and established himself in society through the agencies of marriage, fatherhood, sporting and social achievement and the first flowering of what would become notable political and business careers.

In the early 1930s, Pearman and Dill both started families. In 1931, Dill married Clare Watlington, a cousin of Pearman's and the third daughter of Sir Harry and Lady Watlington. James Appleby Pearman was born on 30 March 1932. He was followed on 20 May by Nicholas Bayard Dill, who would become known as Nicky. Both would go on to a lifetime's professional endeavours with the firm their fathers founded.

Dill and Pearman both rounded out their families with second sons. Richard Shafto Love Pearman was born on 20 September 1934. Known as Dick, he is approaching retirement, after a long and distinguished career with Conyers Dill & Pearman. Conyers was his godfather. Henry David Melville Dill was born on 28 December 1933, his father's 28th birthday, and would pursue a career in acting and hotel management. On Boxing Day 1933, Dill recalled, Conyers brought over to the Dill household a generous Christmas gift of alcohol; Dill's gift to Conyers was a 'push bike'.

If, in sporting terms, Conyers can be described as a cricketer who enjoyed a little sailing, Pearman will be remembered as a sailor, fisherman and bridge player who played a little tennis. Dill, though a racquet man in England, concentrated in Bermuda almost exclusively on sailing. A Bermudian's association with the water is involuntary—no one on the Island can ever be more than half a mile from the ocean.

For years, Pearman had skippered his beloved *Starling* in most of the races of the International Series. In 1932, Dill spent part of his first summer as a father boating in Cowes and on the Clyde, where *Jill*, his brother-in-law John Seward Johnson's boat, won four straight races. In 1933, Pearman played tennis for Bermuda against England, and at the close of that year's season, Dill's *Cardinal* won the Manhasset Bay Yachting Trophy, in races held in Bermuda waters. The following season, Pearman captained the *Achilles* when she won the Prince of Wales Cup.

Conyers was a staple at the Yacht Club. He was often to be found standing at the bar, his left hand planted firmly in the pocket of his tweed jacket, telling long-winded jokes in his unmistakable voice. Over lunch, he would discuss matters of importance, and might from time to time have looked through the windows to catch sight of his partners Dill and Pearman, perhaps involved in more animated conversation with a younger set.

From the first days of the practice, Conyers in particular had wrestled with the idea of forming a trust company to manage the funds of wealthy clients, both Bermudian and non-Bermudian. By 1932, "the partnership had abandoned the idea of trying to organise such a company on its own, but was prepared to co-operate with The Bank (of Bermuda), in return for a proportion of shares and exclusive legal administration, and framing of the trust company bill for presentation to the Legislature," wrote Gordon Phillips in *First, One Thousand Miles...*, his 1992 history of the bank.

The trust company which the bank and the firm started was called the Bermuda Trust Company, and within a year Pearman's cousin, Henry Tucker, was lured back to the Island to manage it. The trust business remains at the core of the international institution The Bank of Bermuda has become. In time, Tucker, who was known to everyone as Jack, came to play such a part in the Island's life that he is now referred to as the architect of the modern Bermuda, which older hands sometimes describe as "the house that Jack built". Tucker became Bermuda's first Government Leader at the outset of Constitutional government in 1968, at the peak of a career in politics and banking which spanned much of the 20th century. He was the key player in almost every development of importance in Bermudian political circles for almost 40 years, and was knighted for his contribution to Bermuda towards the end of his life.

The Bank of Bermuda and Conyers Dill & Pearman were natural allies. Pearman's grandfather was one of the bank's founders; both he and his son, Pearman's father, had served as President of the bank. Conyers was the bank's lawyer; Pearman succeeded him in that role in 1933, when Conyers was appointed Speaker of the House of Assembly. Two years later, the 'special' relationship between the bank and the law firm acquired a physical dimension when the partnership moved into the sixth floor of the pink Bermuda Fire and Marine Building, next door to the bank's head office at Albuoy's Point on Front Street.

In 1936, Dill was elected Commodore of the Royal Bermuda Yacht Club. The position has more to do with sailing than with the management of the Club, and so is traditionally held by an active sailor. Dill brought distinction to his two-year tenure, and was followed into the position in 1938 by Pearman. The two men's portraits hang side by side in a gallery of past Commodores at the Club. Dill's portrait (the photograph was taken 25 years later) shows the man in his three-piece suit and trademark bow tie, with an unguarded smile reinforced by the open book in his hands. Pearman's portrait, taken during his tenure as Commodore, casts a shadow across his face, although his trademark, the chalk-striped, double-breasted suit, is well-lit. Pearman, always reserved, wears a serious expression.

With family life and the law firm flourishing, both men moved into the field of public service without so much as a second thought. In June 1933, Dill was appointed to the Trade Development Board under the chairmanship of H. Villiers Smith. Dill would have been 27 years old when he joined the Board, and was only three days past his 29th birthday when he took the chair on 1 January 1935.

Pearman was appointed to the Board of Trade alongside his partner Dill in 1934, serving for two years before moving on to the Board of Agriculture, of which he was appointed Deputy Chairman in 1939, the year after Dill was elected to the House of Assembly for the first time as a representative of Devonshire, the family seat. Both Dill and Pearman would later hold office at a wide range of Bermudian institutions.

As early as the middle of the 1920s, the revenue earned from the hospitality industry had begun to exceed that derived from agriculture at the height of its success. The Island's well-heeled visitors routinely provided more than 80 percent of Government revenues for most of the 1930s. Bermuda had always positioned itself as an exclusive resort, which protected its tourist trade from the Depression. The Island's exclusivity cut both ways: when times had been good in the 1920s, the wealthy were able to consider Bermuda a home away from home. When the economy turned down, the Island became a place to get away from home for the selfsame travellers. Bermuda advertised itself in those days as "the smartest winter resort west of Biarritz".

For two young men on the brink of their 30s, these must have been exciting and rewarding years. Work, family, social life and a say in matters political all blended into their daily lives in Bermuda. The Depression and the political upheavals which marked the world's progress in the 1930s had relatively little effect on Bermuda. But the grounding both men would receive during this period would serve them well in the disruptions which would mark the decade that lay ahead.

CHAPTER SIX

Innovation

Today, setting up an international company in Bermuda involves little difficulty. Having consulted with professional advisers and weighed the pros and cons of such a course of action, one makes an application, usually through local counsel. The proposed incorporation is then advertised, although this requirement is to be withdrawn for exempted companies in the second half of 1998. The Bermuda Monetary Authority carries out background checks into the applicant's principals, as a formal extension of the less formal vetting already carried out by the potential company's professional advisers. The proposed venture and its management must meet Bermuda's strict background, quality and financial requirements. Those who pass the character examination pay a registration fee, the Bermuda company is formed, and it is ready to carry out its purpose.

But in 1935, all Bermuda companies, whether private or public, were required to be incorporated by an Act of Parliament, which had to be approved by the House of Assembly and the Legislative Council, the forerunner of the Senate. A Bill of Incorporation then as now required the assent of the Governor. Offshore companies, in the way the term has come be understood, did not exist. But the notion, of which companies based all around the world now take advantage, was a-borning.

Tucker referred the American Noble family to Conyers in the spring of 1935. The family operated an international company based in the United States. In assessing its corporate structure, the family sought a headquarters outside that country from which to administer certain non-US interests. Bermuda was on a shortlist of potential candidates the search for a suitable location had turned up.

Conyers was asked for his thoughts on the suitability of utilising Bermuda as a domicile for an international holding company for the family's non-American interests. He pondered the problem and doubtless raised it with his partners. He and Tucker discussed it regularly. It was a tough nut to crack; Bermuda law insisted then, as it does now, that a minimum of 60 percent of the shares of a company registered in Bermuda be beneficially owned by Bermudians. There was no body of law to consult.

The 60/40 ownership rule is a transparently protective measure, designed to keep Bermuda's affairs exclusively in the hands of Bermudians. In 1998, the notion survives as much in the breach as in the observance and is coming under fire from those who see it as a potential roadblock to Bermuda's progress in the electronic 21st century. But back in 1935, when America had yet to introduce social security or electricity to its rural areas, Bermuda businessmen did not dream of competing globally. They were, comparatively speaking, small businessmen. The 60/40 rule was their Maginot Line, their last and only defence against the possibility of being gobbled up by big business interests from the United States. For Conyers and Tucker to succeed, they had to devise a proposal which met the essential requirements of the Law—Bermudian control of Bermudian affairs—and then find a way to persuade their countrymen that it left their defences secure.

The inventive pair came up with the very formula, a way for the family to control its international affairs from Bermuda and yet retain its majority shareholding without compromising the Colony's ownership law. Conyers proposed a Bermuda-resident corporation which would be limited to conducting in Bermuda only those transactions necessary to further its international affairs. Such a company could be owned without restriction by non-Bermudians because it would pose no threat to Bermuda's business interests.

Conyers' proposal must at first have seemed odd and unwieldy. A Bermuda company officially barred from conducting business in Bermuda was an apparent contradiction in terms. That the proposal met with initial resistance is no surprise. "My memory is that it was difficult to get the Bill creating Exempted Companies through the House of Assembly," Dill recalled. The views of the members of the House reflected those of the Bermuda public. Although, today, the members of the House of Assembly are almost entirely in favour of international business, the public sentiment lives on, as was evidenced by the debate in 1996 attending the proposed ownership by exempted companies of the site of the former Bermudiana Hotel. In 1935, however, Conyers was able to persuade his Parliamentary colleagues of the wisdom of his idea with what one imagines must have been the legislative equivalent of a full court press.

The importance of Conyers' and Tucker's revolutionary thinking to Bermuda, to international finance, and indeed to the world, cannot be overstated. Today, hundreds of thousands of offshore companies are incorporated annually in jurisdictions all over the globe. Estimates place as much as a third of the world's private wealth offshore. Exempted companies and their ilk provide owners with a range of advantages such as anonymity, tax efficiency and seamless succession. Almost every large company in the world has an offshore element in its corporate structure;

more than three-quarters of America's 100 largest industrial companies maintain a presence of some sort in Bermuda alone.

On 8 July 1935, Robert and Meta Noble, on the advice of Conyers Dill & Pearman, incorporated Elbon Limited by Act of Parliament. The company's curious name was the family's, spelled backwards. Elbon's capital was set at not less than £5,000 and not more than £500,000. Its activities were restricted to business outside Bermuda except for such necessary matters as currency transactions, local payments and the like. Its commercial business was to be conducted exclusively through Bermudian banks and Elbon was forbidden to conduct commercial banking itself.

These protective measures, which seem so out of step with the *laissez faire* markets of the late 20th century, have served Bermuda well: the two large local banks, which have been among the main beneficiaries, provide several thousand jobs in the local economy in 1998 and a larger number of secondary positions depend upon a healthy banking sector. The banks compete in the global arena and have of late felt the imprisoning effect of the walls put up to protect them. If they are to grow beyond a certain size, they cannot do so without a significant, rule-busting injection of non-Bermudian capital.

Elbon Limited, then, was the first exempted company, conceived as a specific solution to a specific set of circumstances. Only a short period would elapse before other situations called for a similar specific solution, and Acts incorporating Bellevue Limited and the International Match Company Limited followed in short order. International Match was aptly-named: it lit the fire of international business in Bermuda.

A Swedish industrialist named Krüger had made a fortune out of the manufacture and sale of matches. In the early 1930s, he disappeared, or died from a self-inflicted hunting wound—reports vary—leaving behind a tangled web of some 400 companies around the world and scores of angry creditors. In the winding-up procedure which followed his disappearance, many of Krüger's assets were liquidated and the creditors received only partial payment on their debts.

Realisation of certain of the assets, among them a forest in Guatemala and a Turkish tobacco company, proved difficult for the trustee banks who were acting as liquidators. These assets were channelled through a Bermuda company incorporated by Conyers Dill & Pearman by Act of Parliament, The International Match Realisation Company Ltd. Act, 1936. The firm worked closely on the incorporation with Cadwallader, Wickersham & Taft, a leading Wall Street law firm.

By enactment, the company could only deal in real or personal property "outside of these Islands". It was not entitled to hold land, acquire shares issued by any company incorporated locally, nor take a mortgage or acquire bonds secured on land in Bermuda. Any lease agreement the company might execute in Bermuda was to be limited to 21 years. Most of these conditions hold today for exempted companies, although individual exceptions have been, and are increasingly being made as the protectionist sentiment weakens.

Within a year of the formation of International Match, The Bank of Bermuda lent the company $1 million, then virtually the whole of the bank's capital. The liquidation of International Match took almost ten years to complete, but resulted in capital appreciation for the creditors of the company of several hundred million dollars.

The incorporation of International Match created a stir in New York, where an editorial in the *New York Times* railed against what was perceived as tax-dodging. In Bermuda, *The Royal Gazette* reprinted the editorial, with a headline suggesting that the Bank of Butterfield, in any event, would "spurn tax-dodging funds". The implied criticism incensed the management of The Bank of Bermuda. They felt that the Island's tax neutrality, as its lack of corporate, income and capital gains taxes has come to be known, was only one of the attributes which attracted overseas companies. To this day Bermudian service providers and the Government stress the Island's many other advantages to the corporate or individual investor.

Cries of "tax-dodging" are heard no more. Bermuda's international corporate laws, now more than 60 years in the making, have stood the tests of time and international law. The taxation authorities of a number of onshore jurisdictions have passed legislation specifying operational standards which onshore owners of offshore companies must meet, but the offshore principle is accepted worldwide.

No one today adopts a negative attitude towards the legal maximisation of profits through the inclusion of an offshore element. If the word 'offshore', unknown in 1935, now carries any residual taint, it has arisen not because of the behaviour of Bermuda, nor of the great majority of those companies utilising its jurisdiction, but from other offshore locations who have not as jealously guarded the quality of their reputation. The charge, besides, is specious. Corruption and illegality pay no attention to borders.

Conyers Dill & Pearman would never yield the local lead they had established in 1936, when it might be said that they represented the majority of the world's offshore business, such as it was. Today, the firm's market share is a jealously-guarded secret, but perusal of information available from the Bermuda Registrar of Companies places the firm's share in Bermuda, of more than 10,000 exempted companies and partnerships, above 40 percent.

The shrewd insight of Conyers and Tucker spawned an industry, caused governments worldwide to change their laws to accommodate their thinking, and has saved billions, if not trillions of dollars, in taxes. It has provided Bermuda with a significant source of foreign exchange earnings—since 1993, the largest single source—and made of the firm Conyers founded an international corporate presence.

Of course, in the 1930s, the firm remained stubbornly small. Nicky Dill recalls a time when the entire staff was just five: Conyers, Dill, Pearman, Joan McPhee and a Miss Rennick, who was filling in for Isabelle Darrell.

CHAPTER SEVEN

International Intrigue

As the 1930s drew on, the probability of War increased with each passing day. As a British colony, Bermuda would have entered a European war automatically if Great Britain did so. The Island might in due course develop the potential to serve as a strategic staging point, but, as it was, life in Bermuda continued pretty much as usual beyond the start of hostilities.

The visitor total fell somewhat as the shadow of what was to come crept slowly forward, but Bermuda tourism had enjoyed a good run. Having stood at about 43,000 in 1930, the annual number of visitors had risen to 82,800 in 1937, the peak year. The Americans, with whom Bermuda's daily life was and is most closely aligned, did not enter the War, of course, until the attack on Pearl Harbor in 1941, when tourism became virtually non-existent.

In Bermuda, the European war affected people's lives in different ways. Dill's War began early, in August 1939, when his practice of Law was interrupted by affairs of State. His assistance was sought not only in local affairs, in which all three partners of Conyers Dill & Pearman pursued a lifelong interest, nor even in matters regional, but on an undertaking of global importance. Dill's actions that long weekend did not dramatically affect the outcome of the conflict and may have had little to do with the history of the partnership, but they portray an image of swift and competent action which keenly illustrates the man he was.

In the middle of August 1939, he had been preparing to leave Bermuda to sail in a race on Long Island Sound. His family had left the Island ahead of him to stay with his sister in New Brunswick, New Jersey. A decade earlier, Dill had joined the Bermuda Volunteer Engineers, whose main function was to operate the coastal defence battery at St. David's Head and the military telephone system. Like that of the Bermuda Regiment today, the business of the BVEs was mostly theoretical. But just before Dill planned to sail away from the Island to join his family, the Engineers were embodied and all leave was cancelled. The measure was precautionary, but concern and anticipation were in the air. Dill made his way to St. David's by land and sea, and alongside his fellow Engineers began pitching tents and making equipment ready for its purpose.

Not long after his arrival at the eastern end of the Island, a message was received, summoning Dill to see Acting Governor Dutton. Dill duly travelled back to Hamilton, where Dutton quietly introduced him to two men, J.C. Cooper, Vice President of Pan American Airways, and another man, whom Dill perhaps diplomatically recalled only as "a gentleman from the United States Air Force."

The purpose of the call was to request Dill to arrange a lease of Morgan's Island in Bermuda's Great Sound to the United States Government. The reason for the urgency was to allow the officially neutral United States to have secured a lease on equally neutral territory before War, which was looking increasingly likely, broke out.

Morgan's and nearby Tucker's Island were known collectively as the Brother Islands. Dill's Senior Partner, Conyers, traced his familial connections back to ancestors who settled on Morgan's Island more than three centuries earlier. Since then, the islands have been landfilled into singularity, although the restitution of their independence from each other is at the heart of an approved proposal for the redevelopment of the former Naval Annex of which they now form part.

Dill explained that Morgan's Island belonged to his sister Ruth and offered to telephone her at once to secure her agreement to the request. Dutton declined the offer. Given the strength of isolationist elements in the United States at the time, it was felt that the matter should be dealt with as discreetly as possible. The effect in the United States of news leaking out of a lease agreement being made with Bermuda, which was effectively on the brink of War, was described to Dill as "disastrous". He was instructed to fly up to the United States and make the necessary arrangements in total secrecy.

Commercial flight had become part of the Bermuda fabric since regular service began on 16 June 1937, when the first flying boats had landed in the Great Sound. The flying boats live on today largely in monochromatic films and museums, but the introduction of air service brought Bermuda into the modern world, increased its strategic importance and would later enable the post-War development of the tourism industry to take place. Today's regular flights to and from the east and the west are an integral element in the infrastructure which keeps both Bermuda's twin economic pillars of tourism and international business, and its modern lifestyle, alive.

Cooper had been on hand, representing the airline, to greet the very first Pan American flight to arrive from the United States. Also in attendance that day had been Dill's father-in-law, Harry Watlington, then Mayor of Hamilton. Dill had been Chairman of the Trade Development Board, and Pearman a member, when what proved to be a momentous decision was taken to move with the times and open Bermuda up to the advantages of commercial aviation. Under Dill's guidance, the Trade Development Board allied itself to two companies then at the forefront of commercial aviation: Pan American and Imperial Airways, which, after a number of name changes, is today's British Airways.

The journey from Bermuda to Long Island was neither as convenient nor as fast as today's jet-powered flights. The flying boats needed four and a half hours to reach the Eastern Seaboard and considerably longer to fly to England, with a refuelling stop in the Azores, but the graceful clippers served as the forerunners of today's sophisticated flying machines.

The reason for Cooper's presence at the meeting with the Governor was made plain when Dill was told that a Pan American clipper en route from Europe to the United States was to be diverted to Bermuda to allow him swift passage to the Eastern Seaboard, since no flights were scheduled which would permit Dill to discharge his duties before the weekend. But, as circumstances had it on the day, the swell at Horta in the Azores did not permit the diverted clipper to land there and take on the extra fuel which would be required for its new routing. By agreement, the matter was left in Dill's hands. He was requested to secure the lease post haste by any means he saw fit. If at all possible, he was to do so before the coming weekend. It is likely that with the cancellation of the flight from Horta, official hopes of pulling off a lease were all but exhausted.

The next day saw Dill at the Royal Bermuda Yacht Club, doubtless assessing his situation, when he heard the Captain of a vessel named *Corinthia* announce his ship's departure for the Eastern Seaboard ten minutes hence. Dill enquired whether an extra berth might be found for him. A number of potential passengers having declined to travel in the blacked-out condition the times demanded meant that there was room for Dill, but only if he would make himself ready without delay.

He "ran into town" to purchase a toothbrush and some other

necessities and returned in time to board the Corinthia, taking with him only the clothes he stood up in. The vessel docked in Brooklyn on the afternoon of Friday, 1 September 1939. Dill had wired his sister to say that he would be calling that day, although his message was intended to refer to a telephone call. Instead, he was able to take the train from Brooklyn to New Brunswick to pay the call in person.

A good part of that night was spent typing up the lease, to which Dill's sister, then called Ruth Johnson, had assented immediately, once she had been made aware of the circumstances attending it. A Notary Public sealed the lease early on the Saturday morning, 2 September. Now all that remained was for Dill to find a way to return to Bermuda with the lease.

A Pan American clipper was scheduled to leave that day from Long Island, but Dill had already missed the only train connection which would get him to Long Island in time to catch the plane. He therefore hired a private plane—such derring-do!—to ferry him to Long Island. In a development worthy of cheap fiction, a fog arose en route, and the charter flight was diverted to Flushing. The Captain radioed ahead to have a taxi standing by to meet the aircraft. Dill set off for Long Island with his driver's pedal to the metal, only to arrive 15 minutes past Pan American's scheduled departure time of noon. Mercifully, the flight had been delayed—not, plainly, for Dill's benefit, since none but he knew of the importance of his mission.

The clipper arrived in Bermuda at 5:30 p.m. on the Saturday after-noon, completing the journey in just over four hours. Dill telephoned the Governor to advise him that he had secured the lease by the deadline the Americans had given him. Later that Saturday evening, on Dutton's orders, Dill deposited the document with the Governor's secretary and returned to his unit in St. David's, under orders not to refer to the matter in explain-ing his absence. Dill's Commanding Officer, Cecil (Mookie) Montgomery-Moore, D.F.C., asked Dill on his return where he had been. "Oh, I've been around," Dill replied. Sensing something was afoot, Moore let it pass.

Dill's precipitate and adventurous journey had been completed not a moment too soon. Shortly after the Bermuda Volunteer Engineers would have woken to reveille the very next morning, under canvas at St. David's, Neville Chamberlain made the fateful announcement that Herr Hitler had not heeded a final ultimatum to withdraw his troops from the Sudetenland, and therefore the United Kingdom and its possessions, including Bermuda, were at war.

CHAPTER EIGHT

Active Service

Pearman was representing Bermuda on a fishing boat in international waters off Canada, mired in a deep fog, when the message crackled across the radio that War had broken out. Late in the 1930s, he had joined the Bermuda team which fished in the international Blue Fin Tuna angling tournament in the waters off Nova Scotia. Deep-sea fishing had become one of Pearman's lasting passions and for many years the wall of his office at the firm bore testimony to his angling ability in the shape of the tail of a mammoth yellowfin tuna he had landed.

In the mid-1930s, Pearman probably worked harder than either of his partners. Later, his public career would gather steam as Conyers and Dill were appearing on a larger stage. In time, Pearman would become the architect of his own vision, but everyone who knew him remarks that almost throughout his career, he had come to enjoy the work he once disparaged as a younger man.

He had been appointed to the Board of Agriculture in 1936. Three years later he was appointed its Deputy Chairman, in which capacity he served until 1942, the year he was appointed Chairman of the Board of Health. In 1943, he trod in his grandfather's footsteps when he was elected to serve as a Member of the Colonial Parliament for Pembroke North. His election meant that all three partners of the firm now served in one capacity or another in the House of Assembly.

To those unfamiliar with the ways of Bermuda, the notion that the partners of a leading law firm might serve in the legislative and, subsequently, the executive arms of the government might suggest an irreconcilable conflict of interest. That view, however, discounts the stature enjoyed by the professions, Bermuda's tiny size and the grand reach of its institutions. Few towns in Europe or the United States with a population of 25,000, Bermuda's approximate wartime headcount, boast much more than a town council and, perhaps, a regional Fire Chief. Few towns of that size, however, lie nearly 700 ocean miles from their nearest neighbour. Few small communities in the world of any size—Beverly Hills and Switzerland excepted—boast the concentration of wealth which Bermuda has accumulated. Few communities have a Parliamentary tradition dating back 350 years or, perhaps, Bermuda's often unique way of interpreting that tradition.

But while there are times when Bermuda can resemble, even today, nothing more than a small town, it has thrived, arguably, because of the way in which its people have handled their conflicts of interest. Whatever one's political viewpoint, the reality is beyond dispute: despite the conflicts which all Bermuda's most important citizens have had to face, the standard of living in the 22 square-mile country hundreds of miles from anywhere has, over many years, consistently ranked among the highest in the world. What seems hardly possible in theory has worked in practice. Any number of factors may be responsible, but among them is the shared understanding of a sentiment attributed to Tucker, that "a man without a conflict of interests is a man without any interests."

Although Bermudian history has its examples of those who have exploited such conflicts for their own advantage, few of the workings of the Bermudian community go unnoticed. Perhaps it is this enhanced degree of visibility which has ensured that the great majority of conflicts have been resolved—sooner or later—in Bermuda's interest.

Once America entered the Second World War, demands were made of the British to allow Bermuda to fulfill its potential as a staging point. It was the original intent of the Americans to reduce Bermuda to "one gigantic complex in the middle of the main island, ironing out the hills and rewriting Bermudian geography". The idea, expounded to Dill by an American Admiral who visited Bermuda, was to level the hills between Gibb's Hill Lighthouse and the Inverurie Hotel and spread them sideways into the harbour and the ocean. The resulting plain would have been used as a Base by the United States Army and Air Force, cutting the main island in two and displacing its residents.

Looking back, it seems highly unlikely that the relatively insignificant Bermuda should have been able to persuade an American government embroiled in a World War to radically change its thinking. But such was the goal of a delegation to Britain, comprised of Tucker, Sir Howard Trott and John (later Sir John) Cox—and such was their achievement. Dill is said to have personally persuaded Churchill to intercede with the authorities in Washington over the intended size and location of the bases. The American government agreed to site their air base, to be called Fort Bell, on St. David's and the Navy on the Great Sound.

Dill, growing in stature although still not 40 years old, was chosen to come up with a method whereby the lands of the St. David's Islanders could be acquired to make room for the US forces. "I recommended that there be three bodies created to look after the job," he wrote. "The first body would be a legal one to decide who was morally, equitably or legally entitled to the piece of land on which they lived."

The parish of St. David's was an even more independent place in the 1930s than it is today. Many of the St. David's Islanders lived in homes without title to or a lease upon the lands they occupied. The second committee Dill proposed "was to determine the amount of compensation which would be awarded and the third one, named the St. David's Island Committee, would determine how to apply the funds, whether to pay them directly to the person concerned or whether to apply them on their behalf. The first committee was headed by my father, the second by Sir Herbert Henniker-Heaton, who was a former Colonial Secretary in Bermuda, and the third was headed by myself."

The committee work proceeded smoothly enough, but could not keep pace with the construction work at the Base, so that interim lodgings had to be found for a number of St. David's Islanders, "who got so fond of their temporary quarters," Dill wrote, "that they did not want to leave them." Eventually, all the Islanders were resettled. A certain amount of ill-feeling attended these events, but none was directed at Dill. On the contrary, he recalled that Conyers Dill & Pearman gained a number of clients following his regular visits to the eastern parishes.

The accommodations the St. David's Islanders were being asked to vacate were not always palatial. Dill's son, Nicky, who joined his father on these visits from time to time, recalls one man who had raised a family of five or six children in a small shack, probably built and abandoned by the Bermuda Electric Light Company. "It had a cable that went right over the roof to a turnbuckle on the other side," the younger Dill recalled. "He told me that when hurricane force winds came along, he just turned down on the turnbuckle to make sure the house stayed in position."

Bayard Dill and his cohorts went to enormous lengths to ensure that each and every displaced Bermudian ended up in at least comparable surroundings. Prime Minister Winston Churchill visited Bermuda in 1942, arriving in secret by flying boat, to express to the assembled members of the Colonial Parliament his thanks to the people of Bermuda for allowing the construction of the American bases.

Dill's work on behalf of many of those at the East End was rewarded by the Governor, Lord Burghley, when he appointed Dill to the Executive Council, the Cabinet of the day, on 7 August 1944 for a period of three years, "with all the powers, rights, privileges and advantages to the said office belonging or appertaining".

Dill was, at the time, chairman of the Board of Works, the Public Works Planning Commission and the Airport Board. He stood in for the people of Bermuda once again when he travelled to Whitehall in Burghley's company for consultations during the run-up to D-Day, to represent the interests of, and the implications for, Bermuda as a US basing area. In the same year, the wheels of Empire turning yet, King George VI knighted Conyers for his Parliamentary work. To those in his circle, however, he remained 'Reggie' or 'Uncle Reggie'.

By all accounts, the firm's activities during these troubled times were subordinated to the needs of a Colony at war, although the practice continued to service such clients as it had. Bermuda, even with its central hills left intact, proved of great use to the British and the Americans as a refuelling station and also as the home of a troupe of hundreds of military censors. The military uses to which Bermuda was put worried the Germans sufficiently to merit the dropping of propaganda flyers on the City of Hamilton. Headed "To The People of Bermuda", they stated, starkly, if inaccurately:

SURRENDER and save your lives. Bermuda has fallen to the Swastika. Your Defense Forces have been conquered and Hamilton occupied by a Commando sent by the Fuehrer "Hitler", to protect you from your oppressors the British and the Americans. HEIL HITLER.

Only slightly less amateurish tactics had the Nazi propaganda machine reporting at irregular intervals the sinking of H.M.S. *Malabar*, which would have been no mean achievement. Malabar is not a vessel, but the name of the Royal Naval land base near the Dockyard.

The Island emerged from the War at least relatively intact, thanks to the efforts of a community of selfless men and women, among them Dill, who remained throughout a member of his beloved Engineers. Rare indeed is the photograph of him not in his khakis or in his robe and wig. The manner in which he was able to combine his many capacities says a great deal about the way an enlightened person can resolve conflicts of interest in favour of the greater good.

News of the end of the War was relayed around Hamilton by a series of blasts from the siren of Hamilton Fire Station. The Furness Withy liner *Fort Townsend*, alongside Hamilton Harbour, set off a continuous whistle which drew thousands of people to a spontaneous celebration at the waterfront.

CHAPTER NINE

Post-War

By the time the War ended, the partnership Conyers, Dill and Pearman had assembled almost two decades earlier was at best a medium-sized fish in a small pond. Other law firms had come and gone. Pearman's father-in-law, Major Appleby, for one, had started a firm before the outbreak of hostilities that would, in time, approach the size and influence of Conyers Dill & Pearman. But in the years immediately following the War, and indeed for some time after that, the three men had plenty of time for their extra-legal careers.

Pearman was elected to the Board of The Bank of Bermuda on his father's death in 1946. The bank, like the firm, had emerged from the War mostly intact, but in the immediate post-War years, Bermuda's economy was becalmed. Money was tight, and business depressed. Tourism was about to reawaken as Furness Withy chipped the war paint off its cruise ships in favour of more relaxed colours and successors were built, but what was to follow was not yet helping the Island's cash flow. In retrospect, these years can be seen as the lull before the storm, but at the time such a view would have been cold comfort.

Suffering, of course, is relative. Like the United States, Bermuda had not been invaded and had not felt the hand of the oppressor. The buildings and people had weathered the storm, but the Island's economic activity had been seriously curtailed. Just as a renaissance in tourism was beginning, another seed was sprouting which would prolong the Bermudian economic miracle: the servicing of international business.

What the financial world now calls international companies, then just starting to attract the sobriquet 'multi-nationals', were few and far between in Bermuda in the 1940s. Only the oil companies can be said to have been truly global at that time, and even they concentrated their efforts on countries in which their raw materials were found and their headquarters in Europe or the United States. Bermuda figured in very little corporate planning prior to 1947.

Dill had been retained to advise one of the international oil companies on the establishment of a Bermuda presence. Modifying very little the ownership regulations which the firm had pioneered in the 1930s, Dill was able to outline a corporate vehicle which satisfied the requirements of the company's European parent. In August 1947, Conyers Dill & Pearman formed a Bermuda subsidiary company for the oil giant, which remains on the Island to this day. At about the same time as the first of the Seven Sisters were knocking on the firm's door, Dill had also been consulted by an American insurance company which sought a stable environment in which to base the global headquarters of its non-US business interests. The company's long-serving founder was attracted to Bermuda's proximity, tax-friendliness and use of British law.

With Conyers devoting at least as much of his time to affairs of State as to the firm's practice, and Pearman by now a dominant trial lawyer, Dill and Pearman found themselves at the centre of the action. Pearman was shrewd, Dill persuasive and charming. Both had come to enjoy the cut and thrust of the courtroom. The practice settled for a while into a comfortable routine.

By Act of Parliament passed on 16 December 1947, the firm's first insurance client established a wholly-owned Bermuda subsidiary, the very first insurance company of any magnitude to be registered in Bermuda, empowered to carry on its business from, but not within, the Island. Like Elbon, the new company was content to accept severe limitations on the activities it could conduct in Bermuda. The company's first managers, mostly legal and administrative staff, took a suite of offices on the western fringes of Hamilton and began the arduous process, in the days of carbon paper and the need to place long distance telephone calls hours ahead, of rearranging the group's affairs to take account of the new reality of its presence in Bermuda. Once the structure was in place, the company began hiring competent Bermudians.

The oil company began its business in Bermuda a little more quickly than did the insurance company, although the local operations of neither would take on international significance just yet. These two unrelated subsidiaries and all that has followed have between them had the most dramatic and lasting effect on the fate of Bermuda.

Not only *Fortune 100* companies maintain a Bermuda presence, but organisations from every continent on the world. More than half the companies whose stocks are quoted on the Hong Kong index are domiciled in Bermuda. Mutual fund assets managed from the Island approach US$20 billion. One Bermudian bank was last year named one of the two best banks in the world in the field of global custody. The financial scale of the Island's insurance industry makes that of the more widely-celebrated worldwide movie industry, for example, look small by comparison.

Generally speaking, company incorporations create little in the way of public interest. The spotlight tends to shine later, when plans become reality. True to form, the enabling legislation for the birth of the

Island's insurance industry passed through Parliament with a minimum of debate. The international operations of non-Bermudian companies have yet to fully engage the imagination of the average Bermuda resident, to whom the complexity of international high finance remains largely a closed book.

Of far greater public interest was a decision faced by the Bermuda Government in 1947, following a precipitous decline in passenger volumes on the Bermuda railway. The use of the railway by military forces and a lack of capacity for reinvestment in the fast-deteriorating rolling stock had crucially weakened the line's ability to operate. The Government decided to abandon the railway and encourage instead the use of motor vehicles on the Island. The internal combustion engine was an immediate hit with Bermudians, who have maintained their love affair with the automobile ever since. By the close of the year, 352 private cars, 144 taxis and 426 commercial vehicles were officially registered, and a major programme of road improvements was in hand. The railway's time in Bermuda had come and gone.

The number of rail passengers had declined in 1947 to only 41 percent of its level two years earlier. Having purchased the railway for £115,000, Government would have had to make a massive investment—close to US$2 million, according to consulting engineers called in to report on the railway's prospects—to restore the system to operational efficiency. Had the money been found, which was unlikely, there would have been little will to resurrect the Rattle and Shake.

Future historians may well date the beginning of the end of a way of life in Bermuda to the day the decision to close the railway was taken. One can only imagine the effect on tourism and the declining Bermudian landscape which retaining the railway system might have had today, when travelling on Bermuda's roads can be a stressful experience. At midnight on 1 January 1948, the Somerset railway line, the last, was abandoned, and

Rosemary Grissel, Lady Cubitt's daughter, who had driven in the very last spike in the system in 1931, pulled it out again. The railway lines and stock were subsequently sold to the Government of British Guiana, where sections of the railway, at last report, were still in operation.

The loss of the railway occurred at the same time as a dreadful blight began to affect Bermuda's cedar trees, long considered the living symbol of the Island's uniqueness. The blight was so severe that it threatened the continuation of the species. In 1948, a severe hurricane blew down many of the remaining trees, reducing the aspect of the land, in Dill's words, "to an unkempt graveyard". These were serious blows, as was another loss suffered that year.

Conyers' favourite fishing target was the Hog fish, whose unique taste is derived from its own diet of shellfish. Conyers' greatest joy was to catch a large example and supervise the cooking himself, with rashers of bacon on either side of the catch. He would then invite friends to join him at the Yacht Club for lunch, which lasted most of the afternoon. Conyers even named his twin-engined, gasoline-driven cruiser the *Hogfish* in tribute to his prey.

As was his wont, he was out in the harbour one summer morning early in July 1948, anticipating a day's fishing. He pressed the engines' starting button. Gases which had built up in the bilge exploded, and threw him overboard. Conyers was badly burned. After initial treatment at the King Edward VII Memorial Hospital, a mile outside Hamilton, he was sent to Boston for medical treatment.

On his return to Bermuda, he fell ill with jaundice or hepatitis, attributed to a transfusion he had received in Boston. He lingered for a while, seeming to Dill to hold his own and even to recover a little. But on 25 July, Conyers called Dill in to his room at the King Edward and announced: "Bayard, I'm on my way out."

Dill was requested to effect a codicil to Conyers' will, adding various legacies. Dill at first demurred, until Conyers, in Dill's words, "said he wanted it done NOW. Thinking that it would ease his mind, I did as he requested," wrote Dill, "and the codicil was signed that same afternoon. The very next day he died."

CHAPTER TEN

Bermuda's First Citizen

The lead story in *The Royal Gazette* of 27 July 1948 was headlined: "Death of Sir Reginald Conyers; Assembly Pays Tribute to 'Father of House'; Hundreds At Funeral". Accompanied by a report of the funeral and one from the House of Assembly, the news of Conyers' death at the age of 69 took up fully a third of the newspaper's front page. The main report read, in part, as follows:

The Royal Gazette regrets to announce that Sir James Reginald Conyers, Speaker of the House of Assembly since 1933, died in the King Edward VII Memorial Hospital early yesterday morning. He had been gravely ill for several days.

The funeral took place yesterday afternoon at St. John's Church, Pembroke and hundreds of people attended, including representatives of all sections of the community.

In the House of Assembly, earlier, impressive tributes were paid to Bermuda's first citizen and the "Father of the House" before members adjourned as a mark of respect without proceeding with the day's business.

Parliamentarian, lawyer and sportsman, Sir Reginald is believed to have been the first Speaker to die in office. His service in the House—he was first elected in 1904—exceeds that of any other member, and as Speaker he was responsible for the institution of the British Parliamentary practice of a 'question-time', as well as the wearing of wig and robes.

His death necessitates a bye-election in Southampton Parish.

Immediately beneath the report ran the newspaper's formal obituary. In part, it read:

James Reginald Conyers was born in Bermuda on 3 September 1879, one of a large family. His parents were James Adam Conyers and Emma Marie Conyers. His early education was at the Saltus Grammar School. Then he went to London and was called to the Bar at the Inner Temple in 1902. Returning to the Colony in the following year, he was called to the Bermuda Bar and began his law practice in Hamilton. In 1904 he was elected to the House of Assembly, and he remained a member until his death.

For years Sir Reginald represented Pembroke Parish. In 1933 he became Speaker of the House. In the general election this year he was top of the poll at Southampton with 187 votes.

Short, with an abrupt, almost aggressive manner, Sir Reginald was the first Speaker to introduce into the House of Assembly the wig and robe of the British Parliament. He always maintained the dignity of the House and his sharp tap with the gavel and bows to the right and left were a feature of the opening of every sitting. He wore heavy, horn-rimmed spectacles when presiding, which gave his face a studious appearance. His portrait, with those of former Speakers, adorns the north wall of the chamber.

In his modern offices, which he shared with his partners, Captain Bayard Dill, M.C.P., and Mr. James E. Pearman, M.C.P., Sir Reginald conveyed an impression of efficiency with his abrupt, clipped speech. Strangers might at first be inclined to resent his brusque manner, but once they got to know him they appreciated his quality and humour.

He was a familiar and dominant figure at the Royal Bermuda Yacht Club. He was an excellent host and fond of a practical joke. As a golfer he was better than the average; he enjoyed billiards, a game of poker, pottering about in his garden and especially fishing. He used to make several fishing trips a week, and he believed he had caught more fish than any other man in the Colony not fishing for a living.

Alongside the obituary was a detailed report of the funeral, which filled several columns. It read, in part:

The largest funeral seen in Bermuda for many years was accorded to Sir Reginald Conyers when the leaders of the Colony and other members of the public gathered at Blue Waters, his home in Pembroke, and later at St. John's Church, to pay their last tributes.

Long before 5:30 in the afternoon, when the cortège left Blue Waters for the church, relatives, M.C.P.'s, Legislative and Executive Councillors, high-ranking Government officers and friends had made their way to his home.

At 5:30, the pall-bearers—Captain the Hon. N.B. Dill, the Hon. John Cox, the Hon. Hal Butterfield, Mr. H.T. Watlington, Mr.

Owen Darrell and Mr. Gayous Powell—began to carry Sir Reginald on his last journey. They were followed by over three dozen motor cars, moving slowly to the pace of the horses ahead. As they went through the winter lanes, traffic from side roads was held up for many minutes. The route was lined by people watching their leading parliamentarian carried to his resting place.

The journey to St. John's Church took exactly half an hour. Many people who had not gone to Blue Waters were already in their seats as the pall-bearers entered the church. Before the funeral rites began, the pews were full.

The Rev. Eustace Strong and the Rev. David Evans conducted the service, and the address was given by the Right Reverend Arthur Heber Browne.

Dr. Browne said: "The whole community in this ancient and loyal Colony is mourning the loss of one of its most eminent citizens, whose service will long be remembered and whose place it will be difficult to fill. And when I was asked to say the customary few words ere we lay his body to rest, I could but think of Sir Henry Newbolt's *Torch of Life* with its refrain 'Play up, play up, and play the game'.

"For Reggie Conyers, as we called him, loved to revive memories of his youthful exploits on the cricket-fields of England; and as we call to mind the varied activities of his life among us, may we not say that his were the qualities of vigour and straightness which enabled him to 'play up, and play the game.'

The report from the House read, in part:

Sentiments of appreciation for Sir Reginald Conyers' long years of Parliamentary service were expressed in the House of Assembly yesterday when many members paid high tribute to their departed Speaker.

The ordinary business of the day was entirely dispensed with and after the acting clerk had officially informed the House of Sir Reginald's death, the only proceedings were the adoption of a motion by Mr. Ernest Vesey that the House adjourn and record its profound regret.

Stating that Sir Reginald had served in a legislative capacity for one of the longest periods ever known in the history of the British Empire, Mr. Vesey said that he had rendered outstanding service to Bermuda. Although coming to the House meant neglecting his own private practice, his attendance had been constant, the only times he was absent being when it was inevitable. "The public owes a great debt of gratitude to Sir Reginald," said Mr. Vesey.

Stating that he had lost a valued friend, Captain the Hon. N.B. Dill recalled his professional association with Sir Reginald from 1928 and commented that for an older man to take on such young partners as himself and Mr. James Pearman and to operate with them without ever having a disagreement over major matters was an indication of his tolerance. Captain Dill praised Sir Reginald's quickness of mind and clarity of thought, his appreciation for and realisation of the essential truth of matters, his ability to see the viewpoint of a minority, and lastly his great sense of humour.

These were the qualities, Captain Dill declared, that had made Sir Reginald the fine Speaker that he had been.

Conyers left behind him a Bermuda not dramatically different from the world into which he had been born. Dill and Pearman decided to carry on the firm's practice without changing its name, as a mark of respect to the man who had been their Senior Partner for two decades. With the passing of Sir Reginald Conyers, Dill and Pearman, now in their mid-40s, involuntarily reprised the spirit of the compact they had made with each other 20 years earlier to jointly lead their own law firm.

CHAPTER ELEVEN

Long-Distance Information

Enter David Graham, who joined the firm of Conyers Dill & Pearman in the autumn of 1949.

Born on 24 September 1914, the son of Charles James Graham, D.S.O., M.C., Graham had attended Wellington College and Wadham College, Oxford. He was taking his solicitor's law examinations in September 1939, when War broke out. Having enlisted, he was quickly promoted to Second Lieutenant and then to Staff Captain of a Brigade posted to Iraq soon after the Germans were ejected. To reach Iraq required a lengthy boat journey more than half way around the world. From Iraq, Graham and his unit went to North Africa. He was present at the capitulation of Hitler's forces in Enfidaville, standing on the broken bridge, when the first German officers came to offer their surrender.

Graham's Italian campaign took him through Salerno, Anzio and Cassino, the scenes of hellish battles. One set of activities in Italy in particular was officially noted, a fine example of Graham's mind in action and his refusal to automatically follow the obvious course. Instead of attacking the enemy's front lines, he proposed to run jeeps down the flank, using mobility to reach behind enemy lines to attack front-line troops from the rear, relying on speed and surprise. The idea was Graham's, so he was sent in first. It worked. He was awarded the Military Cross.

He was among those who "chased the Vichy French out of Lebanon and Syria," and was despatched with the British Forces who tried to stop the Jews from taking Palestine. His War would have been, as he put it, "a wonderful Cook's tour if there hadn't been any Germans".

Demobilised in February 1946, Graham found himself in the Union Bar in Alexandria, in a scene it is now hard to imagine outside the confines of a black-and-white film. In the bar, he ran into an Oxford crony, David Huxley. Graham was bemoaning his imminent lengthy trip back to Britain, crammed into one troop train after another, when Huxley trumped him by explaining that he had to go to a place called Bermuda, wherever that might be. Huxley's wife, an American, had been forced to travel to Bermuda, the nearest British possession, to collect his Army pay while he was away fighting.

Graham made his way back to England eventually, and in May 1946 married Glorita, his best friend's Argentinean widow, who had three children. Compared to Graham's adventures of the past few years, he found a peace-time England struggling to recover from the ravages of War an especially depressing place.

In the winter of 1947, one of the worst on record in Britain, Graham and his family had travelled to the West Indies in search of a property. They visited Trinidad and Tobago, Jamaica, Grenada and St. Lucia, but finally decided against the idea and made to return to England. The aeroplane developed a problem which made leaving Bermuda after a refuelling stop an impossibility. Stranded on the Island for four days while parts were flown in, Graham looked up his friend Huxley, who was not hard to find: he was the Island's Attorney General. Huxley suggested that

Graham stay on, but with responsibilities to attend to in the UK, he and his family flew back there.

But the Grahams liked what they had seen, and returned to winter in Bermuda in October 1948 with their children, a nanny and a dog. They rented a house nearly next door to Kenneth Trimingham, the elegant and well-liked doyen of retailers Trimingham Brothers, and his wife Dorothy, who was known as Dot. Huxley again urged Graham to stay in Bermuda, but Graham pointed out that he would need work if he were to be able to live on the Island. At about the same time, by coincidence, the Senior Partner of a London law firm, Botterell & Roche (now Norton, Rose, Botterell & Roche), in Bermuda on business, introduced Graham to Pearman.

Pearman and Dill had both taken the title of Senior Partner on the death of Conyers. Less than a year later, while both attended to the needs of their legal practice, they were shouldering considerable responsibility in the public arena. In 1948, Pearman was a member of the Airport Board, the Board of Civil Aviation and the Panel of Assessors of Air Accidents, continuing the developing theme of aviation in both his professional life and the firm's. He was also Chairman of the Board of Works.

Pearman was in the process of becoming a first-class businessman. He knew his own mind and had a stubborn streak. As an attorney, he could be fierce and was mastering a scowl which he would make all his own and use whenever it suited him, along with a noted poker face. He took nothing for granted, and participated actively in running many of the businesses which his family had developed. The problem Pearman faced, as did everyone else in Bermuda in the late 1940s, was that there was not much business to manage.

Graham asked Pearman if there might be a job for him at the firm. As an escape from London, Bermuda must have seemed very attractive to a man who fitted in socially and who, not long before, had been scouting out a place to live in the Caribbean. Pearman and Dill took a while to think about it, and then turned Graham down, by post. Graham kept Pearman's letter for almost 40 years. In 1996, referring to it as "very dear to me", Graham asked the partners if they would frame it and place it by his portrait at the firm as a reminder to history.

On paper still headed with all three founders' names ("Telephone 1264") and the simple address "Bermuda Fire and Marine Insurance Building, Hamilton, Bermuda", Pearman wrote on 26 March 1949:

> Dear Graham:
>
> Dill and I have talked over the possibility of our being able to work out something to the mutual advantage of you and ourselves, but we have come to the conclusion that the volume of the work hardly justifies it.
>
> I am sorry that I have been so dilatory in writing you, and I am also sorry that we cannot achieve a more favourable conclusion for you.
>
> If there is anything I can do for you at any time do not hesitate to ask me.
>
> Yours sincerely,

The letter was "totally correct at the date", Graham recalled almost half a century later. "Bermuda was a threepenny-bit size of a totally unimportant Island, except for the US Bases. There was really not work even for two lawyers. Jim played bridge and Bayard played politics, and at midday the Bar at the Yacht Club was six deep. Afternoon work was not necessary."

Graham considered his options, and he and Glorita opted for South America. Their passage was booked, but Graham had reckoned without the kindness and acuity of his temporary next door neighbour. Kenneth Trimingham had "reintroduced" the possibility of Graham's employment to both Conyers Dill & Pearman and to another firm, the recently-consolidated Appleby, Spurling & Kempe.

In April, as the Grahams were getting ready to leave Bermuda, Pearman offered Graham a year's trial "at a modest salary". What changed Pearman's mind is not known, but Trimingham would surely have stressed Graham's connections, and the probability that so restless a man would not be able to sit idly by and watch the wheels go round.

It surprises almost everyone to hear that the Bermuda Immigration Board turned Graham down the first time around. Bermuda apparently controlled its immigration policy 50 years ago as tightly as it does today. Immigration decisions are not made public, so we shall never know on what grounds the decision to deny Graham permission to work in Bermuda was made, but many an expatriate worker has had his dreams of Bermuda shot down by an unexpectedly unfavourable Immigration decision, only to reapply, often with further documentation, and to be allowed to join the work force without a hitch, as did Graham.

And so, in the autumn of 1949, at the second time of asking, Graham became the first expatriate employee of Conyers Dill & Pearman.

The firm he joined was as small as it had been at any time in its existence. The volume of work was less than impressive. One Mrs. Mitchell was responsible for the book-keeping. Pearman's secretary looked after the administration of whatever legal or criminal work there might have been, while Dill's secretary assisted in the process of conveyancing documents, a far cry from the days 20 years earlier when the prospect of an avalanche of such work had prompted Conyers to cast an eye around for junior partners.

The firm had a total of eight international clients in 1949. Under the circumstances, it is hard to see how Dill and Pearman were making much of a living, yet when Graham came on board, a secretary was taken on for him. Perhaps the Senior Partners were expecting a miracle—which, it could be argued, is exactly what transpired.

In 1950, Conyers Dill & Pearman formed ten new companies, recalls Joan Hebberd, who joined the firm in that year as Dill's secretary and worked for the partnership in that capacity and others for 42 years. Her memory of the firm at the time she joined is permeated by a strong sense of family. Later, a small annual Christmas party was held around the boardroom table. The firm closed at noon to accommodate the event.

Bermuda, becalmed as the 1950s opened, was still a quiet, relaxed environment in which people might anticipate better times to come. Those from remote communities, particularly islanders, carry within them a survival gene adapted to their needs. When times are good, Bermudians live high off the hog, with the finest clothes, regular vacations to exotic and expensive destinations, boats and every amenity. But when the winds blow cold, adjustments are made, plans deferred and the hatches battened down to wait out the worst.

One afternoon early in the 1950s, probably in 1951, an American businessman walked in to the firm's office unannounced, in search of advice. Dill and Pearman were both out of the office, but Graham, who punctiliously stayed until the close of business, was on hand to assist the visitor with his enquiries. Graham sketched for him a broad outline of how a Bermuda exempted company might be used to manage international business affairs. The caller headed back to Boston, leaving Graham with a series of questions and an instruction to telephone Boston when he had the answers.

Graham quickly scouted out the information and then had to ask Dill and Pearman if they would allow him to make a telephone call to Boston on the firm's account. It was duly noted that Graham had permission to telephone the United States. The call lasted only a minute. The potential client was encouraged by what he heard and at once instructed Graham to meet him, his brother and their advisers in New York.

This was a harder pill for Dill and Pearman to swallow, but they finally agreed. Graham went to New York and landed his first client. In the three or four years which followed, he added a small number of other wealthy American clients to his list. He and Pearman broadened the firm's client base a little further with the addition of a handful of substantial individual clients, mostly Europeans looking for shelter against political instabilities as the Cold War started.

Nevertheless, well into its fourth decade, Conyers Dill & Pearman remained a small firm, providing its services to a small market. Graham's pursuit of overseas business promised, at best, to provide a particular solution for a particular client, but there was little on the horizon at the start of the 1950s to suggest that any business other than tourism would ever really take off in Bermuda.

PLATES I

i. The Bermuda Islands

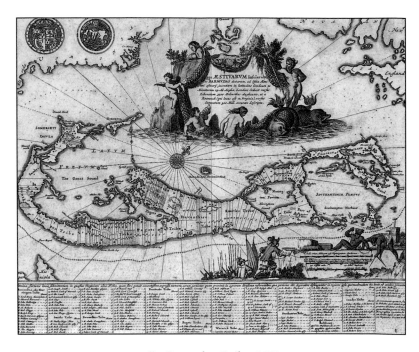

ii.   Bermudas, Ogilvy, 1670

iii.   St. George's

iv.   Bermuda scene, Hallewell, 1848

v.   A slow ride home on coral roads, 1930

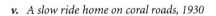

vi.   *Outpost of Empire, 1926*

vii.   *Fishing for bait*

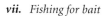

viii. Easter lilies and cedar trees

ix. Heyl's Corner, circa 1920

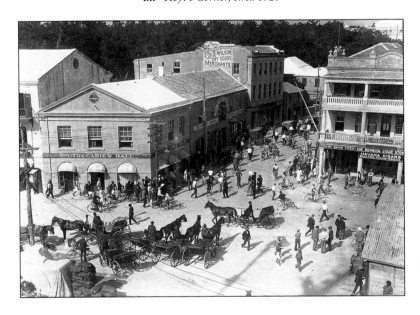

x. *Opening of the railway line over Somerset Bridge, 1931*

xi. *Rattle and Shake, 1941*

xii. *Sir Reginald Conyers*

xiii. *James Pearman fils (second from left); Richard Pearman (third from left), circa 1937*

xiv. *Colonel Thomas Melville Dill, 1934*

xv. *Nicholas Bayard Dill, 1927*

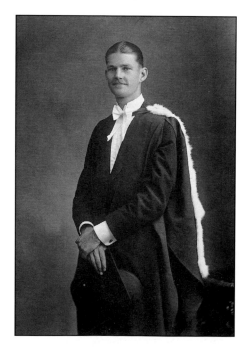

xvi. *James Eugene Pearman, circa 1925*

xvii. *From left: Bayard Dill, Prudence Pearman, James Pearman*
and Clare Watlington, 1929

xviii. *The Royal Bermuda Yacht Club steps, circa 1930. James Pearman (standing front row, left), Bayard Dill (second row, centre)*

xix. *The Executive Council, 1955. James Pearman (left)*

xx. *James Pearman becomes a Commander of
the British Empire, 1960*

xxi. *Sir James and Lady Pearman
at Buckingham Palace, 1973*

xxii. *The 350th anniversary of Bermuda's Colonisation, 1959.*
Sir Bayard Dill (left)

xxiii. *Government House, 1953. Bayard*
and Clare Dill (right)

xxiv. *Development of the United States Naval Air Base*
at St. David's, circa 1942

xxv. *From left: Joseph Laniel, Dwight D. Eisenhower*
and Winston Churchill, 1953

xxvi. *David Graham*

xxvii. *Golden Anniversary of Conyers Dill & Pearman, 1978. From left:
David Graham, Sir Bayard Dill and Sir James Pearman*

xxviii.   *From left: Nicky Dill, Sir Bayard Dill and Nicholas Bayard Botolf Dill*

xxix.   *From left: Richard Pearman and James Pearman, père et fils, 1959*

xxx. *Charles T.M. Collis*

xxxi. *Ronald Reagan (left) and Richard Pearman, 1982*

xxxii. *Harry Chester Butterfield*

xxxiii. *Walter Maddocks*

xxxiv. Michael Woods

xxxv. Alan Brown (left)

xxxvi. *The Conyers Dill & Pearman Classic, 1997*

xxxvii. *Elliott Hubbard*

xxxviii.   *The original Bank of Bermuda Building, Albuoy's Point, Hamilton*

xxxix.   *Clarendon House, 2 Church Street, Hamilton, 1998*

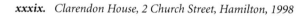

CHAPTER TWELVE

Rise, Sir Bayard

In the first half of the 1950s, the story of Conyers Dill & Pearman, and to a certain extent that of Bermuda, was dominated by Dill's political activities. In four short years from 1951 to 1955, he filled the grandest offices in Bermuda, mingled with the key players on the world stage and won the highest awards. He became during this period the senior Bermudian member of the Executive Council, a role broadly akin to that of today's Premier.

In 1950, the British Government was considering closing its garrison on the Island. Most Bermudians disapproved of the potential loss of the British forces. Governor Sir Alexander Hood's Executive Council persuaded him to allow the Bermudians to take their case for maintaining the *status quo* to the British Government. Dill was nominated to lead the delegation to travel to London. His first act after selecting his team was to cable the United Kingdom to seek the legal advice of Sir Walter Monckton, who had been of service to the British Government during the abdication of King Edward VIII.

At a series of meetings at various branches of the Admiralty, it was explained to the delegation that the final decision rested with the British Cabinet. And so the day came when Dill, Jack Tucker, Ernest Vesey and Hal Butterfield were ushered in to meet Prime Minister Clement Attlee, who was flanked by some 18 advisers. Attlee listened carefully and assured the Bermudians that the position would be looked into most carefully, which some of the civil servants present took to mean a yes, but it was not to be. The British Armed Forces' presence was soon thereafter transferred to British Guiana, where the Bermuda railway had resumed operations.

On New Year's Day 1951, Dill was appointed a Commander of the British Empire. Captain the Hon. Nicholas Bayard Dill, C.B.E., as he was now styled, declared himself "very pleased" and told *The Royal Gazette* his whole family was also delighted. "I believe it has been conferred upon me because of my work in connection with the St. David's Island Committee," he said.

A month later, on 4 Feb 1951, at the annual Assize service held in the Cathedral, Dill was installed as Chancellor of the Diocese of Bermuda by the right Rev. J. A. Jagoe, Bishop of Bermuda. The Chancellor is the senior legal adviser to the Church of England in Bermuda. Dill was following in his father's footsteps. Colonel Tom Dill, when Attorney General, had advised on church matters. Because Bermuda is a small jurisdiction, the Chancellor frequently advises the Synod of the Anglican Church in Bermuda, comprised of elders and Ministers, on matters of importance. He advises the Church Vestries throughout the Island and prepares the oaths for the institution of Ministers, which he attends.

The Royal Gazette reported on the occasion:

Dressed in their official robes and wigs, the Law officers and members of the Bar entered the Cathedral through a Police guard of honour under the command of Superintendent Percy Miller to the installation of Captain Dill, who as a member of the Bar was robed and wigged.

De facto leader of the government and now senior legal adviser to the Church; everyone who knew Dill recalls first his honesty. He was a man in whom, a good friend of his recalled, "you could place your trust completely, whoever you might be".

Among the Dill family archives is a burgundy photo album which serves as a scrapbook of Dill's public life in the period, painstakingly assembled over the years by his wife, Clare. Along with newspaper clippings are personal letters of congratulations from friends, notes of thanks from various organisations and official invitations and passes.

Surrounded by the formal communications, a newspaper clipping from the middle of 1953 throws an amusing light. Dill was one of a number of local notables interviewed for a feature article in *The Royal Gazette Weekly*. Beneath a banner headline, "More Best-Dressed Men Give Views on Clothes", is a rare photo of Dill by the water in his Bermuda business formals: Bermuda shorts and socks, a jacket and the ubiquitous bow tie. The caption reads: "Wife Buys Them". The article, in its entirety, reads:

> Captain Dill takes no credit for his wardrobe. "My wife buys most of my clothes," he said.

More important matters were unfolding at the time the article appeared. Dill wrote that he would "always be grateful, pleased and proud to have been a member" of the Executive Council when British Prime Minister Winston Churchill proposed to hold a tripartite Conference, known in these more utilitarian times as a summit meeting, in Bermuda. Churchill proposed to meet with General Dwight Eisenhower, the 34th President of the United States, and Joseph Laniel, President of France.

In the wake of a World War, summit meetings retained a very real sense of importance, with far-reaching agreements achieved between individual leaders. Today, such meetings are the stuff of the all-news channels and focus the attention of the world on the location where they are held. In 1953, the Conference would have been major international news at a distance, with television in its infancy. The weight of officialdom the Bermuda Conference must have piled on the Island's then-modest civil service would have been fantastic.

Not long before the Conference was due to start, another event took place which captured the world's attention. A few pages from the Dill scrapbook tell the story of a remarkable fortnight in world history from a Bermudian perspective. The first entry is an engraved invitation, eight inches by six, on stiff white card. It reads:

> To have the honour of meeting Her Majesty The Queen and His Royal Highness The Duke of Edinburgh, His Excellency The Governor and Lady Hood request the pleasure of the company of Capt. The Hon. Bayard and Mrs. Dill at a Garden Party at Government House on Tuesday, 24th November 1953, at 4:00 p.m.

The young Royal couple had decided to make Bermuda the first destination on a world honeymoon, which had been delayed until after Elizabeth's coronation on 2 June 1953. A short stay in Bermuda was planned to enable the Queen and Prince Philip to see a little of the Island and meet some of its people. Pearman's invitation to the Garden Party was also among his effects.

On the following page of Dill's scrapbook is glued a photograph of Hal and Florence (Polly) Butterfield and the Dills, culled from a local newspaper, under the banner headline: "They Dined With the Queen at Government House". Beneath it is a draft in Dill's hand of a proposed valedictory note from Hood to the Queen:

> Your Majesty's most Ancient Colony presents its humble due
> to Her Majesty and wishes God's Speed, a happy journey and a safe
> return.

Bermuda has been Britain's oldest Colony since Virginia ceased to
pledge its allegiance to the British flag.

On the right-hand page of the album, folded, is a note addressed
to H.E. The Governor, Government House, Bermuda, in a woman's hand.
It was probably written at the same address. The note reads:

> Please convey to the Government and people of Bermuda my
> warmest thanks for the wonderful reception which they have
> accorded to my husband and myself and which we shall long
> remember. Our only regret is that on this occasion our visit to the
> Island has not been a longer one.

The note is signed Elizabeth R. Governor Hood, in his infinite wisdom, passed it on to Dill in his capacity as the chief representative of the
people of Bermuda.

The very next page of the scrapbook contains four official invita-
tions which, by some magic of the papermaker's art, neatly fill the page.
First, His Excellency the Governor requested the presence of Captain and
Mrs. N. B. Dill at the Civil Air Terminal at 12 noon on 2 December 1953
to have the honour of being presented to the Prime Minister of the United
Kingdom. The next day, at three o'clock in the afternoon, also at the
Airport, the Dills were to be presented to the arriving President of France.
The following day, at 12:15 p.m., the Dills were summoned to meet the
President of the United States of America on his arrival in Bermuda. The

afternoon that Eisenhower arrived, Dill wrote, "the three repaired to the Mid-Ocean Club to consider what arrangements could be made to preserve the peace of the world."

The final invitation in the scrapbook is to dinner at Government House to meet the members of the Bermuda Conference. In his speech that evening, Eisenhower referred to "the tranquillity, the hospitality and the surroundings" of Bermuda as conducive to making possible good decisions for the future. Churchill, in his turn, stood up and "growled away at Eisenhower," in Dill's words. Churchill mentioned that "for 300 or 400 years, Great Britain had been the power, epitomised by the lion, and that the future was in safe hands now that the United States was to take over the lion's job."

On 6 December 1954, Pearman joined his colleague Dill on the Executive Council. Pearman's appointment underlines the eminent levels to which the two school pals had risen in the three decades since they had returned to Bermuda. Both were at the very top of their game and represented the epitome of power in the Colony. The combination of Dill & Pearman had proven to be a formidable alliance, even if at this time their law practice could not be described as a powerhouse.

Less than a month later, Dill received just reward for his services. At the age of 49, on 1 January 1955, Dill became the second of the firm's partners to be knighted. Having visited the exterior of Buckingham Palace, but not its interior, he and his wife and sons Nicky and David opted to travel to London for the investiture.

Dill wrote that he knelt before Queen Elizabeth, "and when the Queen had put the sword on one shoulder and then switched it to the other, she held out her hand and said: 'Rise, Sir Bayard. Do you still live in Bermuda?' I said: 'Yes, Your Majesty, it is my home, I was born there.'" Dill mentioned how much Bermuda had enjoyed the Royal couple's visit. For her part, Her Majesty replied that another visit soon would be unlikely—

20 years would in fact pass before she returned—and closed with "Once again, Sir Bayard, congratulations".

Her Majesty the Queen was therefore the first to call Sir Bayard by the name everyone else used thereafter.

CHAPTER THIRTEEN

No Taxation At All

The firm's premises in the main part of the old Bank of Bermuda building had a languid feel. The offices of Conyers Dill & Pearman were approached by a single set of stairs which overlooked the room in which the bank processed all of its payments. A window opened from the stairs into the banking room, through which the firm's accounting staff would, in the early days, conveniently drop envelopes containing payment instructions. That the bank's manual payments function could fit into a room—today's highly-automated equivalent would fill a whole building—confirms the generally tiny size of Bermuda's international economy in the mid-1950s.

At the top of the stairs, one arrived first in a small, featureless waiting room. Beyond it, separated by Western saloon-style swinging doors known colloquially as 'batwings', lay the legal practice. The whole had a "really, really old-fashioned Caribbean" sense to it, Graham recalls. Bermuda must have been a paradise indeed in the 1950s for those with the means to enjoy it. The qualities which continue to mark the Island today, its undeniable beauty, the general air of friendliness and a community-based way of life, must have been more powerfully in evidence without the hurly-burly and urgency demanded by modern life.

Sir Bayard represented the last of a breed of gentlemen which our world knows less and less. He was a gentleman and a gentle man. Pearman, a year his senior, was also representative of that breed, but with his innate understanding of business and the relish with which he set about creating a larger and larger firm, Pearman acted as a link to a newer breed of legal executives who work in their shirtsleeves. Graham was a breed all his own.

Late in 1955, there occurred a watershed event, the *exegesis kata ton diakonta* of Greek story construction. In Sir Arthur Conan Doyle's Sherlock Holmes stories, the message device which lets the story take shape and introduces the plot occurs almost invariably in the guise of the printed word: an invitation or other document. It was often delivered through newspaper columns. No less so was this true in the real-life story of Conyers Dill & Pearman.

Once again, transportation lay at the heart of the matter; shipping this time. In November 1955, *The Times* of London printed a letter complaining about the shabby treatment being doled out to British shipping in the oil tanker field, compared to the experience of American and Greek shipowners, who used Panamanian and Liberian flags of convenience. The author of the letter was named Graham; not the man employed by Conyers Dill & Pearman, but an entirely unrelated W.M. Graham, a director of a large English shipping company.

Sitting in his office in Bermuda, with the time to read a week-old newspaper, Graham idly decided to respond to the letter. He had no great ambition for his reply, other than to point out errors in his namesake's logic. But everything that Bermuda's international business industry has become dates back to the day when *The Times* published Graham's pregnant response. Not all miracles, it seems, are announced by lightning and thunder. This one began with enlightenment in 'the Thunderer'.

Graham's closely-argued reply must have taken some time to compose, an afternoon's work perhaps, with a final polish on the following morning. Mailed from Bermuda, Graham's response was published in *The Times* in December 1955.

The Letters to the Editor column of *The Times* was in those days a forum for the intellectual pursuit of ideas and nostalgia about the Empire. Graham's thoughts were published beneath a complicated note about negotiating the end of the Indo-Chinese War with Ho Chi Minh and to the right of a letter excoriating Soviet leader Nikita Kruschev for vituperation.

Headlined "Foreign Registration of Ships", Graham's letter ran:

Sir—The recent letters of Mr. W.M. Graham and Mr. G.R. Wright make clear beyond doubt the fact that certain business of an international nature cannot be carried on competitively from a place of business in a highly taxed area.

In no business is this more apparent than in shipping, although the full force of competition from shipping companies operating from Liberia and Panama has not yet been felt. It must be realized that currency exchange control regulations in force at the present time appear to have prevented Liberian and Panamanian companies from entering actively into the Sterling freight market, and when these regulations are removed the position of the British shipowner operating from the United Kingdom will be considerably more adverse than now.

With all due respect I must, however, express the opinion that the attitude adopted by your two correspondents appears to me to be a trifle parochial in that British shipping and United Kingdom shipping appear to be taken as synonymous.

The Imperial Merchant Shipping Act has far wider application:

British ships are not necessarily United Kingdom owned ships and British shipowners are not necessarily United Kingdom companies subject to the penal taxation to which your correspondents refer.

So far as I am aware, no other part of the Commonwealth subjects British shipowners to as high taxation as does the United Kingdom, and certain parts of the Commonwealth, including this island of Bermuda, subject British shipowners to no taxation at all.

It is hardly accurate, therefore, to state that the British Mercantile Marine is not in a position to compete with ships of foreign registry in Central America and Liberia; it is merely true to state that United Kingdom shipowners are not in a position to compete.

The phenomenal rise as a maritime Power of Liberia, where I understand that United States citizens obtained the original charter for the incorporation of companies and the registration of ships, and the currency is United States dollars, is a direct result of the necessity to compete internationally on a tax-free basis.

I would suggest that if the British Mercantile Marine is to survive this competition, the British Mercantile Marine must find the means to conduct its operation in the future from bases more favourable than the United Kingdom. The bulk of the British Mercantile Marine is in the hands of United Kingdom owners; they might well consider the benefits to be derived from ownership and operation elsewhere in the Commonwealth of their new buildings.

The benefits derived by others from operation through Liberian companies and Liberian registered ships can be matched by British subjects operating through, for example, resident Bermuda companies and British ships registered in Bermuda.

The loss to the United Kingdom of this move would consist

merely of the tax on operating companies which is bound in any event to decrease as tax-free competition takes its toll; the profits of a Commonwealth company remitted in the form of dividends to United Kingdom residents would still be taxable in the United Kingdom.

The gain would be a British Mercantile Marine operating from a Commonwealth country under the British flag, able to compete on an equal basis in the world market and continuing to employ British men including Englishmen as now. I suggest that the time has come for this wider approach to be considered in the interests of all concerned.

Yours faithfully,

David Graham

The Chimneys, Paget, Bermuda

His aim was true. *The Times* was known as "the top people's paper". Lawyers are not allowed to advertise their services, but Graham's dry explanation of an esoteric point of law had a far more galvanising effect than any advertisement of comparable size could possibly have achieved. Graham had instinctively selected the one location in which his interpretation of the Law might be brought to the attention of every British shipowner and his professional advisers.

"No taxation at all"—imagine the effect of such a phrase, in the hallowed context of a letter to *The Times*, on a British shipowner enjoying a quiet breakfast. British tax rates on shipping went as high as 48 percent, versus "no taxation at all". Imagine next the warm feeling the shipowner must have experienced when in due course his lawyer confirmed Graham's *bona fides* and the fact that he worked at a respected law firm in the very jurisdiction referred to in the letter.

"Then I was never left in peace again," recalls Graham, a man who would have detested being left in professional peace for a moment and who, in his 80s, remains as active and involved as ever before.

The curtain was about to come down on the First Act of the firm's historical drama and Bermuda's 20th century economy. Side-tracked by War and the austerity which followed, Bermuda's international business industry, so long in the making, was finally beginning a modest boom.

In the business sector, the Bahamas had leap-frogged ahead of Bermuda by this time. Less protective of its banks, the Government of the Bahamas had allowed a number of foreign banks to take up residence. The larger Canadian banks were well-established. Referring their clients to an overseas branch of the bank with which they already had a relationship was the obvious route to take. The Bahamas were less convenient to reach than Bermuda from the north-eastern corner of North America, which probably added to their allure as the cream of the world's wealthiest families looked for ways to protect their family's wealth. The Bahamas' only real competitor was Panama—in practice a paper jurisdiction—and Liberia, whose corporate and shipping registers were controlled from the United States.

What must have amounted to a flood of enquiries followed in the wake of the publication of Graham's letter. His analysis and application of the Law were impeccable, but the general view was that one insurmountable practical barrier existed. If Bermuda were to welcome English shipping, approval for such a move would be needed from the British Government. It was assumed that the Colonial masters would be unlikely to grant the necessary permission for Bermuda to get the business off the ground.

Graham was working at the time with Frank Hayworth-Talbot, a leading English tax lawyer, on the potential move of a wealthy central European family to Bermuda. Hayworth-Talbot pointed out that Treasury approval was necessary before a business could move itself out of British taxation to settle somewhere else, because the move would result in the loss of taxation to the British Government. Hayworth-Talbot could therefore divine no grounds on which the Treasury, not considered the most adventurous of the British Government Departments, might base a request for the approval of the Chancellor of the Exchequer, and ultimately that of the Cabinet of Prime Minister Sir Anthony Eden.

In what followed, a parallel to Graham's rapid flanking manoeuvres in Italy seems unavoidable. Graham proposed to make a series of direct appeals to the British Government, via an introduction by Members of the British Parliament with whom he had an acquaintance. Graham had first to persuade Sir Bayard and Pearman to let him go, which did not take long. With Pearman as his ally, Graham then made his case directly to the Bermuda Government.

The argument Graham proposed to put forward was that Bermuda could not be expected to survive on its tourism business alone. History proves him right; Bermuda's tourism industry peaked and began to decline in the early 1980s. As a Crown Colony, Graham would argue, Bermuda had needed British financial support during and after the War. The chance to enhance its shipping register and develop a secondary means of revenue might reduce the likelihood of the need for British economic assistance in the future.

Aware of Hayworth-Talbot's pessimistic view, and expecting him to achieve little more than a polite welcome and an unequivocal rebuff, the Bermuda Government took the view that the mission was a wild goose chase which could do no harm. It duly sanctioned Pearman to send Graham to London for exploratory talks.

Today, reports on Bermuda's international business sector are routinely delivered in billions of dollars, with nine noughts excluded. Comparative figures from the time Graham flew to London, reported on a similar scale, would be too small to measure; they would show up as zero.

CHAPTER FOURTEEN

Fleet Movements

In short, Graham carried the day.

His plan called for meetings with representatives of interested parties, to sound out their views. In London, he met first with the Ship Owners' Association, and then with the Shipping Council, the Ships Officers' Association and, later, with representatives of the Union of Seamen. Although manning concerns were mentioned, no one turned Graham down, which encouraged him. He then applied to take Bermuda's case, in the company of a friend who was a Member of Parliament, to the Secretary to the Treasurer of the Dominion and Colonial Office.

The request for the meeting produced one immediate result: Raymond Arthur, the British Colonial Secretary, enquired of the Bermuda Government exactly what Graham's credentials might be and, crucially, in what capacity he was acting. Pearman and Sir Bayard were once again able to lend a hand to the endeavour.

It could not be said that Graham, an expatriate employee on a work permit who did not acquire Bermuda status until its introduction in the summer of 1956, represented the Bermuda Government. He most certainly lacked the capacity to bind the people of Bermuda, but Government would be keenly interested in any ground Graham might be able to gain. A telegram was therefore concocted to the effect that Graham's views "represented the views of the Bermuda Government", making him an unofficial ambassador extraordinary. This placed Graham—and Bermuda—in an ideal situation: he had *carte blanche* to pursue his scheme, but any agreements would have to be ratified by the Bermuda Government.

The Cabinet Building on Front Street has few corridors of power. Built in 1838, it has for some time been the most private of structures. The building houses the office of the Premier of Bermuda. The Senate and Cabinet meet there, as did the Executive Council which granted Graham the authority and the leeway he needed to pull together a deal.

Tucker, an early disciple of internationalism, was an avid supporter of the scheme. The benefits for Bermuda, should Graham pull off any sort of coup, might amount to some work and a flow of foreign exchange. At the very least, it would provide economic activity. But it must be said that the greatest factor Graham had on his side was the perception that few, besides Pearman and Tucker, and possibly not even they, thought Graham stood much of a chance of achieving anything at all. Although Britain's power was not what it had once been, Bermuda was still little more than a tiny dot on the map; why would the Treasury willingly forgo taxation revenue and control of a portion of its shipping registry to one of its tinier Colonies?

The Bermuda Government's telegram did the trick. The result of Graham's meeting was another meeting between the British Government and Pat Fitzpatrick, head of Bermuda's Currency Exchange Control Board, in London. Fitzpatrick was accompanied to the meeting by Graham and William Kempe, a founder of Appleby, Spurling & Kempe, who played a key part in the development of his firm's international practice.

Graham argued that the loss of taxation would be minimal because company dividends would be taxable on their repatriation to the UK and that crucial benefits would accrue from the diversification of the Bermudian economy. Leaning heavily on Graham's arguments, the Bermuda deputation somehow achieved the impossible. The Treasury balked at losing the business it already had, so a compromise was reached by which Treasury approval would not be needed if a British company were entering into new business from, rather than transferring existing business to, Bermuda. The importance of that British compromise continues to resound more than four decades later.

The future of the shipping trade, it was widely believed, lay in tankers. Ownership of large commercial vessels is usually vested in individual subsidiary companies; profits are easily fed up the corporate chain, while losses and mortgage liabilities relating to a particular vessel can be segregated from potentially damaging the healthy remainder of the business. The companies which would be formed to own the tankers would undeniably constitute new business. Perhaps the British Government underestimated the coming dominance of tankers. Perhaps Graham, fired up by his mission, was enormously persuasive.

As the Suez crisis was shaking British interests in one corner of the British Empire, a new industry was being seeded in another. Soon after Treasury approval was granted to Bermuda, the P & O line, Britain's largest, arranged for its tanker fleet to be registered in Bermuda. Other British shipowners quickly followed suit. Bermuda's establishment of a brand-new business based on British shipping was demonstrably complete almost as soon as it started.

Instant credibility was achieved. A "high-level" letter was sent by Britain's august Midland Bank on 28 March 1957, to Tucker at The Bank of Bermuda. It read, in part: "I can well understand that the increasing incentive which Bermuda offers to United Kingdom shipping companies may ... lead to (banking) enquiries being made of you." The letter concludes: "We should be able to work out satisfactory arrangements for all concerned."

Six weeks later, British Chancellor of the Exchequer Peter Thorneycroft, in his annual Budget Statement to the House of Commons, announced that he would double taxation allowances for the capital construction of new ships from 20 to 40 percent. The higher the allowance, the more quickly the owner of an asset can depreciate the capital value of his investment. This has the effect of decreasing the amount of tax payable in the early years of ownership of a new asset. It affords owners a little breathing space at a time when interest payments and the stress of running a new venture are at their highest.

Graham landed an equally important American shipping client a few weeks later. A personal memory of Graham's illustrates the regard in which he was held by the international shipping community at the height of the storm of interest he had created. Due to ferry his daughter back to school in America, he agreed to visit the President of one of the very largest US shipping lines during the trip.

When Graham's plane landed in New York, before the passengers could disembark, a number of policemen came aboard, looking for a "Mr. Graham". His client was possessed of sufficient clout to have him transferred from the plane to an "enormous Cadillac waiting outside the door". This was, however, the only occasion on which Graham recalls having received such treatment.

In a very short space of time, Graham was received by, and Conyers Dill & Pearman retained by, a number of leading shipowners. One American tycoon, whose name is now a household word in Bermudian corporate circles, told Graham he wanted to transfer his substantial fleet in its entirety to Bermuda and its British register. That sent Graham back to London for further consultation with the Government, shipowners and unions. He secured for this effort the services of a merchant bank in London, Samuel Montagu. The tanker fleet for whose listing Graham sought approval was one of the largest in the world. If it were approved, there was no doubt that more would follow. Concerns were immediately raised whether the British Merchant Marine could muster sufficient Engineers to meet the mandatory senior officer manning requirements of the Bermuda register. Any vessel which wanted to fly the Red Ensign had to have a British Captain, First Engineer, Radio Officer and Mate.

The British Government had come to understand that Graham's proposal served to extend, rather than curtail, British interests. Allowing the UK fleet to migrate to the Bermuda flag kept the vessels on an ultimately British register, with the Bermuda company providing tax relief. The idea of Bermuda adding elements of the fleets of other nations to the British Merchant Marine extended Britain's interests even further, so the British Government fully supported Graham's latest request. It was the shipowners and the unions who raised objections. The owners raised concerns about the number of new Engineers who would be required to man the fleet Graham's client proposed to add to the register. The unions expressed their concern that non-British officers might be used to meet the anticipated shortfall.

In the end, the American magnate could not transfer his fleet to the Bermuda register. However, the professional relationship Graham established with him lasted for years afterward. At one point, Graham persuaded him to purchase one of the largest companies in the Bermudian hospitality industry as part of an international expansion; the company subsequently consolidated its position as a leader in the local tourism market and the entrepreneur took British citizenship. The size of the Bermuda shipping register may have waxed and waned in the intervening 40 years, but many of the clients Graham landed in an intense few months in 1956 remain with Bermuda and Conyers Dill & Pearman to this day.

The network Graham brought to the cause comprised those with whom he had been at school or at Oxford, and others they knew and recommended. London Chartered Accountants Rawlinson & Hunter were his largest source of personal clients and his friend, the banker Felix Chilvers, was another good source. On the shipping side, Conyers Dill & Pearman worked frequently with the London shipping law firm of Botterell & Roche, initially a contact of Graham's. Accountants Moore Stephens were another key contact; Senior Partner Hobart Moore, who played an important part in directing business to Bermuda, opened an office on the Island as a result.

The bulk of this hectic activity fell into the first nine months of 1956. The Bermudian shipping registry quickly became one of the largest in the world and the practices of Conyers Dill & Pearman and Appleby, Spurling & Kempe, today Bermuda's two largest and most influential practices, were expanded in rapid order. Graham, Kempe and the others were building a franchise which has served Bermuda well over the intervening years. To the Senior Partners of Conyers Dill & Pearman fell the task of pursuing their own political and business careers while dealing with the dramatic fall-out from Graham's hyperkinetic activities.

Now Conyers Dill & Pearman underwent its first great growth phase. In 1956, the firm added staff rapidly to manage the corporate and legal work of the shipping companies which were flocking to Bermuda. Once again, transportation had played a central part in the drama. Founded as a result of the need for a railway, the firm was now compounded to four times its size in the space of a year by the consequences of another shift in transportation, this time global in nature.

CHAPTER FIFTEEN

Westward Ho!

Pearman and Sir Bayard had initially been sceptical of Graham's idea of developing the practice outside Bermuda, but by the end of 1956, they were completely convinced. It was obvious from the level of interest that Graham had engendered that Bermuda was the beneficiary of a sudden and unexpected golden opportunity.

It was also evident that the old ways of the gentleman lawyer were under threat. Few professional people in Bermuda went looking for work, but this sedate way of life was being threatened by a more aggressive search for imaginative solutions, often suitable only on a one-off basis. Further, among an older generation of easy-going legal practitioners, tax work was not considered genteel. Sir Bayard and Pearman, in middle age, were old enough to have lived in a more gentlemanly era, but young enough to be able to change with the times.

Over the years, as Bermuda's international business sector has gathered pace and direction, a consensus has emerged that Graham should receive the credit for starting the whole ball rolling. Phillips sounded no better than almost persuaded in his bank history, when he wrote: " ... through his association with (Conyers Dill & Pearman) and contacts in the City of London, a strong case could be made that Graham was instrumental in initiating the concept of international business in Bermuda."

Really, the case is open and shut.

By the time of the publication of the letter in *The Times*, Bermuda had only established itself in a small way in the personal trust business. World War II had all but dried up the introduction of companies and trusts into the mix. Both Tucker and Pearman, fiercely convinced of the advantages to Bermuda of a more broadly-based international clientele, travelled frequently to New York, Toronto, Montreal, London and other European capitals. "Both men are widely regarded as the founding fathers of Bermuda's international business," wrote Phillips.

Later, when Bermuda had established its international business sector, however rudimentary it may seem by today's standards, others trumpeted the idea of adding insurance to the armoury. *Then* Graham was instrumental, helping a team of committed Bermudians to provide the second-stage boost the nascent industry needed. But at the outset, his interpretation of international shipping law was the one missing element in a stew which had been 20 years in the making.

By taking the idea that Bermuda might be a good location for the provision of financial services and running with it, Graham and the others made it possible for three generations of Bermudians, thus far, to enjoy a standard of living which consistently ranks at the top of the world tables. Bermuda, it should be recalled, is without significant material resources other than the wits of its people and its beauty—and, now, a Gross Domestic Product well in excess of two billion dollars.

Graham's achievement was central and critical. It was carried out first and foremost in the interests of others. He saw what few others saw: an opportunity for Bermuda to be of service to the world's wealthiest community. Graham extended the idea of service to the moneyed, which had been the mainstay of the Island's tourism industry, by offering, in essence, to service their financial affairs. He turned a "threepenny-bit island" into something of considerably greater value.

Of course, to assign the credit solely to Graham would be wrong. The concept had its roots in the thinking others had done a generation earlier. Making a reality of the idea needed the active and continued endorsement, involvement and support of Tucker. It needed the dedication of Kempe, and it needed Pearman's organisational mind. It needed the informed but tacit support of Governor Hood and his successors, the Bermuda Government and, finally the approval of the British Government.

Above all, it needed, and still needs, a Team Effort. There is Bermuda's secret ingredient, laid bare for all the world to see. What has made and kept the Island pre-eminent in international business is not just its British law, not its tax neutrality, nor even the picture-perfect *mise en scène*, the oleanders, beaches and golf courses. In the areas of law, tax freedom, climate and even topography, something similar can be claimed in a dozen other jurisdictions.

What Bermuda mastered effortlessly from the very earliest stages of the development of its new international business activity was the notion of *esprit de corps*. At the heart of all that has followed lies a shared understanding between the Government and the private sector. Each pursues its own agenda, largely without interference from the other, but both fully appreciate that they are the goose and gander of cliché.

Later, when it needed a name, the team was dubbed 'Bermuda Inc.', but in the mid-1950s little public mention would have been made of the merits of pulling together. What transpired was in the interests of the professional class and the politicians who spawned it, but to dismiss Bermuda's achievement as merely a lawyers' or politicians' affair would be to grossly understate the reality. Turning Bermuda into the world's premier international business centre was of major economic importance to all Bermudians. Today's affluent Bermudian lifestyle would not have been maintained by tourism alone.

The success of the private and public sector partnership, to which an educated and friendly English-speaking workforce is essential, has proven hard to emulate because it flies in the face of the antagonistic roles traditionally adopted by government and governed. Bermuda is seen by its clients, particularly those who maintain a physical presence on the Island, as an exclusive corporate club, to which only the very best may belong, a further extension of the Island's traditional top-end market profile. The insurance industry was asked a few years ago to advise on the reclassification of Bermuda insurers to strengthen the jurisdiction's appeal; the industry proposed tougher regulations than Government had anticipated. It cannot be said that the private sector meekly submits to Government's every whim; increases in Payroll Taxes in the mid-1990s sent a shudder down the spine of international business, and a temporary frost in the relationship with Government ensued. Even now, representatives of the Island's international business community regularly warn that Bermuda runs the risk of pricing itself out of the market, as did the Bahamas and, to a lesser, extent, Switzerland.

But if relations between the two estates are occasionally tense, disagreement is over detail rather than grand design. Everyone agrees that while regulation is necessary and desirable, carefully-managed development of the economy is equally necessary and desirable. A graph of the growth in companies and partnerships registered in Bermuda starting pre-Graham and proceeding to today would reveal a gently increasing curve moving relentlessly upwards, despite increases in the Island's level of regulation and monitoring. No wonder few outside Bermuda can fully grasp how it works.

Starting late in 1956, Graham, Tucker, Pearman and others took their message to the world, or more specifically, to North America. Typical

of their converts was a substantial Canadian law firm, whose Senior
Partner reports that he and his partners have always regarded Conyers Dill
& Pearman as a sister law firm. Canadian tax law, at the time, contained
provisions designed to encourage foreign investment by reducing or elim-
inating Canadian withholding tax under certain conditions. Section 4(k)
of the tax code permitted companies to retain a head office in Canada
while doing business elsewhere, without paying Canadian tax. The perceived threat from Russia in the 1950s, combined with Canada's relaxed
attitude to the taxation of overseas activities, offered the Canadians a
notable opportunity to attract nervous European capital. The Canadian
service providers needed a jurisdiction in which to place control of operations such that beneficial European owners were protected from political
instability on that continent.

The Senior Partner of the Canadian firm recalls meeting Graham
in "a small cubbyhole" at the firm's office, overlooking the Yacht Club.
Graham discussed at great length with his Canadian colleague the means
to enable European clients to continue to live in their home countries,
with their assets shielded from taxation. The liaison led to the formation
of a number of Bermuda companies and trusts owned by Europeans,
among them at least one world-renowned manufacturer which has maintained administrative offices in Hamilton for more than three decades.

While Sir Bayard looked after local matters, Graham and Pearman
rapidly developed a busy international practice in personal holding companies, shipping and the general commercial work arising from them. Late
in 1956, Sir Bayard, Pearman and Graham agreed that the volume of work
demanded an additional pair of hands. The pair they chose belonged to a
man who would stamp his personality and his surname on every aspect of
the firm's business in the four decades which followed.

CHAPTER SIXTEEN

A Fourth Lawyer

Charles Theodore Miller Collis joined Conyers Dill & Pearman on 15 October 1956. The practice had by then spread out across 2,000 square feet of office space and undergone a sea change since the publication of Graham's letter just eleven months earlier.

In that short period, Sir Bayard, Pearman and Graham had accumulated a dozen support staff, making the incidence of lawyers among the total staff one in five. (In 1998, the ratio is nearer one in six, thanks to economies of scale and a broadening of the scope of the services the firm offers.) Four staff members were dedicated to the maintenance of corporate records and others to conveyancing, a range of domestic legal work and administration. The firm in which, a few years earlier, Graham could discover only eight Minute Books, had 180 corporate clients alongside its local business by the end of 1956.

In the first six years of the 1990s, an average of 525 international companies and other entities were added, net, to the Bermuda register each year. The modern Conyers Dill & Pearman establishes perhaps 40 percent of them in an average year, which means that the firm is now adding more international clients every year than the total number of active clients it had in 1956. The practice is now able to anticipate and plan for its growth, whereas prior to the publication of Graham's letter, there was no reason to expect to add more than a handful of new clients in the year ahead.

The firm was working flat out; new blood was called for. The partners had been keeping track of the progress young Collis had been making for some time, without his being aware of it. Graham had arranged to meet Collis in London on two occasions in the early part of 1956, although the idea of employment was never mentioned.

Bermuda-born Collis was friendly with Pearman's sons, but had no prior involvement with Conyers Dill & Pearman. Nor did he have any specific plans for a career post-qualification. On 10 August 1956, Pearman wrote to Collis on the firm's Air Mail letterhead which listed Sir Bayard, Pearman and Graham, and a new cable address, Codan. In part, Pearman's frank request for help ran:

> My dear Charles:
>
> I saw by *The Times* earlier this summer that you had got through your Bar finals, and I understand from (my son) James that you are working in London to familiarize yourself with company law and practice.
>
> I am writing to inquire whether you would be interested in a job with us.
>
> We are engaged in a very great deal of business for foreign clients which involves a very considerable amount of company work, and are in need of someone to help us out, in addition to assisting in the general practice.
>
> I believe that you would find it an interesting job and one

which has a bright future.

I think that from the point of view of experience in company affairs that you would probably find the experience which you would gain in this office would be of far more value for practice in Bermuda than working in London, as the Bermuda scene has its own special problems and company law.

You, of course, know that James and Nicky Dill are in the process of studying for their Bar examinations and, when finished, would expect to come back here to the office as well. Presumably in due course Dick (Richard Pearman) may do the same thing. However, it would be our expectation that their return would not in any way detract from your continuance, as I think there will be by that time ample work to go around, as there is now too much to do and the business is rapidly increasing.

When I say that we should like you to come at your earliest opportunity, I mean this in its full sense, in that if you could, the 1st September would be none too early.

Would you therefore give this some thought and let me know by airmail at your earliest convenience.

Yours sincerely,

"It was a case of: 'Tomorrow won't be soon enough,' " Collis recalled, "very much the reverse of the situation in which the firm found itself in 1949." Collis declined the invitation; he was down to spend the balance of the summer in further legal education, and could not join Conyers Dill & Pearman before summer's end. *Nemo dat quod non habet*—no one may give what he does not have. That, said Pearman, would have to do.

Charles Collis' father, also named Charles, came from the Poole area of England's South Coast. Born in 1899, he was not old enough to join the British Army when War was declared in 1914, but, like many young-sters was carried away by the spirit of the times. Adding a fictional year or two to his age, he enlisted and was posted to Ireland with the Black and Tans.

Demobilised at the end of the War into a country deep in reces-sion, Collis *père* had not had time to complete his formal education before taking the King's shilling. He opted to enrol himself in a training pro-gramme at the electronics manufacturer, Marconi, which sent him to sea as a wireless operator. His work took him all over the world, finally aboard a trader sailing between Halifax, Bermuda and the Caribbean.

Within a few years, his mind was made up that staying at sea would deny him the settled future, and the wife and family, for which he longed. Having been around the world, he knew that Bermuda was the only place he wanted to live. In 1927, Collis disembarked in Bermuda from his life on the ocean wave to establish a fruit retailing business, initially in two loca-tions. One he sited next to Bluck's, at Albuoy's Point, making the Bermuda Fire and Marine Building his next-door neighbour. The other outlet, in Lane House on East Broadway, was to prove the more durable. In due course, Collis consolidated his business into Lane House. In 1946, he sold the business to pursue wholesaling. He later set up the Outdoor Living Centre.

Collis had met Mary Alfreda Miller, a teacher, in Nova Scotia. They were married in 1931 and a son, Charles, was born on 23 September 1932. Following preparatory school at Mount Saint Agnes, Collis *fils* attended Saltus Grammar School between the ages of eight and 16. He worked in his father's business from time to time as a young man before proceeding to Dalhousie University in Halifax to earn his Bachelor of Commerce. While there he was awarded the prestigious Rhodes Scholarship.

Cecil Rhodes was the British statesman and tycoon who first opened up Rhodesia to European settlement. He founded the DeBeers

Mining Company in 1890 and, nine years later, formed another company to develop the area that is now Zimbabwe. On his death, much of his £6 million fortune went to found the Rhodes Scholarships, instituted at Oxford University for students in the British Commonwealth, the United States and Germany. Scholarships are granted on general grounds as well as on academic ability.

Collis went up to Corpus Christi, Oxford in 1953 to earn a Master of Arts degree in Jurisprudence. Having taken his Bar finals in London, he was called at the Middle Temple. He returned to Bermuda on 14 October 1956 and started work the very next day at Conyers Dill & Pearman, where he would spend the remainder of his working life. He assumed a capacity equivalent to that of today's associate, albeit with a broader remit. Although he had been called in to work on the burgeoning corporate side, he was expected of necessity to handle matters across the full spectrum of the Law in the firm's continuing general practice.

Collis could be said to have been one of very first to be recruited into the legal branch of Bermuda's new international business sector. He remembered his early days at the firm as something of a baptism by fire, with the other three lawyers all away for lengthy periods, beating the Bermudian drum overseas. He learned the corporate side of the practice, which would become his major interest, with his sleeves rolled up. Joan Hebberd recalls picturing him at the time of his arrival as "a young David Graham—keen, very enthusiastic and gung-ho". Graham and Collis were both called to the Bermuda Bar on 9 November 1956.

Bermudians have become sophisticated world travellers, with Government statistics showing that the average Bermudian travels off the Island twice a year. As a result, the assumption is fairly widespread in Bermuda that everyone in the world is aware of the Island and its economic activities. At the top end of the American and European business community, Bermuda has indeed achieved that profile, but beyond the upper echelons of the business community and in continents farther afield, the general public is most aware of Bermuda in the context of the supposed Bermuda Triangle or the short trousers with which it has become synonymous.

In 1956, Bermuda would have been an almost entirely unknown quantity internationally, but it was possessed, even then, of the four ingredients necessary to allow its international business sector to thrive. These were: a government providing political and economic stability; a legislative mechanism which afforded the basis for the formation and control of companies, trusts and partnerships; good communications and local professional services capable of supporting international companies and trusts.

Bermuda had yet to introduce party politics. There was, therefore, no political agenda to consider beyond the population's internal needs. A corporate tax exemption guaranteed to international companies, initially for 20 years, promised investors the opportunity to plan their Bermuda operations for the medium term.

Even in the 1950s, legislation continued to provide that every Bermuda company be incorporated by Act of Parliament. The careful process of vetting undergone by all potential clients was a Bermudian hallmark from the very earliest days and served to satisfy the requirement that Bermuda would be engaged only in legitimate business. The vetting began in the private sector, with the lawyers receiving instructions to incorporate a new Bermuda entity. The process then transferred to the public sector and the Private Bills Committee of Bermuda's Parliament under the guidance of Sir Henry Vesey and, separately, by Fitzpatrick and his staff at the Currency Exchange Control Board.

Thanks to its geographical isolation, Bermuda has always understood the need for first-class telecommunications. In the days of the telex machine, it had one of the highest *per capita* rates of ownership of such machines in the world; telexes were the preferred means of imparting such corporate information as *bordereaux* (memoranda or invoices pre-pared by underwriters, containing lists of insured risks) from offices out-side Bermuda to local company managers.

In 1998, only a small number of telex machines remain in service, particularly for ship-to-shore communication, but the telephone system is as good as any in the world. Telephone access to and from Bermuda has always been efficient, thanks in good part to Cable & Wireless siting a hub of its worldwide network on the Island.

The same did not initially prove to be the case with the Internet. Given the relatively small size of the population and the inordinate cost of providing Internet access to so small a community, the quality of Internet service in Bermuda initially lagged behind that of other countries. Of late, the Bermuda Government has licensed a second provider, with the prospect of greatly improved service.

In the area of the professional services without which no interna-tional business centre could survive, Bermuda has also been well served. Its banks, accounting and legal firms and company managers have always been the equals of their worldwide counterparts.

At the time Collis returned home, therefore, all the elements were in place. Bermuda was well-placed to develop a second leg to its economy by encouraging international business to make a home for itself in a remote mid-Atlantic chain of islands.

CHAPTER SEVENTEEN

An Unprecedented Rummaging

In April 1958, Nicholas Bayard Dill, Sir Bayard's son, joined Conyers Dill & Pearman at the age of 26. To avoid confusion, the firm has always followed family practice by informally referring to him as Nicky. He attended Saltus Grammar School and then the Forman School in Litchfield, Connecticut before proceeding to Trinity Hall, his father's college at Cambridge. Among Nicky's tutors was one J.W.C. Turner, a noted author in criminal law, who had also taught Sir Bayard. The younger Dill, too, qualified in law at the Middle Temple. It was a proud moment when his father called him to the Bar.

It went without saying that Nicky would join the firm. He had spent a number of summers as the firm's office boy, running errands around town and helping out with filing. The title of office boy has fallen out of favour in these politically correct days, although the job, whatever its name, remains the entry position to the world of business for any number of young hopefuls. As a result of his exposure to the firm and the inner workings of Bermuda's legal system, the younger Dill knew people in "the

Supreme Court Registry and all sorts of areas of town".

And so it was that Nicky Dill became a general practitioner of the Law, the equivalent of the friendly medical G.P. to whom we first report our ailments. Bermuda lawyers of the 1950s and 1960s differed from their medical equivalents in one key area: where a G.P. must refer specific problems to a specialist, in law the generalist must become at least an intermediary specialist as and when specific questions arise.

Just as Collis had been two years earlier, Dill was introduced to the full breadth of the firm's practice. Legal aid cases, divorces, property matters and disputes made up the bulk of the ever-changing roster of a young lawyer's work. With a degree of certainty probably not available to his father, Dill would have made the assumption that he would spend the balance of his working life with the firm he joined. He has become an expert on matters of shipping law, particularly with regard to the Protection and Indemnity clubs—universally referred to as P&I clubs—and for many years has driven the firm's practice in that area. At the start of the 1960s, he married Norwegian Bitten Brodtkorb.

The Colony of Bermuda in which the couple set up home was less pressured, less sophisticated, more mannered, and more isolated than the United Kingdom Overseas Territory of Bermuda has become four decades later. In this regard, Dill recalls a story from his days as a young lawyer. Conyers Dill & Pearman had a client for whom it conducted a great deal of litigation. The matter of paying his bills did not exercise his attention as much as did his litigiousness. One day, Dill proposed that the client settle some of his outstanding fees. The client returned a day later and pressed a £5 note into Dill's hand. It transpired that the client had borrowed the sum from Dill's uncle.

On a broader stage, at the time Dill joined the firm, preparations were well in hand for celebrations of the 350th anniversary of Bermuda's discovery by Sir George Somers.

Early in June 1609, a fleet of nine ships, under the flag of the Virginia Company, set sail from England, to carry supplies to the struggling Colony of Virginia. The Sea Venture was the fleet's flagship, with Admiral Sir George Somers in command. On 23 July, near the Azores, a heavy storm scattered the fleet and drove the *Sea Venture,* with 150 aboard, far off-course to the south. For four days, the crew battled to keep the wooden ship afloat as the storm drove it who knew where. On Friday 28 July, Somers spied land, so close that trees could be seen bending in the wind.

The Admiral brought his ship to within a mile of the *terra incognita,* but with the water, even at that distance, at only four fathoms deep, he decided to run inshore as close as possible and then abandon ship. The vessel foundered on the Island's coral reefs, the world's most northerly. By nightfall, William Zuill wrote in his *Bermuda Journey,* every man, woman and child had been safely landed. Bermuda, also known as the Somers Isles, had been settled by Act of God and duly inspired Shakespeare to site *The Tempest* in the "still-vexed Bermoothes".

The sesquitercentenary of the fortuitous landing was celebrated throughout 1959. Bermuda brought the year in with a parade and a ceremony of commemoration, attended by large crowds on Front Street. All year long a variety of events marked the Island's remembrance of its humble beginnings and long history.

Once again, the Dill scrapbook tells the formal story. In mid-February, Sir Bayard headed to England to represent Bermuda at two key ceremonies. The main event was the religious service in the very church in London at which the first settlers had worshipped before leaving England, with a simultaneous and matching service held at the Anglican Cathedral of the Most Holy Trinity on Church Street in Hamilton. The other ceremony, a more relaxed and modern occasion, took place only in London: it was one of Bermuda's very first international Press Conferences.

To place the celebrations of 1959 in context, it is important to bear in mind that the international media coverage which today we take for granted was undreamed of at the time. Those who had televisions, a tiny minority, enjoyed flickering black and white images on small screens. The fragility of the images added a sense of excitement lacking in today's high-quality colour pictures. Live international television coverage existed, but was broadcast only on extraordinary occasions. In the dissemination of news, print reigned supreme.

The Press Conference came first, on 18 February 1959, at the Savoy Hotel on London's Embankment. London at the time had a magic few cities could match and the Savoy was the acme of the world's hotel establishments. The scrapbook contains Skeleton Programme Notes for the Press Conference:

> Abraham Lincoln Room laid out for Conference. Speakers, Mr. Steel, Sir Bayard Dill and Mr. Selley. Lady Dill seated to side near other Bermudian guests. Press seats arranged in two blocks each approximately 60 with centre gangway. Press release sets plus calendar tied with Bermuda blue ribbon on seats (120). Spares (100) on small table at side for News Bureau staff.

Also in the scrapbook is the script of Sir Bayard's address to the Conference. The pages are unmarked, making it impossible to say whether or not they contained the final text. The speech began:

> I bear greetings from Bermuda. I have come here to take part in the first of the celebrations of her 350th anniversary to be held in this country, a commemorative service attended by the Lord Mayor in State. Much depends upon those two words, which mean that the Lord Mayor and the other officials of the City of London

will attend in full regalia and that there will be an unprecedented rummaging in wardrobes for tail coats.

Sir Bayard pointed out, and rightly so, that Bermuda felt highly honoured that the City of London had turned out in full array for the historic occasion. In 1998, as Britain attempts to re-brand itself for the 21st century, much of the panoply of state seems likely to be abandoned forever. The loss to Britain of the wig and robe of the Speaker of Parliament and the Judges' finery, it is argued, will somehow enrich its citizens. To the historically inclined, however, such changes amount to throwing out the baby and jealously guarding the bathwater.

Sir Bayard continued:

My home, Bermuda, might well be called the enigma island. We produce literally nothing—apart from a minute quantity of perfume and some really beautiful Easter lilies. Yet we are one of the biggest dollar earners in the Sterling area, certainly for our size. We earn about two dollars per square yard per year.

That is an extraordinary statistic, which it is possible to update by making a few assumptions. It seems likely that Sir Bayard had rounded off the precise figure for the sake of simplicity. It must be also be assumed that he was referring to the Colony's Gross Domestic Product, the largest standard measure of earnings. On this basis, the comparative figure for the year ending 31 March 1997 was $36.22 per square yard per year. Taking Sir Bayard's figure as exactly $2.00, the figure represents a compound growth rate of just a little under eight percent for each of the intervening 38 years. Although the Bermuda economy has always grown at a fairly smooth and well-managed rate, it has not achieved eight percent in every year, but rather has grown in fits and starts.

Sir Bayard continued:

We have our equivalent of the House of Lords and the House of Commons, but with one great difference. Your members of Parliament are forbidden to have any interest in the affairs which they debate (in case I am taken wrongly, financial interest). Our M.P.s in contrast each have a stake in the trade of the Island.

It is, in fact, governed by traders.

Following questions from the floor, Sir Bayard directed the attention of the journalists gathered at the Savoy to the next matter of business, a sumptuous Bermuda birthday cake. "And now I understand that I have to blow out 350 candles before we can all have a drink," was his scripted closing remark at the formal conference. The Press, a body notoriously dedicated to the recreational consumption of alcohol, must have been enchanted by this informality on so august an occasion.

The following day, at 3:30 p.m., a service was held at St. Lawrence Jewry-next-Guildhall in the City of London, and simultaneously at 11:30 a.m. at the Cathedral in Hamilton, to commemorate a service held by the original settlers. After the hymn *O God of Bethel*, Sir Bayard read the second lesson, St. Matthew 6, verses 25-34. The words must have been of peculiar comfort to the original venturers:

Therefore take no thought, saying What shall we eat? Or What shall we drink? Or Wherewithal shall we be clothed? ... for your heavenly Father knoweth that you have need of all these things. Take therefore no thought for the morrow: for the morrow shall take thought for the thing of itself.

In the year 2009, Bermuda will celebrate its 400th anniversary, an

occasion which might merit a soundbite or two of coverage on the night-
ly newscasts if the future shape of world history permits. It might be
argued that more of note has happened in Bermuda in the years since 1959
than had taken place in the 350 years preceding them.

CHAPTER EIGHTEEN

Brothers In Law

A Pearman family tradition was begun in 1959 when James Pearman's sons James Appleby Pearman and his younger brother Richard Shafto Love Pearman joined the family firm. Both have made Conyers Dill & Pearman their life's work. Richard stands second in seniority only to Nicky Dill, and James remains a Consultant after a career spanning 36 years, in which he became Minister of Transport, continuing his father's interest and record of achievement in the field. With James' son, Peter Pearman, working at the firm, the tradition continues.

Brothers James and Richard Pearman joined the firm on the same day in the spring of 1959. Although their official capacity was simply that of lawyer, contemporaries at the firm describe the two Pearmans, Collis and the younger Dill as "partners in waiting". As any young lawyer who finds himself in that position will tell you, that phrase translates, loosely, as 'doing the lion's share of the hard work'.

The brothers Pearman had gone to Saltus Grammar School—almost a Bermudian given, in this context—and when each reached 13, they attended Stowe, a public school in Buckinghamshire, England. Despite the distance from home, their being Bermudian was no exception in rural England. A number of other Bermudians attended Stowe when the brothers were there: among them, Eldon and Andrew Trimingham, David Gilbert and Eugene Harvey. A formidable crew they must have made, and still do, one might say. They comprised almost the entire Stowe swimming team during their years there.

The Pearman brothers followed in their father's footsteps by going up to Merton College, Oxford, from which Richard's son Scott graduated in 1997. Richard also followed in his friend Charles Collis' footsteps by receiving the Rhodes Scholarship the year after Collis. The Pearman brothers were called, in turn, at the Middle Temple and returned separately to Bermuda, Richard breaking his journey to honeymoon. The brothers were later simultaneously called to the Bermuda Bar. Both have spent their entire working lives at the firm, members of a backbone of half a dozen partners who have been with Conyers Dill & Pearman throughout its most dynamic years.

Soon after joining the firm, Richard was involved with his friend John Profit in starting the Bermuda Ballet Association, initially a loosely-formalised organisation which existed primarily to assist interested dancers in financing their tuition. The work of the BBA, and that of Pat Gray and Lonnie Jackson, led to the formation of the Bermuda Civic Ballet.

At Conyers Dill & Pearman, following another tradition, the brothers joined the circuit being plied by Collis and Nicky Dill through Magistrates Court, divorce and general law. The emphasis on general practice is worth underlining, since today the generalist has become something of a dinosaur.

In any profession, however, it surely makes sense for a newly-qualified professional to try his or her hand at a range of work. For one thing, how else would the undecided discover which branch of the work most appealed? Yet many of today's lawyers and accountants claim to know with certainty where they intend to spend their professional lives. The majority of those who qualify in the professions rarely venture from the path once selected. With age and the accumulation of experience in a particular field, such manoeuvring becomes less feasible.

The firm the young Pearmans joined was growing, in the younger James Pearman's words, "like Topsy". Another tradition enjoyed by the Senior Partners at the time has gone the way of the generalist. Sailing or golf on Thursday afternoons was an adaptation of the continental system of an early-closing day in mid-week, which is no more. Offices opened on Saturday mornings, a practice which has also disappeared. The 'partners in waiting' worked their Thursday afternoons and found other opportunities to sail and play golf or tennis.

Both Pearman brothers were keen sportsmen, like their father. Both represented Bermuda on more than one occasion in the Eisenhower Trophy, the World Amateur Championship of golf, held every two years since 1958. Richard was the United States' National Champion at croquet, and runner-up four times in the US Championship doubles, with John Young. James' prowess at fishing eclipsed that of his father. Both father and son were selected for the British Empire fishing team in their respective days, and James *fils* held several world fishing records.

Plainly, the partners of Conyers Dill & Pearman could not be described as lazy. Far from it. Pearman *père*, particularly, undertook considerable business travel, and in the years to come was almost constantly on the road, a more cumbersome pastime than it is now. In Bermuda's small circles, Government committee work and social occasions, which were anything but, kept Pearman and Sir Bayard fairly constantly at work, in the broader sense of the term. That they deliberately balanced themselves by getting out in the fresh air is symptomatic of a civilised way of life that we appear to have forgotten to our detriment, as anyone who works for 50 weeks straight before taking a ten-day break will confirm.

On New Year's Day 1960, Pearman *père* was made a Commander of the Most Excellent Order of the British Empire and became, formally, the Honourable James Pearman, C.B.E.

The office world at the time continued to exist in what may be described as the Ice Age of office technology. Asked on one occasion to produce "one copy" of a complex 12-page document, Joan Hebberd did so, only to discover that what was wanted was the document *and* one copy— resulting in her having to type it all over again. Corrections were often made by retyping the entire document. She also recalls the first photocopier the firm used as a complicated device which required cameras and liquids and hanging the result on a line in a darkroom to dry.

Today, drafts of important documents can be changed as often as necessary before any but the writer's eyes see the first fruit of such labour. American author John Steinbeck, by contrast, wrote that he never shook the habit of writing his 600 words a day in longhand, and then tearing the pages off the pad to be sent to the printers. Were professionals and other wordsmiths more efficient in the days of three drafts, or was the quality of their work less sophisticated? Perhaps a blend of both.

But if its ways were prehistoric by comparison with today's high-speed office gadgetry, Conyers Dill & Pearman had already reached a size and complexity which required it to commence the process of sloughing off much of its *ad hoc* nature and to begin to take on the shape of a legal corporation.

In 1962, Collis was admitted to the partnership, joining Sir Bayard, Pearman and Graham on the letterhead. In the same year, Scottish Chartered Accountant Roger Younie joined the firm to come to grips with its financial and administrative side. By then, the firm employed 28 people, including the partners. The simple Cash Book which Miss Lusher took two years to fill would no longer have been the most efficient way to process the data.

Younie's appointment marked a stepping stone in the firm's development. Three partners in two rooms, with a secretary apiece, had no need of a financial manager. Their records could be maintained in two or three ledgers, and billing might have taken a secretary half an hour a day, if that. But a firm with upward of two dozen employees created the need for financial and administrative procedures and controls, the direct issue of which is today's time sheets.

Younie recalls the firm he joined as being rather like a family. Most evenings, the younger employees would congregate in someone's office to discuss current events, with a smaller set drifting off to the Yacht Club to pursue a similar agenda. The socialising continued in people's homes at weekends. Partners might on occasion be missing from these gatherings because they were overseas, marketing Bermuda and the firm, laying the foundations for what was to follow.

Younie had been working in Canada for a drug company and had spent his summer vacation in Bermuda in 1961, staying with an old school friend. He had met the senior Pearman socially once or twice, and when the partners decided that their accounting and administrative systems needed full-time professional attention, they interviewed Younie in January 1962. He was ready for a move: he had booked passage on a French freighter from Panama to Tahiti, planning to work his way around the world, as one could in those days of less red tape.

Pearman wrote to Younie to offer him the job, but the letter was sent to Toronto, Ohio, rather than to Ontario, by mistake. Pearman's offer, when it finally reached Younie, caught him rather unawares, but eventually he accepted and joined the firm. His role, in due course, would encompass more than finance and administration, as he lent his efforts to managing companies and other non-legal aspects of the firm's work.

Younie's appointment, nevertheless, can be seen as a milepost. As the 1960s, a decade of unimaginable change, began, the small country practice had set out its stall in the marketplace, where a new line of business was about to enter the Bermudian vocabulary: insurance.

CHAPTER NINETEEN

Captive Insurance

Graham cannot lay claim to having introduced captive insurance to Bermuda, although he and Pearman were among a small group who were the very first to try. Frederick (Fred) Reiss of Youngstown, Ohio had pioneered the idea of captive insurance, and coined the term, in the process of forming an insurance subsidiary for an industrial client in the United States as early as 1952. Reiss is known as 'the father of the captive'. His legacy to the corporate world includes International Risk Management Group which, from its Bermuda home office, operates 39 offices in a dozen countries around the world as part of the Swiss Re group. Reiss' son and daughter, Jonathan and Nicolette Reiss, are both now accountants in the insurance field.

Graham had established a useful relationship with Samuel Montagu, the London merchant bank he had engaged in the mid-1950s to help with his shipping proposition. Montagu's owned two large insurance broking firms in London. In 1962, at Graham's suggestion, Reiss expounded the notion of establishing a captive insurance market in Bermuda. The bank responded favourably and proposed that Reiss join one of its broking subsidiaries.

Although this was no mean offer, Reiss sensed that he could develop the business on his own. He, Graham, Pearman and Tucker formed a Bermuda company to begin the promotion of captive insurance business in Bermuda. Its prospects looked bright, but to the principals' consternation, the new company completely failed to get off the ground. Insurance companies have always been of necessity the most conservatively-managed organisations, and everyone in their networks to whom the four men spoke replied that only when others had shown an interest and backed that attention with capital, would they follow suit.

At exactly the time that Joseph Heller was writing *Catch-22*, Graham and Reiss found themselves caught in a classic example of the conundrum. Everyone agreed that captive insurance was a good idea, but no one was prepared to take the first step toward making it a reality. Reiss remained utterly convinced of its feasibility and bought out the shares of the others in the newly-formed promotional company.

A captive insurance company, at its most fundamental level, is a vehicle designed to underwrite the risks of its parent corporation, which is not itself an insurance company and, often, the risks of fellow subsidiaries.

Over the years, this basic principle has been embroidered somewhat, with esoteric derivatives such as association captives, which insure the risks of groups of people or organisations, and agency captives, formed by brokers or intermediaries to participate in programmes put together for clients. But, like all great ideas, the initial concept Reiss formulated was simplicity itself. It is said that there are no new ideas, only new connections. The connections Reiss made between existing insurance industry processes contained the seed of what has become a multi-billion dollar international industry, now carried on in more than 40 jurisdictions, of which Bermuda is the undisputed leader.

If the parent company were large enough, Reiss argued, and its captive insurance subsidiary sufficiently well-managed, it would be possible for the subsidiary, in the fullness of time, to retain for its owners the brokerage fee and the element of profit contained in every insurance premium, instead of letting others earn that profit. If the captive were managed by insurance professionals, the service Reiss proposed to offer in Bermuda, the captive's economic activity could effectively mimic that of the outside insurer who had hitherto received the premiums and provided the coverage.

The captive's efficiency would be even greater than that of established insurers, mostly North American and European companies, if the captive were located in a jurisdiction with a low incidence of, or no, direct taxation. The company's tax-free status would act to speed up the rate at which the subsidiary retained its profits and enable it to build more quickly a core of capital to meet future contingencies.

No profit comes without risk, but a captive company, like any other properly-established insurer, need not bear the brunt of the risk it accepts in return for the premium it receives. Reinsurance is a device by which companies, for a price, can 'lay off their bets' with other insurance companies. The overall risk a captive company, or any insurance company, actually lives with can thus be reinsured down to a manageable size. The average buyer of insurance has no idea that the coverage he has purchased might be carried by a dozen or more companies.

What Reiss had crystallised was a system which promised very real enhancements to the profitability of larger companies around the world. With hindsight, it seems remarkable that the idea did not catch on at once. Reiss was undeniably its architect and driving force. Those who knew him speak of his intense drive to succeed and an unshakable—and entirely justified—belief in the merits of captive insurance. Tucker, Pearman and Graham shared the view that captive insurance would work and that

Bermuda would prove an apt cradle. Unlike his Bermuda associates, however, Reiss was essentially broke and therefore, one might argue, better motivated to succeed.

The idea was as good as money in the bank, but was not producing any. In the early 1960s, Reiss, lawyer Sidney Pine and others could not convince a single company to be the first to step into a new age of Bermuda-based self-insurance. Tucker, Pearman and Graham, each a pioneer and a man of proven vision, all reluctantly turned their back on the idea of captives and sold their holdings to Reiss in what would become an extraordinarily profitable enterprise indeed. Each of the three came to benefit in other ways from captive insurance, but as late as New Year's Eve of 1962, there was no such thing as a captive insurance company in Bermuda.

If companies could not be persuaded to insure their interests in Bermuda, the insurance establishment quickly enough saw the threat if the idea caught on. The mechanics of reinsurance suggested that the real danger would accrue to the brokers who earned a fee for bringing clients' business to the insurance companies.

In an odd episode, Graham was summoned to the US by the founder of one of that country's largest insurance brokers, a man he knew through his connections to Montagu's. Graham was told in no uncertain terms that the idea of Bermuda establishing its own insurance business as Reiss had suggested was out of the question and was to be curtailed forthwith—or else. The broker told Graham point blank that it and another major broker were considering the formation of a Washington, D.C. lobby group specifically intended to kill Bermuda's inchoate captive insurance industry before it could establish a foothold.

Graham returned to Bermuda to consider and share with others the ultimatum he had been given. Following consultation with his colleagues, he returned to the States and spoke, not to the founder of the company, but to a man one or two rungs lower down the ladder, with whom he had done business in the past—was there anyone Graham did not know?

He patiently explained that the combination of captive insurance and Bermuda was too powerful an idea to simply be ignored. Given the strength of the concept and capital's inexorable demands for better returns, captive insurance would take hold, sooner or later, somewhere in the world, with or without interference from this quarter or that.

Graham argued that, given the specific nature of risks which could suitably be transferred to a captive, the idea was unlikely to affect the ordinary insurance business of the large American insurance companies. And then Graham played his trump card, in a suit the insurance industry understood only too well: reinsurance. Business written in Bermuda, he pointed out, would eventually work its way back to existing insurers through the medium of reinsurance.

So, Graham argued, why not drop this opposition to the inevitable, get on board and, in his own words 30 years later, "join the party"? The idea could not have been an easy sell to the brokers, the intermediaries who collect and deliver premiums to the insurance companies. But once again, Graham carried the day, and the idea of a full-time anti-Bermuda lobby attempting to sway United States politicians into legislating against Bermuda's interests passed into history. The presence on the Island today of many of the giant international brokers shows Graham's arguments to have been exactly on the mark. Most of the brokers manage captive insurance companies for their non-Bermudian parent companies. By having the brokers join the party, Graham enabled them to increase their wealth and reach.

The next to cry foul was one of the largest insurance companies. This time, the call came from a representative of a company who had been advised by his Head Office to have nothing to do with captive insurance. He had taken the time to understand the workings of what Reiss had proposed and saw that it would catch on regardless of any opposition. Would Graham care to discuss the ramifications?

Unbeknownst to Graham, the company had been considering terminating its Bermuda-based operations, since they had proved thus far to be a solution to which no one could define the question. Graham and Reiss travelled to New York to meet with the company's second-in-command.

Again, Reiss proved persuasive on his favourite subject, pointing out that the insurer had little to lose, and that by becoming a player in the proposed captive market, it would be able to monitor developments from the inside and direct its Bermuda operations in a more useful and profitable manner. Reluctant initially, the company—or, more specifically, its dynamic second-in-command—took the advice and is now counted among the leading captive insurance company managers.

Reiss succeeded in setting up the first Bermuda captive insurance company in 1963. The business grew slowly and six years later he was managing just 14 captives. The oil companies were among the first to incorporate their own captives; the parent companies' size all but ensured the success of the subsidiary.

History records that captive insurance came into its own in the 1970s and has retained its attraction ever since. Captive insurance now accounts for six percent of the property/casualty premiums written each year in the United States and is as unexceptional as any other form of insurance. Several thousand Bermuda captives of one sort or another were in existence at the end of 1997, representing better than 40 percent of the global total. Of these, about 60 percent are beneficially owned by American interests, 17 percent by Europeans and 10 percent by British principals. Bermuda has never given up the lead it established in the captive industry as a result of the pioneering efforts of Reiss, Graham and others.

CHAPTER TWENTY

Temporary Quarters

John Anthony Ellison was born on 19 January 1932 and, following his father's death before his first birthday, grew up "all over England". Until he was seven, that meant Yorkshire; during the War, it was Cornwall, on those occasions when train travel and other restrictions permitted. As a boy, he had wanted to join the Navy and had been destined for Dartmouth, but at the last moment, he opted instead for school, where he would concentrate on science, particularly chemistry.

Ellison attended Charterhouse, which had been established in the City of London in 1671 and moved, just over 100 years later to Godalming, in Surrey. Famous Old Carthusians include Roger Williams, founder of Rhode Island, the Methodist leader John Wesley, composer Ralph Vaughan Williams and the novelist William Thackeray. After the War had ended, Ellison spent a few years in Kent with his guardian, his mother having died during the month he reached 16 years of age. He went up to Christ Church, Oxford to read chemistry.

His great-grandfather had established a family business in chemical engineering, which his grandfather managed, but Ellison knew that avenue was not of interest to him. He toyed instead with a career in the Royal Air Force, but during his second year at Oxford decided to pursue the Law. The decision came too late to enable him to change his degree, but on going down from Oxford, he took the Bar examinations—with the help of that well-known cramming establishment, Gibson & Weldon, then patronised by Nicky Dill and the Pearman brothers, as it had been earlier by Collis.

After passing his exams, Ellison was claimed by his country for National Service, which had been deferred to allow him to complete his education. National Service has since been discontinued in Great Britain but Ellison describes his time as "18 delightful months in the Royal Air Force". For if he had no desire to join his family's formal business, he was quite happy to play his part in the family hobby, flying. His aunt Margaret Ellison, later Fenton, had been among the first half-dozen women in Britain to earn a pilot's licence; indeed, Ellison learned to fly before he learned to drive.

While still serving in the R.A.F., and having eaten his qualifying dinners, Ellison was called to the Bar by the Inner Temple in May 1957. When his National Service was completed, he became a pupil of Bernard Caulfield, who later, as Sir Bernard, became a High Court Judge. After completing his pupillage, Ellison became a tenant of John Hobson's chambers shortly before Hobson became England's Attorney General.

In 1962, Ellison was a junior for the defence at the celebrated 'A6 murder' trial of James Hanratty, a petty burglar. The Crown argued that Hanratty had kidnapped a man and his mistress at gunpoint and forced them to drive aimlessly for hours along the A6, a main arterial road, until at some point Hanratty killed the man and assaulted the woman.

Hanratty went to the gallows proclaiming his innocence on 4 April 1962, despite the conflicting evidence Ellison's team presented in court.

Hanratty was the last to be executed in Great Britain before public doubts about his conviction played a major part in the abolition of capital punishment in 1965. A Home Office review of the Hanratty case was started in January 1997.

In 1963, Ellison went to prosecute the summer Session in the Bahamas as Acting Solicitor General at the request and on the suggestion of Hobson, in whose gift such appointments lay. At the suggestion of Nicky Dill and the Pearman brothers, Ellison had already bought a holiday home in Bermuda in 1958, following his first visit to the Island a couple of years earlier. The three months in Nassau were enough to awaken the thought that, quite apart from holidays, working outside England had its attractions.

The idea became a reality when Pearman first discussed and then proposed that Ellison lend his effort to the increasing workload at Conyers Dill & Pearman. Ellison was the fourth, after the founders, to join the firm as a partner, and the last. Less distinctively, like his colleagues, Ellison started his career at the firm as a generalist.

Pearman was by now the driving force of both the partnership and his family's businesses, encouraging and cajoling his forces into action. Always direct, Pearman had acquired great confidence from his corporate and governmental experience and was a man who succinctly expressed what he wanted, without ornamentation. Sir Bayard continued to appear in court on behalf of clients and to bring his efforts and experience to bear on the firm, but where he had by now achieved the great majority of his goals, Pearman's star remained on the ascendancy. In some ways, the best of Pearman was yet to come.

For Graham, however, the nature of the game had changed. He was by nature an innovator rather than a consolidator; a tenacious contact-maker rather than a manager. Possessed of a keen nervous energy and an inventive intellect, Graham might have successfully pursued a career as a

concert pianist, and was altogether too dynamic an individual to be stim-
ulated by the routine imposed by the steady growth which followed his
earlier endeavours. With Bermuda's international business industry established, the element of challenge necessary to everything that Graham did
had begun to evaporate from his work with Conyers Dill & Pearman.

It is axiomatic in business theory that the managers who take a
venture from its inception to a certain initial level of success are often not
the men and women possessed of the skills or interest to build on their
achievements and take the company to its next level. The relationship
between Graham and his colleagues and partners deteriorated somewhat
as he assessed the impossibility of his situation, early in 1965. How was he
to follow the exhilaration of the past few years? How was he to propose
new ideas in a firm, or a Colony, already devoted to expanding the new
market he had created? Like others who have achieved outstanding success
in Bermuda's greenhouse atmosphere, Graham turned his sights on the
outside world. Simply put, in his own words: "I'd done all I could do in
Bermuda, really."

While Graham pondered his future, the firm moved out of the
Bermuda Fire and Marine Building. The Bank of Bermuda had grown
apace with the Bermudian economy and needed more space than was
available in its headquarters building. In 1964, it had opened a new building on Church Street, complete with drive-through banking windows; the
new building was more impressive than its headquarters. The bank then
purchased the entire site at Albuoy's Point, and construction of a new
building was scheduled to start in 1966 and take three or four years to
complete. Bermuda Fire & Marine moved half a mile down the road to the
site it now occupies on Pitts Bay Road.

Conyers Dill & Pearman intended to move in to the new Bank of
Bermuda building, which meant that temporary accommodations had to
be found. In the end, the old ZBM building on Par-la-Ville Road, a stone's

throw from Albuoy's Point, was selected. The firm christened it the Rosebank Building.

Those of the firm's staff who worked there describe the conditions as cramped, but adequate on a temporary basis. The firm's complement would have totalled about three dozen by 1965. Conyers Dill & Pearman had established a solid foothold in an ascending market. A little over half way through its first 70 years, the firm could no longer be described as a small country practice, but it was still modest in comparison with its New York and London counterparts. Its practice in the mid-1960s entailed a mix of advising clients on exactly what they could and could not do and the execution of the paperwork and detail which followed decisions based on that advice. Those decisions were usually taken elsewhere, with the firm responsible for due diligence at the Bermuda end.

Later that year, as the firm unpacked its papers at the end of its second move across Front Street, Graham resolved his situation by accepting an offer to join Samuel Montagu, of which he would later become Chairman. Within three years, he would engineer its sale to the Midland Bank, one of a handful of retail banking giants in the United Kingdom, of which he in turn became a Director.

Among Graham's final contributions to Bermuda's international business industry in this period was the establishment of two professional organisations, one local and one international. The local group would in due course become established as the Bermuda International Business Association. Younie recalls the initial conversation on the idea of setting up such an organisation taking place in his office prior to Graham's departure from Bermuda.

Separately, Graham helped found Multinational Fiscal Associates, an informal legal network spread across the world's financial centres. When the needs of a client with far-flung interests exceeded a member's ability to provide a complete service, the member could freely seek the advice of other members. The gentlemen's agreement called for any work resulting from the referral, naturally, to be passed on to the member who had provided advice. In time, as many as 25 top international lawyers became members of MFA.

Not even in London or New York was there a firm with the reach of MFA. The organisation anticipated in an informal way the globalisation of professional services being experienced today. MFA was not intended as a supra-national partnership, but as an understanding that enabled each member to provide the best possible extended advice and service to individuals and client companies with interests in several countries. When MFA was established, its clients were, for the most part, genuinely high net worth individuals, possessed of old money. For their international lifestyle they were continually referred to by the media as the 'jet set'.

It is often said that it is easier to make a fortune than to keep one. For an accumulation of wealth to last for generations requires constant attention and an unending spring of the best legal and financial advice money can buy. All too many forces act to dissipate capital. In the second half of the 20th century, inflation has come to affect the world's major economies as it once ravaged smaller fry. In the mid-1960s, it was generally held that a developed economy could not sustain annual inflation much beyond two and a half percent, but time and circumstance have changed economic thinking beyond recognition since then.

Inflation, however, can be managed. What is much harder to contend with is political risk, wars, imprudent spending, market declines, the changing structure of economies, crime, legislative changes, accidents, Acts of God, bank failures and a hundred other such agents. Few and far between are the weapons available to those who seek to conserve and build on a fortune; good legal advice is among the most important.

Heward Stikeman, a top Montreal lawyer and author, co-founded MFA with Graham. Its members were spread as far afield as the Philippines and Hong Kong. Although avowedly international in flavour, MFA maintained a strong Bermuda connection for many years. Collis became a member, as did Ellison, who served as Secretary of the organisation until his retirement in 1997.

In the years after 1965, Graham would direct a stream of business in the firm's direction. He had opened up Bermuda's future, and made possible much of what Bermudians enjoy today. His departure from the firm and Bermuda in 1965 was, symmetrically, a false exit, since he would reappear, briefly, in 1970. But when Graham stepped onto the plane which was to carry him to London and the start of his career in banking, an era drew to a close for the firm he had joined 17 years earlier.

Exit David Graham.

CHAPTER TWENTY ONE

Administrative Discipline

Enter Michael Esmond James Woods.

A lawyer by training, Woods was working as a management consultant when he was referred to Conyers Dill & Pearman in 1968; the partners had realised they would need professional help in administering the growing enterprise for which they had responsibility. Over the course of a 27-year relationship with the firm, Woods was to put in place what is today referred to as its corporate architecture. The term does not mean buildings, although he took charge of those, too, but the firm's infrastructure.

Woods was to propose and implement how the firm's work would be processed, who would do it, when it would be done and where it would be done. Like a fort, a successful business enterprise is constructed brick by brick. Woods was to build a modern law firm and imbue it with the policies and procedures which would let its staff complement multiply fivefold in the first decade of his association, and then grow twice as large again during his 17 years of full-time stewardship.

Following a detailed assessment of the firm's prospects, it had become obvious to the partners of Conyers Dill & Pearman in the mid-1960s that continued growth was more or less inevitable. The firm, then 40 years old, had lengthy, often pioneering expertise in the local and international sectors, both of which were exhibiting continuing strength. Internationally, Bermuda had generated an expanding trust business and with Reiss at the forefront, was building a captive insurance industry numbering hundreds of companies. Government adopted a generally benign view towards its business sector, continuing to co-opt the probity of the professionals and bankers who were the conduit for new clients.

By 1968, a view had taken hold that the development of the captive industry to that date might well prove to be merely the tip of an iceberg. Particular solutions to particular problems were turning into general solutions for a market which Bermuda had barely begun to tap. Reiss had been spot on; the possibilities were tremendous. On the trust side, growth had been equally impressive, even if its more discreet nature had kept it out of the international spotlight.

If captive insurance and trusts were such good ideas for the development of Bermuda, who was to say that other good ideas would not come along? No one could have foreseen the entirety of what was to follow, but when the partners of Conyers Dill & Pearman assessed their prospects, it was obvious that professional attention would be required to manage the expansion of the practice which undoubtedly lay ahead. In general, the firm had coped well with the changes it had experienced this far, but growth brings its own particular demands and was tugging at the shape and culture of a business enterprise which remained, at heart, an association of friends.

The partners' review suggested that the firm was not especially well positioned to manage the next wave of its development; a surge of new business, entirely feasible in an industry bubbling along like Bermuda's, might even have threatened to scuttle the ship. Although not without busi-

ness acumen—the Pearmans in particular ran successful family businesses alongside their interests in the firm—the partners had not the skills,
time or interest to devote a significant part of each day to managing the
legal enterprise they were building.

The seven-man partnership was established and well-balanced by
1968. Sir Bayard and James Pearman *père*, in their 60s, were legal ambas-
sadors and missionaries for Bermuda's international business sector, both
held in high regard locally and internationally. Pearman *père* was a
Freeman of the City of London. Collis, the Pearman brothers, Nicky Dill
and Ellison, all in their mid-30s, were the workhorses. But being lawyers,
not managers, they called in a firm of management consultants, a step
taken by most intelligently-run firms at a similar point in their development.

Bermuda has a long tradition of importing experts. The population is so small that it could not reasonably be expected to produce all the
men and women needed to people its ambitions. Since the first settlers
washed ashore, legions of foreigners have been drafted in to the Bermuda
workforce, bringing with them the technical skills or strong backs unavail-
able on the Island.

In that no Bermudian law firm had ever gone where Conyers Dill
& Pearman was heading, no one available in Bermuda would have had the
skills and experience needed to create the administrative structure for
what was to follow. A great friend of Ellison's from his University days had
joined P.A. International, a substantial management consultancy in a
range of disciplines, including marketing, administration and production.
When the partners of Conyers Dill & Pearman concluded that they had
need of the services of a management consultant, Ellison approached P.A.,
who assigned Woods.

Woods came from a military family. His father was a Wing
Commander in the Royal Air Force, his grandfather and great-grandfather

soldiers both. His mother was a school Headmistress. Born on 21 September 1934, Woods grew up in Oxford, the city of dreaming spires, with a fierce regard for learning. After schooling at St. Edward's, he entered National Service in the Royal Air Force and served as a Movements Officer in Malaya, when the British were dealing with the insurgency there.

Demobilised, he returned to Oxford, to Worcester College, where he read Law. From there he set his sails for the Bar at Gray's Inn. As a 'scholarship boy', his economic circumstances did not permit him simply to study the Law; he was required to work by day and study in the evenings. He was offered a position as a management trainee at Shell, the petroleum giant, and became the company's representative for the county of Northamptonshire.

Of the various routes one may take to enter the world of business, the scholarship student is among the luckiest, although he, or increasingly she, may not feel quite so fortunate at the time. The work required is prodigious. Fresh out of University, one holds down two jobs simultaneously, one in the very real world of commerce, the other in the less tangible zone of theory. The experience, which lasts a few years, tends to produce realists. It must count as the best possible foundation for a career in which theory will be applied to practice.

Having been called to the Bar, Woods wanted to marry, which meant plunging headfirst into the waters of commerce, rather than joining Chambers and earning a relatively small income for the first several years. Woods joined P.A. International, where he was the only member of the team with a legal qualification. Among a wide range of clients in diverse industries, he consulted with a number of law firms in the City of London and others as far afield as Hong Kong and Jamaica, who had reached a certain stage of development.

Woods was assigned to spend seven weeks in Bermuda in 1968, reviewing the firm's practice. His initial recommendation was the formulation of a detailed plan, the first plank in the introduction of management accounting techniques, with ongoing organisation and methods oversight. Alongside the tangible structure he put in place, Woods would also prove to be the filter through which the firm's future would pass.

He had what he describes, with a grin, as "the great pleasure" of introducing time sheets, and with them a routine of tracking billings and expenses, in an administrative database system known as a Matter Ledger, in which every piece of work undertaken is referred to as a 'matter'.

Time sheets are considered a mixed blessing by some professionals, who argue that life, particularly professional life, does not always proceed in the linear manner of the relentless march of little time boxes to be filled in all day, every working day. Neither can time sheets reflect the thinking process carried out at the back of one's mind on an almost continuous basis, which may result in only an hour's billable work once the thinking has fallen into place. Time sheets, however, are essential to the modern legal practice and unlikely to disappear any time soon. Without them, lawyers and other professionals would have to estimate their time, an impossibly erratic process.

The firm Woods reviewed was also administratively well-balanced, thanks to the efforts of Younie and Alan Brown, a fellow Chartered Accountant, and a small staff including Audrey Horseman, who joined the firm in 1962 and has remained with the practice ever since. She recalls the first accounting machine the firm used, a Kalamazoo system which had trouble getting its lines straight. Kalamazoo has manufactured a range of accounting machinery over the years, much of it worthy, but from today's perspective, the office equipment which predated the age of the computer can now only be viewed as Heath Robinson-style gadgetry.

For seven weeks in 1968, Woods swarmed all over the firm's procedures, looking at how money was processed, how work was allocated and at the growing battery of equipment … but his most important contribution remained his first: the institution of a plan for the firm's development. In time, he presented a five-year plan, which went so far as to allocate particular partners to the promotion of the firm's business in different sectors, both geographically and along business lines. The firm has had a rolling multi-year plan ever since Woods helped create the first in 1968.

He arrived at an historic moment for the Island. Until 1968, Bermuda lacked a Constitution. Although it had been entitled to make its own laws since the 1600s, Bermuda was still very much run by a British Governor, who chaired the Executive Council. Without political parties, government was, in Sir Henry Tucker's words, "by personality—or personalities—and not by political parties". Tucker was of the view that "in theory, such a form of government ought not to have worked at all, but in practice it worked well enough for the needs of those days."

All that changed on 8 June 1968, when a new Constitution was adopted, following a London conference two years earlier and a spirited public debate. The new Constitution preserved the centuries-old titles of Legislative Council and House of Assembly, but beyond the names, change was both sweeping and fundamental. The introduction of political parties allowed voters to look at issues rather than individuals.

Under a banner headline, *The Royal Gazette*—price 9d.— announced that a Cabinet had been named and that "Mr. James E. Pearman, a former Executive Council member with much experience on Boards during his 25 years in the House, will be the Member for Ports and Civil Aviation. There had been speculation that he was an alternative as Finance Minister." Pearman was also appointed to the Advisory Committee for the Prerogative of Mercy.

A few days later, he was formally put in charge of two government Departments: Marine & Ports Services and the Civil Aviation Department. His lifelong interest in transportation issues, from the days of the railway onward, had been suitably rewarded. Upon being sworn in to his new Cabinet position, he became The Honourable James E. Pearman, C.B.E., M.P.

The appointments capped his political career. In his day, he had been a Member of the Board of Trade and the Board of Agriculture, Chairman of the Board of Health twice, Commissioner of the Public Works Reserve Fund, Chairman of the Board of Public Works, a member of the Board of Civil Aviation and the Public Transportation Board, Chairman of the Transport Control Board and a Member of the Trade Development Board. In addition, he served as Bermuda's Honorary Consul for Bolivia.

For his part, Sir Bayard had retired from political life. He told a reporter: "I've had a long innings—almost 30 years now—and I feel that the time has come to make way for a younger man. It is very easy to keep putting the decision off, but I think it right to let some new blood into the House." He was not among those who felt that the move to party politics was necessary.

In 1968, Sir Bayard was 62 years old, and still a comparatively young man, but politics had changed. Sir Bayard was always and ever a man for consensus. Where Pearman relished the cut and thrust of political debate, Sir Bayard performed his best work in the more predictable realms of personal persuasion. Besides, he had held almost every post in government, including that of *de facto* leader. He was reappointed to the Legislative Council, one of five non-elected positions in His Excellency the Governor's grant, at the time when Pearman was appointed to the Executive Council.

The 1968 Constitution, having now lasted three decades, must be counted a success, although a few key anachronisms have survived. The practice of each of the 20 constituencies into which Bermuda is divided electing two Members of Parliament produces what some see as an overabundance of Parliamentarians. Others feel that the Parish boundaries remain in need of reform.

The new Constitution placed in the hands of Bermudians responsibility for all the Island's affairs, excepting (in real terms) only internal security, external affairs and defence, which remain the bailiwick of the Governor and, by extension, the British Government. The Governor may, in Tucker's words, "counsel, advise and warn" the Government of the day, and often does so, but in a day-to-day sense, Bermuda is master of its own internal affairs.

The Constitution mandates an independent judiciary, which is achieved by vesting in the Governor the power to appoint the Chief Justice, Judges and Magistrates, ensuring that no political pressure can be brought to bear on such appointments. The same provisions apply to the appointment of the Attorney General, in whom is vested absolute discretion in deciding whether or not to prosecute. Similar provisions apply to the appointment of the Commissioner of Police and in line with these provisions, the Constitution also established a Public Service Commission, responsible for the appointment, promotion and discipline of nearly all other public officers.

The Constitution itself comprises 63 closely-printed foolscap pages, written in a style the layman might not find easy to follow. But its enduring success over three decades has made the 'Bermuda model' one to which many other small island nations aspire. Bermuda has its own flag and an infrequently-heard National Song, although little of this concerned Woods as he set about the business of creating an infrastructure at Conyers Dill & Pearman.

CHAPTER TWENTY TWO

The Art Of Insurance

Alternative Risk Transfer was invented in Bermuda when the first captive insurance company was created, although the term did not gain currency for more than two decades. ART was initially a process by which an offshore insurance company allowed corporations to finance elements of their insurable exposure in such a way as to reduce the ultimate cost of such coverage. Subsequently, ART has come to connote a range of insurance techniques beyond the traditional.

By the end of the 1960s, Bermuda insurers had begun to experiment with various forms of captive insurance. In so doing, they attracted the attention of the commercial insurance market in the United States. The constituents of the first wave of Bermuda captive companies are today referred to as 'pure' captives. They were established to meet the needs of a single parent, required low levels of capitalisation and carefully limited the risks they accepted. Pure captives continue to this day to represent the largest single category of Bermuda insurance company. The single-parent captive remains the bread-and-butter vehicle of Bermuda's international business industry and is enjoying a new vogue in the late 1990s, following a surge of interest from companies in Latin America and the Far East.

As Bermuda's captive industry matured over its first decade, it became plain to the parent companies that their position and profitability might be strengthened if the captives were to write some non-related, third-party business, at a time when the insurance market was expanding. This natural fit of supply and demand meant more work for the companies' lawyers, onshore and off. In this era, the parent company's lawyers would draft the necessary documents and ask Bermuda lawyers to confirm that the proposed transactions were sound in the context of Bermuda law.

As a result, Conyers Dill & Pearman began to intensify the ongoing search for new blood. The first of three lawyers to join the firm in the space of less than a year at the end of the 1960s was Charles Forster Alexander Cooper, known as Alex.

The name Cooper is one of Bermuda's oldest. It is prominent in the business community in the local accounting firm of Cooper & Lines, which by a nominal coincidence, is part of the larger international firm known, until recently, as Coopers & Lybrand, now styled PricewaterhouseCoopers. The name is probably more widely associated in Bermuda with the retail sector, for the Front Street department store of A.S. Cooper & Sons Ltd., which celebrated its centenary last year. A.S. Cooper was Alexander Samuel Cooper; Alex is one of his grandchildren.

Born on 12 July 1942, Alex was what the British press once referred to as a 'war baby'. His education began in Bermuda when his parents, Charles Forster Whitter Cooper and American Mary Louise, *née* Kean, enrolled him at Miss Pitt's Nursery School. Cooper *père* had served in the Canadian Navy during the War, after which the family moved to the United States. Alex was to finish his education in North America, thereby acquiring what might be termed a 'Western trans-Atlantic accent'.

In Oakville, Ontario, a northern suburb of Toronto, Cooper

attended Appleby College, another nominal coincidence, since a Bermuda law firm containing that name would later offer him a job. Head Prefect Cooper captained the football team and enjoyed mathematics and science. He went on to gain a Bachelor's degree in General Arts at Trinity College at the University of Toronto, with a major in philosophy.

He chose the Law by a process of elimination, influenced by a background of lawyers and Judges on his mother's side. At the University of Toronto Law School, he earned his Bachelor of Laws degree and was subsequently articled for a year in Toronto, to John D. Clements, Q.C., at the firm of Lash, Johnston, Sheard & Pringle. Qualified, Cooper was admitted to the Canadian Bar and shortly afterwards, moved back to Bermuda early in 1969.

Stable economic conditions attended the 1960s in Bermuda for the most part; the Island had managed to hit the right note on both sides of its business. Tourism was enjoying a heyday. Bermuda was no longer quite the 'Isles of Rest', but for a generation which had fought the Second World War, it remained an up-market destination, with a friendly reputation and an air of exclusivity it retains to this day in many of its European markets. The international business sector acted as a healthy adjunct to the tourism trade.

On his return to Bermuda, Cooper was offered a full-time position with his family's law firm, Appleby, Spurling & Kempe. He had, however, spent two University summers working for Conyers Dill & Pearman, "down among the cobwebs" in the basement of the Bermuda Bakery building, where the firm stored its older records. The Pearman family owned the business and allowed the firm to use its excess storage space. Those subterranean summers were time well spent: as a result, Cooper implemented the practice of maintaining a corporate information sheet on each client, now the firm's standard policy.

After talking to Appleby, Spurling & Kempe, Cooper met Sir

Bayard and James Pearman *père*, friends of his parents; Cooper's experience as a teenager informed a "straightforward" decision. In March 1969, he joined Conyers Dill & Pearman as an associate. The seven-partner firm he joined—two Dills, three Pearmans, Collis and Ellison—had anticipated and was starting to face the broadening of the insurance market into unrelated business. The earliest-established captives were beginning to accumulate meaningful capital and surplus, money which had to be put to work in the narrow range of low-risk activities to which insurance capital is committed. As the 1970s dawned, Bermuda began writing a little reinsurance of its own, tens of thousands of dollars' worth, perhaps, rather than today's billions.

Side benefits attended the broadening of the Bermuda reinsurance business: it cemented the legitimacy of the captive, preserved its tax efficiency and held out the possibility of the company gradually emerging from its cost-control chrysalis to become a profit centre. Bermuda captives did not race headlong into writing third party business. Insurance companies make long-term promises, one of which is to be around decades from now to fulfill the other promises it has made. Capital is at risk the moment it is created, and retains its value through the years only with constant attention.

Two incidental but particular dangers attend the accumulation of offshore capital; they are known colloquially as 'the pump' and the 'dollar dollar'. One arises from an offshore company's success, the other multiplies its potential for failure.

Generally, profits accumulated outside the US from business transacted beyond its shores are not subject to US taxation until they are remitted to the US. The exemption has been a factor in Bermuda's success in attracting its international business industry. But offshore companies can be too successful, effectively stranding offshore profits which might be needed to fund onshore growth. Offshore profits are effectively inviolate.

Even their indirect use, say as collateral in an onshore loan arrangement, could destroy their non-taxable status. Having turned on 'the pump', some US companies—usually those whose forward planning has been less than thoughtful—have found themselves with little choice but to remit the necessary capital back to the parent company, after paying Uncle Sam his share.

Tax deferred for eight years or so, thanks to the concept of Current Purchasing Power, is much the same as tax not paid in the first place, so the effects of 'the pump', while an irritant, need not be fatal to a corporation's forward motion if onshore cash flow needs can be satisfied by other means.

The 'dollar dollar' effect, however, can exacerbate failure. If US corporate taxation runs at 50 percent, a profit of a dollar made in the US would be worth just 50 cents at the end of the day. A profit of a dollar earned outside the United States, in a tax-free zone, would be worth a dollar as long as it stays offshore. Bermuda profits are therefore made in what some American businessmen refer to as 'dollar dollars', rather than in '50-cent dollars'. But offshore losses cannot be offset against prior earnings for tax purposes. While business conducted offshore is inherently likelier to be profitable than its onshore counterpart, American corporations keen to expand their offshore interests nevertheless do so with 'dollar dollar' caution.

The Internal Revenue Service requires that an offshore company's "mind and management" be and remain offshore if profits earned by such a venture are to be excluded from onshore taxation. "Mind and management" is an ill-defined phrase which American courts have had occasion to test and interpret. Many smaller US corporations, often the creation of a single founder, have found difficulty cutting a subsidiary free of individual control to allow the subsidiary's management to genuinely dictate its fate, as tax law dictates it must. *Pour encourager les autres*, the IRS has made a habit of coming down with an iron fist, and heavy penalties and interest, on those who deliberately fail to follow the rules. Companies which meet the tests of the Law, however, and assign key responsibilities to Bermuda-based personnel, may legally escape the iron press of the IRS. The personnel need not all be insurance executives. Directors of the company, or its Secretary, for example, can be non-US resident professionals. The best qualified to supply such services are the accounting and legal professions.

Just before Woods joined Conyers Dill & Pearman, the firm had acknowledged the diversity of its professional services and established two companies as subsidiaries of the partnership. North Rock Enterprises would in time provide Corporate and Secretarial services. The name was taken from a part of the coral reef representing the northern rim of the mouth of the volcano atop whose southern rim Bermuda now sits. In time, North Rock became Codan Services, named for the firm's telegraphic address.

Westbroke Limited, which was to provide accounting and management services, was named as a play on Pembroke Company Ltd., which the firm had previously established. The City of Hamilton lies in Pembroke Parish.

The partners had seen far enough into the future to establish these companies; now, with Woods' guidance, they set about establishing the companies' individual identities.

CHAPTER TWENTY THREE

The Mancunian Candidate

The plan the partners of Conyers Dill & Pearman had drawn up at Woods' behest took note of the fact that the practice earned its fees from different sources: transaction-based legal work, which generated the lion's share of the practice income; corporate representation, which required a steady stream of attention, with a client base numbered at the end of the 1960s in the hundreds; and private client work, largely based on trust law. Litigation and Property were still considered part of the general practice. If the firm were to grow, even comparatively slowly, separation of its functions would soon become a necessity.

Doubtless at one of the partners' meetings held every Monday morning at 8:30 a.m. sharp, Woods, on an interim visit, proposed to recognise the different streams of work by breaking the practice into segments, each with a corporate identity of its own. The firm would not change its name, but the elements were to be more efficiently organised along individual and separate lines. To Westbroke and North Rock would eventually be added a licensed trust company, which is today Codan

Trust Company Limited.

Before any of this was to happen, however, a more urgent matter required attention; the firm's local practice needed beefing up. A month after Alex Cooper joined Conyers Dill & Pearman, Englishman Walter Maddocks came on board in April 1969.

Maddocks was born on 27 March 1930 in Manchester. His father, Edgar Shotton Maddocks, was an electrician, who died when Walter was two years old. His mother, the former Annie Mosley, brought Walter and his older sister up in the suburbs of Manchester, where Walter attended Urmston Grammar School. Thereafter, he served articles—a form of apprenticeship not unique to the legal profession—with a local firm of solicitors, Bernard, Kuit & Steinart. Barely 20 at the time, Maddocks started his period of apprenticeship in the time-honoured manner: licking postage stamps in the general office.

The notion of the apprentice dates back to antiquity, with religious temples managed along hierarchical processes which stressed the relationship between master and pupil. In mediæval times, the craftsmen of the Trades Guilds were responsible for ensuring the skill and aptitude of newcomers, initiating them into society and bringing them up in ways of godliness. Tools and work methods were prescribed by the Guild. A master would accept no more apprentices than he could train.

Upon the completion of training, a student would not necessarily become a master immediately. A interim period of indeterminate length might ensue, in which the newly-qualified artisan would work for a day's wages, as a journeyman. These ancient professional principles all have their counterparts in modern professional practice.

By the Middle Ages, universities had adopted a similar system with a master's degree, which has the meaning of a degree taught by a master as well as the process by which the student becomes one. The lawyer of the Middle Ages served an apprenticeship by working in close association with a master of the profession. The practice persists in jurisdictions which base their legal systems on the English model.

For a fixed period—in Maddocks' day, six years was the standard term—a school-leaver was bound by a legal agreement to work exclusively for the solicitor to whom he was articled. In return, the lawyer agreed to school the student and make it possible for him to gain the necessary training and ethical understanding, confirmed by examination, to enable him to practise Law. For the greater part of the 20th century, an articled clerk paid his master an annual fee for the privilege of serving articles. Articles were available to anyone whose family could pay for the minimal costs of tuition and the chance to earn the licence to practise. The term 'articles' has fallen foul of political correctness in certain corners of the world. Blaming word rather than deed, society has renamed the articled clerk a student lawyer. Nothing is improved by this process: he or she remains at the lower end of the totem pole in an office staffed by qualified professionals.

To those who served articles in any profession in the middle of the 20th century, the period of indenture led, with a degree of certainty and the accumulation of acceptable examination results, to a professional career. Eventually, the premium paid by articled clerks or their families was phased out, and by the end of the 1960s, clerks were receiving a few hundred pounds a year towards the cost of living. Today's students are paid a small salary, with the best in Bermuda often the beneficiaries of significant scholarship largesse on the part of Bermuda Inc.

Maddocks emerged from his six-year articles exactly as the system intended he would: versed in all facets of the Law. An application to the Law Society followed the completion of his articles, as did the also then-traditional interview at the Law Society Hall. At the age of 25, Maddocks was enrolled as a solicitor in England and Wales. He set up his shingle and opened his own office to become what is known in professional circles as a sole practitioner, in Urmston. Later, he moved the practice to Cornwall, that most charming of British counties at England's south-western extremity, its winding, hedged roads so reminiscent of Bermuda's. In all, Maddocks spent 11 years in private practice.

An advertisement in the *Law Society Gazette* caught his eye and his attention, one day in his mid-30s. Bermuda was in need of an additional Magistrate. Bermuda's legal system follows the English model and has retained the right of appeal to the Judicial Committee of the Privy Council, comprised of Judges from the House of Lords. Given the Island's relatively small and comparatively law-abiding population, the judicial system is simply structured. Bermuda is a common law jurisdiction, with Magistrates' Courts and a Supreme Court. Proceedings are avidly reported in the media and widely debated. Bermuda's Judiciary is headed by a Chief Justice, appointed by the Governor. Puisne Judges serve with him in the Supreme Court.

To Maddocks, the post of Magistrate in Bermuda was of great interest. His application joined a long list of others. Following a series of interviews, the then Governor of Bermuda, Lord Martonmere, duly appointed Maddocks as a Magistrate. Bermuda's Chief Justice at the time was Sir Myles Abbott.

Towards the end of his three-year Magisterial contract, Maddocks met Pearman *père* at a cocktail party, that essential building block of Bermuda's social relations. Not entirely by way of small talk, Pearman asked what Maddocks planned to do when his contract was up. Maddocks replied that he had no particular plans. A further contract was a possibility, but, inspired by his move to Bermuda, he was intrigued by the new and the different. Pearman suggested lunch, at which, as usual, he came straight to the point.

Conyers Dill & Pearman had concentrated on the international business sector with such success that, as a consequence, the firm's local practice had not kept pace. Would Maddocks consider joining the firm to help build up the local practice? His experience in the courts would prove invaluable. Maddocks gave the matter some thought and in April 1969 joined Conyers Dill & Pearman as an associate, working alongside Cooper, the only other individual in that position at the time.

CHAPTER TWENTY FOUR

His First Case

In December 1969, Chet Butterfield joined Conyers Dill & Pearman as an associate at the age of 42. Harry Chester Butterfield was born on 19 October 1927. His father, Sir Harry Butterfield, ran the Bank of N.T. Butterfield and Son Ltd., which his own father had founded in 1858. Sir Harry was an indomitable character, the classic patrician with a helping hand in almost every endeavour in Bermuda. He served alongside Sir Bayard and Pearman in their time on the Executive and Legislative Councils.

Sir Harry and his wife, Florence, had three sons, of whom Chet was the eldest. Chet Butterfield was a partner in Conyers Dill & Pearman from not long after he joined the firm on 1 December 1969 until his untimely death in 1987, which robbed the firm of a man who had helped lead and shape it, and of his fine legal mind. Butterfield is remembered with great affection today for his charm, acumen and sense of humour.

He attended Saltus Grammar School and Trinity College School in Ontario and graduated from McGill University in 1948 with a Bachelor of

Arts honours degree in English Language and Literature. He served as a Lieutenant in the Canadian Army Reserve, and spent four years in the Royal Air Force Voluntary Reserve.

Chet's father had been a Rhodes Scholar, and when Chet was similarly honoured, he proceeded to Oxford to earn an honours degree in Jurisprudence at University College. Butterfield appeared out of the blue on Ellison's first day at Oxford and insisted on pointing out some of the sights to the newcomer. Butterfield, Ellison and James Pearman *fils* all flew in the Oxford University Air Squadron. Butterfield was called to the Bar at the Middle Temple. His background thus eminently suited him for a career in the Law, but he was a Butterfield and chose to join his family's bank as a messenger, intending to work his way through the ranks.

After 16 years, he had risen to become the bank's Assistant Manager in charge of Foreign Business Development in the Overseas Department. On the way, he served two terms on the Public Transportation Board. But the Law was Butterfield's calling, and banking, he had begun to realise, was not the lifetime's work he craved. Following conversations, presumably with Pearman and Sir Bayard, who were his parents' contemporaries and friends, a brief notice appeared in *The Royal Gazette*, placed by the firm in late November 1969, announcing that Butterfield was to join Conyers Dill & Pearman.

His arrival cemented relationships between the firm and the Bank of Butterfield. The practice now had familial links to both the Island's large banks, although more by accident than design. What was gained by design was Butterfield's infectious enthusiasm, his *joie de vivre* and his legal mind. Now seven lawyers had become ten. With only a single further addition, this team would stay together for 18 years.

On 12 January 1970, Butterfield and Cooper were admitted to the Bermuda Bar in the company of Ann Cartwright, who, as the Honourable Ann Cartwright DeCouto, subsequently rose through the ranks of the

United Bermuda Party to become Deputy Premier before resigning over the issue of Independence in the choppy waters of the 1995 referendum on the subject. The day after Bermuda's three newest lawyers were called, *The Royal Gazette* carried a lengthy, unattributed article on the event, which read, in part:

> The Colony's legal profession turned out in force yesterday to see three new lawyers admitted to the Bermuda Bar in Supreme Court. Miss Ann Frith Cartwright, Mr. Charles Forster Alexander Cooper and Mr. Harry Chester Butterfield were welcomed to the Bar by the Chief Justice, the Hon. Sir Myles Abbott.
>
> The Hon. Sir Bayard Dill, moving for the admission of Mr. Cooper and Mr. Butterfield, said it gave him great pleasure "because both are sons of very old Bermuda families.
>
> "I am proud that both have agreed to join our firm," Sir Bayard continued. "Mr. Butterfield started maybe in the wrong direction. Having been called to the Bar in England, he then decided to become a banker. However, his leaning has always been toward law, and he has decided to follow that profession."
>
> Sir Bayard said he and Mr. Cooper's father had been friends for many years. The candidate for the Bar had followed legal training in Canada, gaining a B.A. at Trinity College of the University of Toronto and subsequently becoming articled in a substantial firm in Toronto.
>
> The Chief Justice said he was "very pleased to accede to all three applications". He asked the three applicants to retire to the robing room and put on their robes and wigs.
>
> Upon their return, Sir Myles complimented Miss Cartwright on her academic background and told Mr. Cooper: "I knew your father and was proud to know him. I look forward, and so does my broth-

er Judge, to having you appear in these courts frequently."

The Chief Justice told Mr. Butterfield: "I know you, and I know perhaps even better your mother and father. I hope you too will appear frequently here."

Addressing all three new barristers, Sir Myles continued: "Don't forget, please, that your first duty as members of the Bar is to the Court: first because it is essential that a court has every assistance from members of the Bar in order to secure justice and the proper administration of justice in the Colony. Without proper administration of justice, no community can survive for very long. Your duty to your client comes second—a bad second, but nevertheless it does come second."

The Solicitor General, Mr. A.G. Sedgwick, said it was a very great pleasure to see all three new barristers admitted.

Mr. Peter Smith, as "the senior member of the Bar who isn't involved", said it was a privilege and pleasure to welcome the trio to the Bar.

The admonition by Sir Myles was not idle. Butterfield, a banker all his life, had never appeared in court. In the fullness of time, his name showed up on the roster and he was assigned the case of a woman accused of smuggling drugs into Bermuda, who had requested Legal Aid. Butterfield asked the Chief Justice if he might be excused; the Chief Justice insisted.

The case, by all accounts, looked hopeless for the woman and for Butterfield in his first courtroom appearance. But with an impassioned defence, he won the day and the woman walked free from the room. Butterfield might have celebrated the verdict with a glass of brandy.

In 1969, the firm was re-embodied in 10,250 square feet of space in The Bank of Bermuda's new building and Head Office at Albuoy's Point. The move was slated for a weekend, over which the firm regained its cherished view across Hamilton Harbour from the fifth floor of the new building. Its rectangular lines have since become a symbol of the strength of Bermuda's business sector.

A familiar name rejoined Conyers Dill & Pearman soon afterwards: in 1970, David Graham returned to Bermuda after five eventful years in London. He had retained an active association with the firm throughout this time. His tenure at Montagu's had been planned to last five years, with a view to heading back to Bermuda when the quinquennium was complete. On his return in 1970, Graham had planned to spend part of the year in Bermuda and part working from a European base. The notion sounded good, but Graham was soon to learn the truth of the saying, 'you can never go home again'. Within two years, he had left Bermuda permanently, but not before he had played his part in the establishment of the Bermuda International Business Association.

BIBA was formed initially as a lunch club, meeting at the Royal Bermuda Yacht Club, an informal network of senior people meeting at the traditional locale for such activities. Among BIBA's founders were Richard Pearman and Chartered Accountants Richard Butterfield of Coopers & Lybrand and Donald Lines of The Bank of Bermuda.

BIBA has developed into an association of more than 50 of Bermuda's service providers to the international business industry: banks, law firms, accountancy practices and management service companies. In the early 1970s, it was an informal grouping of executives who met to discuss matters of mutual interest. Today, BIBA is a fully-fledged trade association, representing the interests of Bermuda Inc. locally and internationally. BIBA has become an integral part of the private and public partnership which makes Bermuda tick. It has a full-time staff, based in offices

next door to the Bermuda Stock Exchange, at work in the areas of education, marketing and media relations. Its many committees are often the
seeding ground for potential changes in legislation affecting the international business sector.

Graham may not have played the pivotal role in the development
of BIBA—his final stay in Bermuda was too short to enable him to do
much more than suggest the idea—but he was there at its beginnings, and
one imagines him in his element as the association moved from pipe
dream to concept and, finally, just prior to his departure, to reality.

Given what Graham had already done for the well-being of the
Island, BIBA can be regarded as icing on the cake. At the start of the 1970s,
Bermuda had yet to fully digest the results of his earlier contribution.
There was little further scope at the time for an inventor. What was need-
ed, at least in the legal profession, was skilled labour.

CHAPTER TWENTY FIVE

Currency Crisis

On 6 February 1970, a year ahead of Britain, Bermuda decimalised its currency, abandoning the British system of Pounds, Shillings and Pence in favour of a Bermuda dollar of one hundred cents. The transition went smoothly. Decimal currency is a better option for an international community, without a doubt, but something was lost when the old system was left behind. The move to a Bermuda Dollar proved inspired, for unexpected reasons.

Having added Maddocks and Butterfield to bolster the firm's local practice, the next area of focus for Conyers Dill & Pearman became the structure of its Corporate Secretarial activities. An English Chartered Secretary, J. Douglas Robinson, answered a Conyers Dill & Pearman advertisement and moved to Bermuda to establish North Rock Enterprises, as its first Managing Director, in the early months of 1970. Robinson and a secretary, given a small corner in the firm's offices, set about transferring to North Rock and their stewardship the corporate and administrative responsibilities which the firm routinely carried out for many of its clients.

Each attorney was on the Board of as many as a hundred companies. Each company was required to hold at least an Annual General Meeting; many held meetings with greater frequency. Although most of these meetings were a matter of form, with simple agendas prepared and agreed in advance, a provider of legal services owes each and every client the duty to provide a comprehensive service. Those who administer the corporate affairs of so many companies cannot afford to make a single mistake, since reputation is their mainstay. A missed statutory meeting, no matter how formulaic in nature, may jeopardise the affairs of a mighty international enterprise. Above all else, therefore, the Chartered Secretary is a methodical animal.

Over his 13-year tenure with the firm, Robinson was to build North Rock's clientele from small beginnings to a base of more than 2,000 companies by the time he retired to West Sussex, to be near his children. He was a great club man and a proud member of the Rotary Club and the Bermuda Maritime Museum Association.

Bermuda's international sector at this time was a secondary market. Its insurance industry, and to an extent its trust business, continued to rely for the source of its work on professionals in the cities which referred clients to Bermuda. A handful of top-flight insurance executives lived on the Island. Young Bermudians such as Brian Hall, Frank Lancaster and Robin Spencer-Arscott were learning the business at American International on Richmond Road; each went on to manage an insurance-related group of international significance. The Island, nevertheless, was a referral market in both insurance and legal terms.

At the end of 1971, Sir Henry Tucker retired as Government Leader, citing age, and was succeeded by Sir Edward (E.T.) Richards, who had come to Bermuda from Guyana to teach mathematics at the Berkeley Institute. Established near the end of the 19th century, Berkeley has long been one of Bermuda's leading educational establishments, and is today a

Government-aided senior school of excellent repute. Sir Edward served in the House of Assembly for 28 years, four of them as leader of the United Bermuda Party and Premier of Bermuda. He was the first to use the title of Premier and achieved distinction as a teacher, a businessman and a practising lawyer. His son Robert, known as Bob, a UBP Senator, is in 1998 the Minister for Telecommunications.

With North Rock established and growing, like every other part of the firm it served, Conyers Dill & Pearman expanded its partnership on 1 April 1972 with the admission of three new partners. Cooper, Maddocks and Butterfield, associates for just three years, joined the two Dills, three Pearmans, Collis and Ellison to form a ten-man partnership.

Graham was in the process of leaving Bermuda for the last time, perhaps a little disenchanted, to remain with Conyers Dill & Pearman as an honorary consultant-at-large for a further 20 years. Travelling on his own account, he saw hundreds, if not thousands, of potential clients around the world and referred many to the firm until 1990, when he formally retired— although to a man of Graham's energy the concept has no meaning.

Jo Marshall, who later helped set up and then for many years headed the Liquidations Department of the firm, first came to Conyers Dill & Pearman to act as Graham's secretary during his final four months in Bermuda. He fell ill during this period and was forced to spend time at the Hospital and at home. Marshall recalls taking dictation from him in both locations. His departure meant his retirement from the many companies on whose Boards he served. That, in turn, meant a personal letter to the beneficial owner of each company, and Marshall retains the sense of amazement she felt at the way in which Graham rattled off letters, aware of the name of every single beneficial owner and details, in every case, of families, professions and occupations.

That summer, Cooper represented Bermuda at the Munich Olympic Games, as a sailor. The 1972 Olympiad will always be remembered for the massacre of the Israeli team, but Cooper was away from the horror, competing in Soling races held in the city of Kiel.

He was even further away from Bermuda when the currency crisis hit on 24 June 1972. Without warning, the British Government, under Prime Minister Edward Heath, allowed the Pound Sterling to float against the US Dollar and a basket of currencies, without prior warning to the Sterling area. Four days later, the British Government abandoned the Sterling area altogether, leaving the Island to the mercies of the markets.

A Bermuda delegation made its way to England to meet with Bermuda Governor-designate Sir Richard Sharples to express their "concern and resentment at the lack of notification and consultation with Bermuda" on the decision to abolish the Sterling Area. The outcome was never really in doubt. Shortly after the Sterling Area was dissolved, the Bermuda dollar was pegged to the US Dollar. In the process, Bermuda became the world's smallest independent monetary area.

Once again, Bermuda had stared down the barrel of a gun and emerged with real advantage. The hyperinflation which wracked Sterling and the European currencies at the end of the 1970s and during the early 1980s did not inflict such damage on the US Dollar. Prices in Bermuda, which have grown high enough, would have been all but ruinous had the link to Sterling been maintained.

Against this backdrop, in July 1972 Frank Mutch joined Conyers Dill & Pearman at the start of a 22-year career. He remains with the firm today as a consultant, with an office on the second floor of Clarendon House and the physical appearance of a man half his age.

Mutch was born on 14 March 1936, in Liverpool, England. The city, perhaps now best-known as the home of the Beatles, sits at the mouth of the River Mersey and has long been one of Britain's most important ports, the point of entry for generations of immigrants. Frank's father, John, was an administrative officer with a large UK coal company, and his mother, Gladys, raised Frank and his older brother, John.

Frank attended the Liverpool Institute and, open to suggestions as to a career, left school to join the Canadian-Pacific Shipping Company, Ltd. in its Liverpudlian offices, as a trainee. National Service was still the order of the day in Britain, and Mutch served for two years in the Army. Thereafter, he held several corporate positions in quick succession, learning different aspects of business affairs before taking a post with a family-owned dairy business.

He was a runner long before the exercise became a public entertainment, a wiry fellow with an excess of energy. Mutch was destined to be a late bloomer, one of those fortunate individuals who, in the search for a definitive direction in life, explores a range of possibilities. The exploration, for a while, becomes the vocation. The broad general knowledge such people acquire on the way makes them, in later life, richer characters, possessed of a broadly enquiring nature and a dislike of the repetitive.

Like Maddocks, Mutch's life was changed in his early 20s by a newspaper advertisement. The Crown Agents were looking for candidates for the Police Force, to serve in a number of overseas locations. Mutch chose Bermuda, because "it sounded right." He enrolled in the training programme at the Police headquarters in Prospect, at the top of an imposing hill overlooking Hamilton and the waters of the North Shore.

Bermuda's Police Service traces its origins back to the very earliest days of colonisation, when Parish Constables enforced the Law and kept the peace. Today's Police Service numbers more than 400 men and women. The Service has contributed a considerable number of worthy individuals to Bermuda, whose careers after leaving the Service have blossomed in other directions, becoming Corporate Secretaries, civil servants and advertising and public relations advisers.

Mutch served his two years in Bermuda, but then returned to the United Kingdom to join Westminster Bank Ltd., back in the City of

Liverpool. Westminster Bank merged in 1967 to become part of what is now National Westminster Bank plc, one of the three remaining major British retail banks.

At Westminster Bank, Mutch started on the lending and security side, and found there his calling in corporate financing and investments. The 'art of the deal', as financing has been called, is attended by its own tensions, often culminating under the most ferocious time pressure in last-minute negotiation and, finally, documentation. Not every transaction is attended by quite such high drama, but each is different and therein lies the appeal of corporate finance.

Mutch had married Bermudian Helen Pitman not long after leaving the Police, and within a couple of years, they moved back to Bermuda. He joined the Investment Department of The Bank of Bermuda. Like Conyers Dill & Pearman at the time, the bank was in temporary accommodations, in the A.S. Cooper Building, while its old headquarters made way for the new.

Already a Member of the Institute of Bankers, in Bermuda Mutch studied for and earned his qualification as a Chartered Secretary. A short time later, he joined Conyers Dill & Pearman and was assigned to work with Robinson in North Rock.

The addition to the firm of Mutch, who would become a partner, put in place the team of principals which would guide the firm's development over the next 15 years. The firm Mutch joined in July 1972 numbered about 50, in addition to the partners. With Younie and Brown handling the administration and Woods coaching from the sidelines, the principals and the structure were in place. Woods had woven his spell well.

Now, as is always the case with recommendations from management consultants, it was time to put Woods' ideas to the test.

The French have a saying: *jamais deux sans trois*—things go in threes. On New Year's Day 1973, the senior Pearman was created a Knight Bachelor by Her Majesty the Queen. Each of the firm's three founders had now been knighted.

The Royal Gazette's front page for 2 January 1973 carried the news, with a picture of Sir James Pearman prominent among a distinguished collection of honorees. The report, headlined, "New Year's Honours for 11 Bermudians", led with:

A distinguished Parliamentarian who has given nearly 30 years of outstanding public service to Bermuda becomes a Knight Bachelor in the New Year's Honours List, issued last night.

The new Knight is the Hon. Sir James Eugene Pearman, C.B.E., who has had a long and distinguished connection with the political, public and legal life of these islands.

For very many years, he was a valued and active member of the House of Assembly, was twice a member of the Executive Council and is a former Member for Marine and Air Services.

He retired from the House of Assembly and the Executive Council six months ago but, following the general election at that time, was nominated as a Member of the Legislative Council and is continuing his long record of public service in that capacity.

Sir James, who was awarded the C.B.E. in 1960, is senior partner of Messrs. Conyers Dill & Pearman.

Born into an old Bermudian family, he first entered the political arena as far back as 1943, when he was elected Member of Parliament for Pembroke West.

For nearly 30 years, until his retirement, he served that constituency with diligence and dedication—and, in a wider context, served the whole of Bermuda as Member of the Executive Council from 1955 to 1963 and from 1968 to 1972 as Member for Marine and Aviation Services.

Sir James has served on the Board of Health, the Board of Agriculture, the Board of Trade, the Transport Control Board and the Public Transportation Board. He has been Honorary Consul for Bolivia since 1967.

During his long years in Parliament, Sir James built up a reputation for being a practised debater on a wide range of issues coming before the legislature.

If, at times, he was somewhat controversial, few denied the sincerity with which he held tenaciously to his principles and beliefs—even when they most disagreed with them.

The measure of the work he did over the years for his Pembroke constituents was proved by his return, as Member, in successive elections and also by the fact that today his son, Mr. James A. Pearman, M.P., is the sitting member for that constituency—so that the 'old firm' of the Pearman clan are the only father-and-son combination to be members of the House of Assembly and the Legislative Council simultaneously.

When the news of his elevation to Knight Bachelor was officially released last night, Sir James was the recipient of many congratulatory messages.

Sir James was pleased and delighted at the honour conferred on him by Her Majesty and made no secret of his pleasure.

"I can only say that I am very pleased indeed by the honour which has been bestowed on me," was his comment to *The Royal Gazette.*

He agreed he was looking forward to visiting Buckingham Palace for the investiture ceremony in due course.

He has met the Queen once before. "But that was quite some

time back, about 15 years ago, when Her Majesty and the Duke of Edinburgh visited Bermuda and I had the honour of being presented to her," Sir James said.

Though the Pearmans have been closely linked with Bermuda and its affairs over many years, Sir James is the first member of the family to be knighted.

Truth is, indeed, stranger than fiction. Much as people love a good legal drama, no John Grisham best-seller, nor episode of *L.A. Law*, would dare propose so outrageous a conceit: a law firm, each of whose founders earned the distinction of knighthood, with so diverse a range of achievements. Such a firm, in real life, is Conyers Dill & Pearman.

CHAPTER TWENTY SIX

Golden Anniversary

Nicolas George Trollope joined the firm in February 1975 as a Chartered Secretary, assigned to North Rock's burgeoning operations. Born on 24 June 1947 in Chelmsford, Essex, Trollope grew up in England's Home Counties. His father, George, was an engineering salesman and his mother, Jean, a home-maker. After attending Leiston Grammar School in Suffolk, Trollope enrolled in the Army at the age of 17, in search of a commission but without a clear idea of what his life might hold in store. He did not succeed in his military quest, and instead entered the hospitality industry, which "turned on a light," he recalls.

At Bournemouth College, he earned his National Diploma in Hotel Care & Management and joined a company which played its part in the story of the Bermudian hospitality industry: Trust House Forte, a major, publicly-held international hotel and leisure group, which was later purchased and broken up by Granada, a British public company. At THF, Trollope entered a management training scheme which exposed him to a number of the company's hotels and the group's London headquarters.

Eager to gain overseas experience, he worked at the George V Hotel in Paris, an experience fondly remembered.

Trollope was offered a position on the staff of the Company Secretary of THF, in a busy office responsible, inter alia, for the group's adherence to statutory requirements in the many countries in which it had operations. Trollope learned first-hand the nuts and bolts of the practice of corporate administration, which led him to successfully sit the examinations to become a Chartered Secretary.

As had Maddocks and Mutch, he saw an advertisement in an English newspaper, in this case in *The Daily Telegraph*, seeking the services of a recently-qualified Chartered Secretary. The advertisement was placed by P.A. International on behalf of Conyers Dill & Pearman, whose identity was not revealed, but the location was, which gave Trollope a notion as to who the interested party might be. He knew of, and had on occasion dealt with, the firm.

Paris had given him the taste for the expatriate life, and when he glanced at the advertisements in the *Telegraph* that day, Bermuda was the first word to jump off the page. Woods interviewed him, and Trollope duly took his place alongside Mutch and Robinson at North Rock in February 1975.

The mid-1970s saw a series of political shifts in Bermuda, with the Premier, Sir Edward Richards, resigning after four years, to be replaced by businessman John Sharpe, known as Jack, who led the United Bermuda Party to its second re-election in May 1976 and was later knighted. Sir John and his wife Eileen have a son and daughter, both attorneys at Conyers Dill & Pearman. Sir John's Premiership proved an inter-regnum, and he was replaced as Premier by Finance Minister David Gibbons, who held both posts for a period during which the UBP was re-elected for a third time. Gibbons was also later knighted and served for many years as Chairman of the Bank of Butterfield. His nephew, Grant, is now Minister of Finance.

By the time of Sir John's appointment, Conyers Dill & Pearman, in good measure through the efforts of Nicky Dill, had become well-known in shipping insurance circles. Many of the P&I clubs that had moved to Bermuda had done so because the Island more suited their newly-international character, and to avoid the currency risk which UK companies had to face at a time when Sterling was entering an extended period of weakness. Taxation was a subsidiary aspect in many of these cases, and Bermuda was able to accommodate either the clubs themselves or the reinsurance subsidiaries of existing London-based clubs.

Of late, the British have come to an arrangement with many of the clubs on the payment of a nominal level of taxation, which has had the effect of revitalising the industry. The added complication of the regulations of the European Economic Community has also changed the equation for the P&I clubs, making the practice of shipping law once again of one of the more vibrant aspects of the legal work of Conyers Dill & Pearman.

The record suggests that the mid-1970s were a relatively calm period for the firm, although Sir James, Richard Pearman, Butterfield and others, continued to travel overseas, building the network from which the firm derives its referrals. The Incorporations Department, set up by May Coye in this period, was growing particularly quickly as business was referred to it from within the firm.

Coye recalls a steady flow of work and the need for an area in which to meet an increasing stream of clients. Changes in law in any one of a number of jurisdictions could require feverish work on the part of Conyers Dill & Pearman to bring clients' complicated corporate structures in line with the new legislation. The work required a room in which to meet clients. A small space was chosen and partitioned, but the noise generated by the busy surrounding office—the click-clack of manual typewriters, telephones ringing—called for soundproofing. Younie and Brown hit on the idea of carpeting the walls and matched them to the existing carpeting, creating an accidental but not overwhelming 'padded cell' effect which lent the room something of the feel of an oasis.

Woods paid the firm an annual visit to ensure that all was proceeding according to plan, but the mid- to late-1970s was that most unusual period at Conyers Dill & Pearman, when the firm generally was able to catch its breath and settle into something approaching routine. That this relative tranquillity was not to last was confirmed in 1978, when a familiar name joined the firm full-time in the capacity of Partnership Secretary: Michael Woods.

Persuaded that his expertise was needed full-time, Woods moved to Bermuda and began working alongside Younie and Brown. It was a natural development; the firm already bore Woods' stamp throughout. His timing was immaculate. The firm was about to enter another period of intense growth as the Bermuda captive market began the strongest phase of a seven-year growth cycle.

The Bermuda market had graduated. Captives routinely wrote third-party business and reported solid earnings. A number of captive companies, seeded with greater capital, were writing third-party business just about as fast as it could be signed up. Interest rates were steadily climbing, to peak beyond 20 percent *per annum*, masking, in a few cases, a lack of underwriting quality. Capital and surplus in the Bermuda market approached US$5 billion. In the midst of this boom, the firm of Conyers Dill & Pearman celebrated its 50th Anniversary.

Sir Bayard hosted a celebration at his home, Newbold Place, on the North Shore in Devonshire, featuring what *The Royal Gazette* referred to as a "sumptuous multi-course dinner". Graham attended. In a photograph much cherished in the Dill household, Sir Bayard, Sir James and Graham, reunited, are all smiles. On a golden anniversary in the 'golden age' of captive insurance in Bermuda, smiles were in order.

To mark the occasion, the *Gazette* ran a memorable photograph of Sir Bayard and Sir James standing in front of a portrait of Sir Reginald. In the accompanying interview, Sir Bayard did most of the talking and mentioned that the firm's complement had reached 102.

This was too many to accommodate in the Bank of Bermuda building, just eight years after consolidating there. The operations of North Rock and the Conveyancing Departments had spilled over into the Vallis Building across the road, and at about the time of the firm's 50th anniversary, the Litigation Department moved out of the bank building and into the Rosebank Building. Both the firm's overflow offices were within a stone's throw of the partnership's headquarters, but it was becoming increasingly spread out.

The *Gazette* article on the firm's anniversary ran in a short section of the Island's daily newspaper referred to as *Business Week*. It is a sign of how far Bermuda has come in the 20 years since the article ran, that the newspaper now features a daily business section and employs two reporters full-time to cover the business beat. The *Bermuda Sun* runs a 12- to 18-page business section twice a week. Business-related stories routinely make the front pages of all the Island's newspapers, even the *Mid-Ocean News*, the *Gazette's* sister weekly, although its focus is more community-based. Two quarterly business magazines, *Bermudian Business* and *The Bottom Line*, are widely read and contain well-written contributions from individuals across Bermuda's business sector. A dozen other regular publications service the tourist market. Perhaps two dozen books have been published in Bermuda in the past year, including guide books and notable contributions on the coins and roses of Bermuda and some of the Island's more important political figures.

Bermuda has a high rate of literacy and Bermudians have an insatiable appetite for news. A greater percentage of Bermudians read the daily paper than in just about any other community in the world. For that matter, a greater percentage of Bermudians read their daily paper thoroughly, surveys show, than read a daily newspaper at all in most countries in the world.

Reports of legal matters retain a particular fascination. The modern practice of law has changed somewhat the degree of confidentiality attorneys afford themselves and, sometimes, their clients. In the United States, for example, Johnnie Cochran has become more famous than many of his clients, thanks to the experiment of broadcasting once-cloistered legal proceedings and the modern habit, at least in North America, of trying cases in the media. The British legal system is less susceptible to such behaviour.

To the founders of Conyers Dill & Pearman, these developments would have been anathema. There was a time, not long ago, when no aspect of one's business affairs was a matter for public discussion; even acknowledging a client's identity would have been regarded as sacrilegious. Sir James Pearman was famously reticent in discussing clients' affairs. He took the view, then widely accepted, that his activities, and those of his clients, were not open to discussion. His direct approach was, on occasion, taken for brusqueness, but among those who knew him well, he was always regarded as courteous.

For many years, American writer Suzannah Lessard had combined her trips to Bermuda with the preparation of an analytical article on the Island for *The New Yorker* magazine. Her extended research introduced her to a broad spectrum of Bermuda's diverse population. She arranged to meet and interview Sir James.

Published in *The New Yorker* on 16 April 1979, Lessard's *A Close Gathering* was the centrepiece of the issue, covering 39 pages. In a small stand-alone section in the body of the text is a record of her meeting with Sir James, who was 74 years old at the time. The excerpt read:

From his rather different perspective, Sir James Pearman is also inclined to see forces allied against him. Sitting in the air-conditioned, carpeted offices of Conyers Dill & Pearman, one of the two law firms that have managed to corner the profitable custom of companies for which Bermuda is a tax haven, Sir James has a British air about him, though he comes of old Bermudian stock. Brittle, unsmiling, he made it very clear that he had granted an interview because he thought he ought to, but that he did not intend to be forthcoming. If a foreign journalist comes to Bermuda, word gets around fast. If the journalist, for no other reason than orderliness, decides to work from the bottom levels of the society up, it is automatically assumed in some quarters that the journalist is anti-establishment. For the duration of the interview, Sir James sat with his body pressed forcefully into the back of his chair, his expression that of endurance.

How might the social effects of the economic slowdown be handled?

"I don't know," said Sir James.

Did he have any thoughts about the future of Bermuda?

"I don't know," said Sir James.

"Thank you," I said at last, rising to go.

"I can't imagine what for," said Sir James, letting escape his first hint of friendliness as he showed me to the door.

Sir James, entirely on top of his game, would have been delighted by the sub-text. Happily, the partners of Conyers Dill & Pearman no longer treat enquiring journalists with quite the same degree of reserve.

CHAPTER TWENTY SEVEN

A Matter Of Curiosity

By the start of the 1980s, it had become apparent to the partners of Conyers Dill & Pearman that the firm was outgrowing its tripartite accommodations. The main body of the practice remained at Albuoy's Point, the firm's home for most of the preceding 45 years, but the overflow offices in the Rosebank and Vallis Buildings were themselves filling up. A decision was called for.

A few hundred yards to the north, straight up Par-la-Ville Road, stood Masters' Clarendon Building, between the Rosebank Theatre on Bermudiana Road and Par-la-Ville Gardens on Par-la-Ville Road. The undistinguished but cavernous building had served as a warehouse and was now a vehicle showroom and storage area.

The partners of Conyers Dill & Pearman entered into an arrangement with Masters Ltd., in which the Pearman family had an interest, for co-ownership of the Clarendon site and building. A complete reconstruction, adding a fourth and fifth floor in the process, would permit the firm to concentrate its Bermuda practice under a single roof once again. A two-year programme was laid out for the redevelopment of the site. In the spring of 1980, as Collis began his Presidency of the Bermuda Chamber of Commerce, contracts were signed and work began on a brand new headquarters for the firm.

The choice of Clarendon House would reconstitute the firm just across the road from what had once been the Richmond Road railway station and is now the 24-hour Esso City Service Centre. The Station stood at the mouth of a railway tunnel under Par-la-Ville Gardens, and was the next stop down the line from Pond Hill en route to Front Street and the water.

The bank buildings to the west of Clarendon House are both relatively new. The Bank of Butterfield's Rosebank centre was formerly the Rosebank Theatre, a cinema and a prime entertainment venue. Next door, The Bank of Bermuda's new Compass Point building houses its Treasury and Investment Departments. Where once the American International Group's purpose-built headquarters—itself the subject of extensive renovation and refurbishment last year on the occasion of the company's 50th Anniversary in Bermuda—stood in solo splendour on the edge of things, it is now merely the furthest outpost of a congregation of office buildings in which are housed some of the world's largest insurance and reinsurance companies and the professionals who support them.

When construction booms, real estate law in Bermuda is as lively an occupation as any. Michael James McCabe, who today heads Conyers Dill & Pearman's Property Department, joined the firm in May 1980. With hindsight, it seems that he was destined to extend a family tradition in the Law, although he did not realise it until he had finished school and was contemplating what might follow. Both his grandfathers had served on Police forces, and his mother Maureen McCabe, née James, was a legal secretary and, later, executive. McCabe was born in Liverpool on 7 July 1953, the first of four children, but his father Stephen's career in management in the motor vehicle industry took the family briefly to London and then to Bedfordshire, where McCabe attended Challney High School for Boys.

He left Challney with no definite career plan, but agreed with his parents on a course of action which might open up possibilities: he joined Lathom & Co., a small firm in Luton, Bedfordshire, an hour's fast drive north of London. His mother was a legal executive at Lathom's at the time.

McCabe was to spend a total of eleven years with the firm, including two and a half years at the College of Law in Guildford, Surrey. The full-time programme led to what was known as the solicitors' qualifying examinations, which McCabe successfully negotiated, entitling him, after all that hard work, to serve articles with a firm of solicitors. He returned to Lathom & Co.

His experience there provided a thorough grounding in the practicalities of the profession in a general practice with an emphasis on Criminal and Property law. Although, in another context, the word property can mean an asset of any description, Property in this context is what is known in Bermuda and the United States as real estate. In due course, McCabe spent as much as three-quarters of his professional time on Property work, with the balance spent in general practice. Having completed his articles and become a solicitor, he remained with Lathom & Co. for a year, and then found himself, in his late 20s, at a crossroads.

To stay much longer would have meant a permanent choice and a predictable lifestyle. McCabe felt he was too young to make that sort of commitment, and wanted to find out what he might be made of. He considered his options. He had for many years had a hankering to travel and to work overseas. A clause in his employment arrangements with the provincial firm meant that, were he to leave, he would be unable to practise law within a certain distance of his former employers. McCabe used this prospective disadvantage as a springboard to take a look at what might be on offer elsewhere.

Glancing through the *Law Society Gazette*, his eye fell upon an advertisement placed by Conyers Dill & Pearman. He answered it "as a matter of curiosity" and was first interviewed by Woods at P.A. International's offices in Knightsbridge. Without revealing his hand, Woods left McCabe with the suggestion that he research Bermuda. A second meeting followed, with Collis and Woods. It was more of a social occasion, at which McCabe recalls Collis outlining the firm's ethos. Neither side had trouble making a decision, and on 21 May 1980, McCabe joined the firm of Conyers Dill & Pearman as an associate. He was assigned to the local practice, then headed by Maddocks, to concentrate on real estate law and was quickly appointed Head of the Property Department.

Circumstances, it might be said, made McCabe one of the firm's early specialists. At the time he joined the firm, Bermuda real estate law, by a quirk of fate, predated English property law. Bermuda's legislation dated back at the time to the 1860s. English law had been updated and radically changed in 1925, but Bermuda Law was not consolidated and amended until later.

When he arrived in Bermuda to start work, McCabe was put up at the Royal Bermuda Yacht Club. During his stay, the Club was the destination for the 1980 Newport-Bermuda yacht race. The race was a favourite of Sir Bayard's and vice versa, as Kyle Hunter reported for *The Royal Gazette*. Hunter was on assignment in Newport for the start of the 1980 race and filed the following front page report of a special occasion:

One of the most emotional scenes in all the Newport-Bermuda races happened yesterday when the Governor of Rhode Island, Mr. J. Joseph Garrahy, declared 19 June 1980 as Sir Bayard Dill Day. This was the second time Sir Bayard has been honoured in this historic sailing port. Two years ago, he was presented with a tile from

the Mayor of Newport, the Hon. Harp Donnelley, for his outstanding participation in the Newport-Bermuda race.

Although Governor Garrahy was not on hand to present Sir
Bayard with his certificate, the Senator from Rhode Island, Mr.
Robert J. McKenna, was at the Ida Lewis Yacht Club in Newport.

And presenting Sir Bayard with his certificate, the Senator said:
"To call Sir Bayard a gentleman is an understatement."

Sir Bayard, with tears brimming in his eyes, was clearly overcome by the honour.

He told *The Royal Gazette:* "This is a complete surprise, and a
wonderful surprise. I am very grateful."

But Sir Bayard added that it was a pity that his crewman,
Bernard Nelles, could not be on hand for the occasion. Mr. Nelles,
who suffered broken ribs and a punctured lung while making the
crossing from Bermuda to the United States last weekend in hor-
rendous weather, was in hospital, but by all reports he is in a satisfactory condition. He is expected to be flown back to Bermuda this
weekend.

Sir Bayard will be racing his 45-foot sloop *The Duchess of
Devonshire* with the other 164 yachts when the race begins tomorrow.

The Bermuda team, who have been in high spirits, were completely overjoyed with the honour bestowed upon Sir Bayard, who
is taking part in his 13th Bermuda race.

To those who knew him, Sir Bayard's concern for his crewman,
expressed at a time when he was himself being fêted, was typical of the
man. McCabe vividly recalls seeing the *Duchess* arrive, with the great man
in command.

CHAPTER TWENTY EIGHT

A Further Affidavit

In December 1980, what has become an 18-year tradition began with the publication of the first edition of *Briefcase*, the Conyers Dill & Pearman newsletter. *Issue No. 1* carried a photograph on its front page of Sir Bayard and Sir James, both in their mid-70s, surrounded by the recipients of long service awards made earlier in the year. Sharing the inaugural cover with the firm's senior partners were Joan Hebberd, then celebrating 30 years' employment with the practice; Carrie Musson, 25; Janet Mackay, 22; Audrey Miller, 21; Peggy Edmead, 20; Audrey Horseman, 18; Daphne Smith, 17, Sue Simmons, 16; and Cleo Davis, 15 years.

Hebberd was the first editor of *Briefcase*. In 43 issues to date, the in-house staff newsletter has chronicled the comings and goings and the internal and, often, external activities of the firm and its people. In its early days, the tone was light and enthusiastic. Messages of goodwill from the partners were followed by reports from members of staff on changes within the firm, vacations they had taken in unusual places and matters of the day. Staff functions, milestones and anniversaries have been grist for the

Briefcase mill, and always and ever the newsletter contains pages of photographs of new members of staff, often unflattering mugshots which at least serve to introduce the newly-hired to old hands.

As it developed over the years, *Briefcase* was overseen by Woods, and later taken in hand by John Ellison, who brought to it his own élan and dry sense of humour. Today, the firm's Manager of Human Resources, Sandra Cann, edits *Briefcase*. From an almost determinedly amateurish start, well before the age of desktop publishing, the magazine today is a professional notice board for matters relating to the practice. Back issues afford an inside look at those who worked for the firm and, on a detailed scale, who they are and what matters to them. The newsletter encouraged constructive criticism and, perhaps a little surprisingly, the firm occasionally came in for some stick from staff members with ideas for ways to improve systems or procedures.

Today's *Briefcase* continues to record the minutiae of an extended legal practice, from matters as mundane as contest winners at the annual Christmas party to meatier announcements, such as changes in the Law or the appointment of new partners. It has been joined by *Bulletin*, a client newsletter published on hard copy and the Internet, which is a forum for outlining changes in Bermuda law and other matters.

The third issue of *Briefcase*, dated June 1981, welcomed John Morrow Sharpe to Conyers Dill & Pearman. His sister, Kathy, would later join the firm and is today Head of the Wills & Estates Department. Sharpe's middle name was his mother Eileen's maiden name. His father is Sir John Sharpe, the former Premier of Bermuda.

Born on 15 May 1954, Sharpe attended Warwick Academy, on Middle Road in the Parish named for the Earl of Warwick. The Academy is the oldest continuously operating educational establishment in the western hemisphere, founded in 1662. Sharpe then proceeded to Malvern College in England to complete his studies for his O- and A-level examinations, national programmes which identify and grade, at 16 and 18, those who are University material.

Having passed his examinations, Sharpe opted to study at the Law School of the University of Kent at Canterbury. The city, probably best known for its Cathedral and Archbishop, lies about 90 minutes south-east of London by train.

Established in 1966, the Kent Law School almost immediately acquired a reputation for its innovative approach to the Law, offering a multi-disciplinary degree and a law clinic. The proximity of London afforded students the chance to gain a rounded education in a suburban setting while allowing them to stay in touch with big city life. In the early years, students were afforded the opportunity to help shape the pro-gramme. As the first Bermudian to graduate from Kent's new Law School, Sharpe unwittingly established a Conyers Dill & Pearman tradition which extends to this day. The University has so far produced for the firm three partners and several associates, as well as a number of other Bermudian lawyers.

Sharpe spent one summer working at Conyers Dill & Pearman to add practical experience to the Law School theory he was learning, and emerged from Kent a Bachelor of Arts (Law). He then spent a year at the College of Law, run by the Law Society in Chester, a mediæval walled city which lies on a bend of the River Dee, south-west of Manchester. Sharpe knew at this point that the Law would be his calling, but he had no fixed ideas about the direction in which it might lead. Neither side of his fami-ly had a background in the Law, but he felt that it might offer him "the best chance to do something else" if his interest transpired not to be all-con-suming. The thought was *à propos*, given what followed.

His studies at the College of Law led, after a year, to success at examinations for eligibility to serve two-year Articles of Clerkship. Sharpe sought employment with Wedlake Bell, a broad commercial practice in

London's Covent Garden, situated on the borders of the financial district known as the City of London and its more familiar heart, the West End.

Upon completing his two years of articles, Sharpe was admitted as a solicitor of the Supreme Court of England and Wales. Subsequently, he became, quite possibly, the first Bermudian to qualify as a solicitor. The admission of lawyers in Bermuda is governed by the Island's Supreme Court Act. Bermuda law, drafted in an earlier era, required a solicitor to have served three-year articles. Following a meeting between Maddocks, Sharpe's proposer, and then Chief Justice Sir James Astwood in his Chambers, the matter was resolved by the filing of a further affidavit. Sharpe's qualifications for the call were more than adequate as he had already been admitted in another Commonwealth country. The Supreme Court Act was subsequently amended to remove this anomaly. A considerable number of Bermudians have followed Sharpe into the Bermuda profession as solicitors. Indeed, it has become the preferred route of qualification for those not intending to practise before the courts.

The decision Sharpe faced, to return to Bermuda, was not an easy one. He had become accustomed to living in London, but he felt that his future lay at home, so home he came. To best assess his options, he applied to The Bank of Bermuda, to Conyers Dill & Pearman and to the small but growing legal practice of Bermudian lawyer Julian Hall, a beneficiary of Conyers Dill & Pearman's legal awards programme and a former associate in the firm, who had branched out on his own. Sharpe had met Woods earlier, when summering at the firm. Now the two men met again and an offer of employment was made.

When Sharpe joined the firm as an associate in June 1981, he started work as a litigator. He recalls being one of just three associates, along with Alastair Gunning and Gerald Collett. Sharpe found that he did not enjoy the courtroom experience as much as he had thought he might and within a year, at his first annual review with Woods and Cooper, discussed his ambitions and the firm's needs, and was, as a result, transferred to the Corporate Department.

Sharpe was not destined to spend the remainder of his working career with the firm. Although today he remains with Conyers Dill & Pearman in a consultancy role, his interests outside the Law, principally a wine-importing business, now claim his attention for half of each working day.

CHAPTER TWENTY NINE

Poetic In Appearance

In the spring and summer of 1981, work on the firm's new building was proceeding apace. The fourth and fifth floors were going up and some of the roofing structure was in place. An article contributed to *Briefcase* on the subject read, in part:

> To those who daily pass this concrete monster, it would appear that only a few more bricks have been put in place each day, but somewhere, somehow in that conglomeration of steel and mortar, great things are slowly but surely happening.

Photographs show a skeleton-like apparition with a dark interior. The building's structural steel had proven to be of a quality too good to waste, so the edifice was being recreated, as it were, from the inside out. The menacing air evaporated pretty quickly as the walls went up. Today it is hard to recall a time when Clarendon House, for such the building was renamed, was not there.

As the firm was preparing to move to its new location, so Bermuda might have been said to be preparing itself for new management. Realtor and businessman John Swan was appointed Premier on 15 January 1982 on the resignation of David Gibbons. Swan was the youngest Premier and party leader, representing a nominal handover of power to a new generation. Initially regarded as Gibbons' protégé, Swan would serve for more than 13 years as Premier, leading the United Bermuda Party to victory in four elections. Knighted for his services to the country, Sir John presided over a remarkable period in Bermudian history which saw the insurance industry expand fivefold during his tenure and the overall number of companies on the Bermuda register soar likewise. His propulsion of Independence to the front of the political agenda caused his downfall in 1995.

Collis, whose political career unfolded largely during the Swan years, was appointed a Senator for the United Bermuda Party in 1981. Not long afterwards, he completed his two-year presidency of the Bermuda Chamber of Commerce. The Chamber is different in style from its overseas counterparts, with local and international divisions, a heavy emphasis on education and the ear of Government. For a long time, the Bermuda Chamber was perceived as a trade organisation for Bermuda's merchants, but by the time Collis left the presidency, the Chamber had more than 600 members, all corporate or professional, organised in seven divisions representing every facet of Bermudian business. Collis had acted as the organisation's spokesman, which brought him greater visibility in the community.

To mark the occasion of his retirement from the presidency, *The Royal Gazette* interviewed him, running the article under the title: "Putting 'his way' to the ultimate test". The unattributed feature offered Collis the chance for self-assessment. In part, it read:

Almost two years ago to the day, Senator Collis—he was then plain Mr.—settled back in his office chair and described himself as a man of compromise, favouring a moderate, reasoned approach to problem solving, rather than the heavy-handed techniques of the radicals in the community.

In that interview, the 49-year-old lawyer expounded the belief that Chamber presidents need not court popularity, but should have a reasonable personality and a degree of confidence.

Little did he know then that his philosophies would soon be put to the ultimate test and that his intervention in the 1981 labour dispute would make him one of the most popular figures on the Island.

Last week, seated in the same office, Sen. Collis said that although those crisis-ridden days had undoubtedly been the most difficult of his presidency, they led to what he now regards as an unequalled high spot.

"I think the real high spot of the past two years came when people demonstrated their apparent goodwill towards me after I intervened in the conflict. I received dozens of phone calls and telegrams from friends and Opposition and Union members who felt that I had acted in an effective manner."

Their reaction, he recalls, placed him in what many lawyers would feel was an unusual position at the centre of attention, a position he has tried to avoid during a 26-year career with one of Bermuda's leading law firms.

"I was quite surprised at the response," said Sen. Collis. "I'm a self-effacing sort of person and, as is common in my profession, am not given to looking for publicity."

Publicity, of course, can work both ways. It might have been sharply critical of the Senator had his attempt to ease mounting tensions been considered imprudent. The fact that it wasn't says as much for the Chamber's decision-making process as it does for Sen. Collis' conciliatory style.

The presidency has placed considerable pressure on his working day, 20 percent of which he was already devoting to community activities, well before he took over the presidency from Mr. Jack Outerbridge.

Said Sen. Collis: "Apart from last year's labour dispute, I think that perhaps the most difficult task I encountered was trying to adjust my working life to meet the demands of the post."

The Conyers Dill & Pearman partner is certain that he would not behave otherwise if he had to relive his term as president. 'Different' was the word he used last week to describe his approach to the job and it is probably the most accurate way to sum up his contribution.

Yet the approach could hardly have been anything but different. As the first lawyer in the president's chair, Sen. Collis would have found it difficult to emulate the thinking of his trade-oriented predecessors, even if he had wanted to.

Instead he adopted a broad overview of local issues, often linking them to world events and giving regular Chamber newsletters a distinctly international flavour.

Said the Senator: "I don't think I can say whether I have been a good president or not. I have tried to focus the Chamber's attention on general economic and commercial trends rather than concentrating on narrower affairs of trade, as my predecessors have tended to."

Whatever Sen. Collis may have done for the Chamber and its members, he feels the presidency has done much for him.

"I must say I have enjoyed the last two years," he said. "It has allowed me to see that there are no absolutes on any question and that in this position, you have to be concerned with both sides of an argument and try to follow a middle path."

Two weeks later, the partnership of Conyers Dill & Pearman was reduced to ten when Walter Maddocks retired from the practice and opened a thoroughbred horse-breeding farm just outside Lexington, Kentucky. Something of a nomad, Maddocks' travels would later bring him back to Bermuda to serve for three years as Attorney General. Among other achievements since leaving the firm, he was in charge of a Rotary fund-raising programme aimed at ending poliomyelitis, which set out to raise US$120 million to fund a World Health Organisation programme. In the end, more than twice that amount was raised.

There was little time for the firm to reflect upon the loss of Maddocks; in the months which followed, Conyers Dill & Pearman would change its shape almost completely as it underwent another burst of growth and the nature of the practice of corporate law in Bermuda changed altogether.

In the first week of May 1982, the staff completed the move inland to Clarendon House. The firm occupied most of four floors and sub-let superfluous space on staggered lease lengths, in case additional space were needed in the future. Clarendon House is a boxy, limestone building, which makes maximum use of space. Its straight, clean lines dominate the crossroads on which it stands.

Vivian Young wrote for *Briefcase* of the atrium connecting Clarendon House and The Bank of Bermuda's building which stands behind it. Young wrote:

Original in design, poetic in appearance, sturdy of frame (and long in execution!), the atrium is the creation of the local firm of

Onions, Bouchard & McCulloch. Stuart Galloway and Ed Jones are the architects supervising construction; the ultimate responsibility rests with Fraser Butterworth, partner-in-charge.

In Roman domestic architecture, the atrium was the interior court, surrounded on all sides by the rooms of the house. It evolved from the main room of the earliest Roman houses, which usually had at its centre the family cooking hearth. Larger homes had several atria—the largest serving as a formal reception area, often colonnaded.

Our atrium is the first of its type in Bermuda, although they are becoming very popular in the United States. World travellers who have visited Spain may have seen the beautiful example in the Alhambra in Grenada.

A structure known as a 'space frame' makes up the roof of the atrium. Explained in simple terms, it consists of a series of aluminium-tube trusses placed at right angles to each other and inset with pyramids of polycarbonate, a high impact-resistant glazing material.

The side walls are set with panels of glass tinted for solar control and although the structure gives an appearance of airiness and delicacy, it has been built to withstand winds of up to 135 m.p.h. Hot air, which rises naturally upward, will be dispersed through louvres strategically placed at the tops of the side walls.

The north side of the atrium has as a focal point a 'wet-wall', constructed of natural limestone. Although not the first in Bermuda (the lobby of the Hamilton Princess has one similar) it certainly is the tallest, rising 45 feet. The wet-wall has been studded at intervals with plants—the vivid emerald of the foliage offering an appealing contrast to the soft grey of the natural stone. The fall of water, which will be regulated according to weather conditions, will flow into a series of three cascading pools.

History records that the firm's gamble in creating 60,000 square feet of first class office space in Clarendon House paid off. The new building was expected to cope with the firm's potential growth over the succeeding 15 years. From a vantage point in time 17 years later, it can be seen that Clarendon House has exceeded its specifications.

The move to the new building ended one tradition: the tea break. A veritable institution in British business, the tea lady made twice-daily visits to those in her charge, retailing 'cuppas', perhaps some watery coffee and sugary biscuits. Her arrival once announced the only permitted breaks in a day's office labour—15 minutes in the morning, known as 'elevenses', and tea at four o'clock in the afternoon. At least one large insurer in Bermuda has retained the trolley and the tea lady. Here it might be said that Conyers Dill & Pearman took a wrong turn, but the firm appears to have survived the loss of its tea lady as well as could be expected.

Exit the tea trolley.

CHAPTER THIRTY

Breathing Space

At about the time the firm moved into Clarendon House, a collection of maps and other Bermudiana came on the market. The collection belonged to the late Helene Montgomery-Moore, an American who lived in Bermuda and who married Sir Bayard's former Commanding Officer, Major Cecil (Mookie) Montgomery-Moore. Among the collection's 41 Bermuda maps were 30 which Conyers Dill & Pearman added to its permanent collection.

The firm agreed to display the collection to interested members of the public in open, air-conditioned rooms, and to properly care for the maps. Visitors to Clarendon House can see that the firm has been as good as its word. The walls of almost every meeting room bear the Montgomery-Moore maps and others from the firm's collection of maps and watercolours of Bermudian interest. Woods described the collection, later, to senior reporter Robin Zuill of *RG Magazine*. In part, her account read:

The collection includes a 1760 map, called *City of Bermuda,*

Metropolis of the Summer Islands, a proposed street map of Hamilton. It is a favourite of Michael Woods, Conyers Dill & Pearman's Partnership Secretary, who is responsible for the collection. The map lists proposed features in the city, including a steeple, fish market, herb market and flesh market, public parks and groves, public baths for men, baths for women, a theatre and an academy of music.

The earliest is a 1548 Giacomo Gastaldi map of the *Tierra Nueva* (New World), called *La Bermuda*. The next earliest is a 1561 Ruscelli. The most valuable map is by Capt. John Smith, dated between 1624 and 1632. The Smith map, called *The Summer Ils.*, is surrounded by scenes of Bermuda, mostly forts and bridges.

The collection also includes several maps derived from Norwood's original survey of 1618. Three are by John Speed, dated 1626 and 1676, while another is by William Blaeu, dated 1635. Norwood divided Bermuda into 50 strips of land of 25 acres apiece, owned by the Somers Isle Company. Maps based on Norwood's survey also include a list of shareholders and the number of shares they own in the company.

The smallest is a 1740 Desbruslins, which measures 15 cm by 13.5 cm. That map was featured on a 1984 Bermuda stamp. Other maps include a 1729 van de Aa with fanciful scenes of Indians measuring and surveying land. One of the most fascinating features of the maps is the cartouche, an embellishment which often encompasses the name of the map, the scale and other information about the map.

Others in the collection are a 1692 map called *Le Bermude*, by P. Coronelli of Venice, dedicated *Al illustrissimo Sig. Abbate Isidoro Bernardi*; an 1860 A. Fullerton & Co. map of Bermuda set with Jamaica; and a 1727 Herman Moll map of the *Island of Bermudos*, which shows Pembroke as Penbrock Shire; and a 1778 Venezia with contemporary colouring.

The firm has continued to add to its collection, which now numbers more than 50 maps and 30 watercolours, prints, etchings and the like. Although not enormously valuable, the collection is numbered among the more interesting with a specific focus on Bermuda. The maps and paintings add a uniquely Bermudian touch to meetings held at Clarendon House and were later joined, on the fifth floor, by some of the fine underwater photographs of Laurence Gould, who, before he was killed in a road traffic accident, was a pharmacist at the Clarendon Pharmacy on the building's ground floor. Bermuda is home to a surprisingly active art world. It is entirely in keeping with its dictates that Mrs. Montgomery-Moore would have asked that the collection be made available to the public. Hamilton boasts several art galleries, among them that of the Masterworks Foundation, whose goal is the return to Bermuda of works created on the Island by visitors to Bermuda who fell under the Island's spell. Richard Pearman has been one of the organisation's trustees since he assisted in its establishment.

By the summer of 1982, the newly-consolidated firm of Conyers Dill & Pearman was sufficiently comfortable in its fresh surroundings to consider its future. The competition was no longer that other firm across town, but the larger firms in New York and London, who were accustomed to earning the lion's share of the fee. The partners of Conyers Dill & Pearman discussed the establishment of a European presence; Bermuda would serve for the North American markets. The logic was solid enough. The firm's domestic market had been conquered. The largest Bermuda law firm could grow locally only at the expense of the other large firm or the smaller practices. The partners of Conyers Dill & Pearman had decided, more or less explicitly, to limit their market share in Bermuda and to seek to attract new clients from outside the Island.

In the autumn of 1982, the firm asked McCabe, who had spent a couple of years as Head of the Property Department, to take on an altogether different property assignment. Having proven admirably well suited to the firm's ethos as Collis had described it to him, McCabe was asked to set up and run a new venture: the firm's first overseas office, in Guernsey. The second largest of the Channel Islands, Guernsey lies some 20 miles off the coast of Normandy. An hour's flying time from London, but in the same time zone, Guernsey owes its allegiance to the British Crown, but has its own Legislature. Its legal system is based on the ancient customary Law of the Duchy of Normandy, although English law is increasingly applied when the old system needs alteration or amendment.

Office space had been rented in a converted Methodist chapel in the town of St. Peter Port, and a management company formed. St. Peter Port is a tiny town, really, not unlike many areas of Devon and Cornwall in England. Guernsey boasts some light industry, but has to a significant degree based its international sector on the Bermuda model. The islands share similarities; the populations are well-educated and of about the same size, and their economies rely on similar sources of revenue. At 24 square miles, Guernsey is only slightly larger than Bermuda. When McCabe arrived at the office, he found three carpeted rooms and little more.

A professional firm in Bermuda opening an overseas office was a grand reversal of the tradition by which Bermuda routinely imports business and staff from overseas. Nowadays, the announcement of the opening of a new Bermudian-owned overseas office has considerably less impact, since the major law firms, the banks, Government and many of the larger Bermuda insurers have between them some three dozen offices in operation around the world.

But late in 1982, when McCabe set off to establish a Guernsey presence from scratch, "paperclips and all", the firm crossed a Rubicon. It became an international practice not only in the nature of its business, but in its infrastructure. Having earned as large a share of the Bermuda pie as was good for the firm or the Island, the partners looked outside the parameters of home turf, out to sea, as had generations of Bermudians before them. The initial objectives of practising Bermuda law in Guernsey were to establish a European presence, to provide Bermuda legal advice to European clients and friends, and to manage companies and trusts established in jurisdictions other than Bermuda.

McCabe scared up some office furniture and gradually accumulated the thousand and one necessities that all offices require to conduct business. Without a client base, life proceeded quietly enough at first and McCabe recalls with some satisfaction the day, early in 1983, when the Guernsey office received its first instructions, which would have clattered out over the telex machine. Telex messages were printed on a small yellow tickertape, a predecessor of today's more sophisticated electronic back-up techniques. The tape copy allowed the message to be forwarded by running the tape through a different part of the machine. It took thousands of years to devise a machine as sophisticated as the telex, and less than 60 years for it to become all but obsolete.

The sound of that first incoming telex at the Guernsey office was the opening shot: Conyers Dill & Pearman had begun to take on the world. But this internationalisation did not mean that the firm was ready to ignore the legal needs of the community from which it sprang.

In February 1983, Narinder Kumar Hargun joined Conyers Dill & Pearman as a litigator. He was born on 10 December 1954 in Punjab, India. His father, Mula Ram Hargun, was a teacher, who moved to England in the late 1950s. Once Hargun *père* was established, his wife, Kaushalia Devi, followed with the children. Having completed his secondary education in Yorkshire, Narinder proceeded to read Law at the London School of Economics & Political Science, known as the LSE, where he earned his

Bachelor of Laws and Master's degree.

Hargun then served his pupillage at 2, Crown Office Row and was called to the Bar in England and Wales at the Middle Temple. He had his eye on the Law from an early age. The role he always envisaged for himself, and has achieved, is that of advocate. Although he briefly considered an academic career, the man who today heads Conyers Dill & Pearman's Litigation Department gave little thought to any other career.

To Hollywood, the image of the trial lawyer in full swing has proven irresistible. The dynamics of courtroom drama make for more riveting viewing than the back-room labours of the solicitor or the corporate lawyer. As a result, when people think of attorneys, they tend to imagine the impassioned advocate in the manner of Gregory Peck's portrayal of Atticus Finch in *To Kill A Mockingbird*, Paul Newman as Frank Galvin in *The Verdict*, or any other of a dozen other fictional trial lawyers. The law office has, of late, proved a useful locus for American and British television series to house their soap operatics, although the drama in such settings stems more from the relationships between lawyers than from that between lawyers and the Law.

The reality of the modern practice of law is, of course, more mundane than that depicted in the breathless melodramas. A portion of every litigation lawyer's day is spent dealing with relatively minor affairs. The more interesting cases, which comprise the majority of the litigation practice of Conyers Dill & Pearman, are corporate disputes, often complex and opaque international matters. These arcane proceedings are of the greatest interest to the parties to the case and those in their industries, and would not lend themselves well to the tight confines and emotional requirements of cinematic treatment.

In London, Hargun fell in with a group of young Bermudian professionals-in-training such as the Pearman brothers had encountered at Stowe. Among Hargun's circle of Bermudians were Julian Hall, David

Kessaram and the Scott brothers, Larry and Michael, now leading lights in the Government and Opposition, respectively. Hall was a year or two senior to Hargun, but on his return to Bermuda to set up his own firm, Hall invited Hargun to join him. Hargun had visited the Island before, but the idea of two or three years overseas to broaden his experience of work and life sounded attractive and sensible.

Like so many who leave home for a year or two abroad, Hargun never went back. There are those who complete an overseas contract and return to the country they never really left, in their mind's eye. Their careers at home are duly enhanced by what was learned elsewhere and the memory stays with them for a lifetime. The British excel at this rite of managerial passage, rotating, for example, their Foreign Service staff into and out of postings worldwide.

A smaller number who venture overseas stay there for the remainder of their working lives and beyond. A comfortable expatriate life places a physical distance between past and present and can open vistas of opportunity unimagined by those pursuing more traditional career paths back home. Popular wisdom suggests that expatriates work harder than those whose society they join, whether to justify their presence or to prove a point to those left behind. This must be a canard; there must be lazy expatriates.

Almost every Bermudian professional has been an expatriate at some stage of his or her life. Schooling, university, work experience; perhaps one of the reasons that many expatriates have been able to enter the fabric of Bermudian society is a shared sense of internationalism.

Within two years of Hargun's arrival in Bermuda, Hall dissolved his practice. Hargun joined another of his Bermudian friends at Kessaram & Co., but the work of greatest interest to Hargun, it seemed, was the preserve of the large firms. Conyers Dill & Pearman placed an advertisement in *The Royal Gazette* for a litigation lawyer a year later, looking to replace Gerald Collett, who had gone on to become a Judge. Hargun was interviewed by

Ellison, then head of Litigation, and Woods, of course. In February 1983, Hargun joined the firm as an associate in the Litigation Department.

Among the tools Conyers Dill & Pearman brought to the fray at around the time Hargun arrived were its first word processor and its third or fourth accounting system, far removed from the days of the hand-written ledgers of the 1920s and '30s. The word processor more or less filled a room and users had to book it in advance, like today's conference rooms. Its application was unofficially limited to large and important work. Computers were becoming a part of the business landscape, with 1984 still two years away.

Installed in its new fortress, armed with the latest in technology and with a new breed of lawyer aboard, the firm of Conyers Dill & Pearman watched as the Bermuda insurance industry paused, unexpectedly and unusually, to catch up with itself.

The reinsurance market in the United States grew 'soft', an industry euphemism for supply exceeding demand. Some captive companies became excess to their owners' requirements and entered into run-off. Others found third-party business less predictable, and less profitable, than they had anticipated. Several folded their tents and left Bermuda. But to interpret what happened in the middle of the 1980s simply as bad news would be to undervalue the lessons Bermuda and the insurance industry have learned from the experience. The soft market by which the industry is afflicted in 1998 has seen considerable merger and acquisition activity, aimed at diversifying Bermuda's insurance sector away from over-reliance on any one form of insurance.

The firm used the mid-'80s slowdown as a breathing space of its own. Moving and merging offices are changes best swallowed at their own pace. Had the Bermuda insurance industry instead put on one of its characteristic spurts at that moment, the wave of new business might have made Conyers Dill & Pearman a less comfortable place to work and placed impossible demands on lawyers and staff at a time when a considerable infusion of new blood was needed.

CHAPTER THIRTY ONE

A Complicated Itinerary

In October 1982, Richard Pearman and his wife visited Washington, D.C. with about 40 other couples from the International Chapter of the Young Presidents Organisation. The theme of the trip was 'The World According to Washington', and its purpose was to bring together outstanding young managers to exchange ideas and to catch up on international developments in management.

YPO was founded in the 1950s to gather together the young presidents of companies and to allow them to meet regularly. In time, the organisation coalesced around a mission statement: "To become better presidents through education and the exchange of ideas". To belong to the organisation, one has to head a business enterprise and be under the age of 50.

During the Washington visit, YPO members were taken on a tour of the US Capitol building, culminating in a question and answer session on the floor of the United States' House of Representatives. Attendees listened to, and were able to ask questions of, a number of decision-makers in the Republican administration, on topics such as the economy and international relations and trade.

Later that afternoon, YPO representatives were taken in a London double-decker bus, painted green, to the State Dining Room at the White House, where each was introduced individually and had a few moments to chat with the senior official in the Administration, the 40th President of the United States, Ronald Reagan. The day concluded with a black tie dinner at the State Department, following a tour of some of the 18th and 19th century rooms which had recently undergone redecoration.

Pearman's meeting with Reagan was not the first between a partner and the President of the United States, both Sir Bayard and Sir James having met President Dwight Eisenhower on his visit to Bermuda three decades earlier. The YPO has since gone from strength to strength, and in 1997 some 1,700 members and their families visited Bermuda for their annual excursion, with almost all having the opportunity to meet Premier Pamela Gordon.

Premier Gordon had not yet entered politics in January 1984, when Brian Smedley, Q.C. joined Conyers Dill & Pearman as an associate. Educated at London University and Gray's Inn, Smedley had been appointed a Recorder of the Crown Court. Having taken Silk, he had been seated for three years prior to joining the firm, mainly at the Central Criminal Court in London, more widely known as the Old Bailey. His arrival in Bermuda further strengthened the firm's Litigation Department.

Three months later, John Charles Ross Collis joined the firm as an associate. History records that the oldest son of Charles and Margaret Collis, née Ross, was the first corporate specialist at Conyers Dill & Pearman, in its 56th year of operation. Today, the firm's Corporate Department, which John Collis heads, is the *force majeure* of the partnership.

The firm had developed other specialties before John arrived, notably in the areas of the P&I Clubs, shipping law and real estate. Those in the firm who were litigators cannot rightly be called specialists, since the practice of litigation is more than a specialisation; it is a separate branch of the Law, quite different from the work of solicitors. Litigators, it is said, look backwards, at what happened, while solicitors look forward, to anticipate what might go wrong. The two English legal professions, barristers and solicitors—Americans make no such distinction—attract two distinct breeds of legal minds.

Under the British system, barristers generally engage in trial advocacy and solicitors in office work, but their duties overlap to a considerable degree. Barristers are often called upon for an opinion or to draft documents and solicitors may appear in the lower courts. Only barristers, however, may appear before the High Court. From their number are made the most important judicial appointments. Barristers are members of one of four Inns of Court: Gray's Inn, Lincoln's Inn, the Middle Temple and the Inner Temple.

The early history of the Inns is obscure, but since their inception in the Middle Ages, they have taught English Law, rather than Roman, which was taught in the universities. By the middle of the 13th century, there arose a class of men who created and dominated the modern legal profession, who established the Inns of Court as a means of education.

The School of Law at the Inns of Court, known colloquially as 'Bar School', traces its origins to the establishment of the Council of Legal Education in 1852. The present School consists of 45 staff, most of whom are qualified barristers. The Bar Vocational Course prepares students for the more specialised training to be given in pupillage and lays the foundations for future practice, whether in Chambers or as employed barristers. The course teaches seven skills: Advocacy, Conference, Drafting, Fact Management, Legal Research, Negotiation and Opinion Writing. It also covers the knowledge areas of Evidence, Civil Procedure, Criminal Procedure and Sentencing.

A prospective barrister must pass a series of examinations established for the Inns by the Council of Legal Education and satisfy certain traditional requirements, perhaps most famously eating at least three dinners at the chosen Inn per term.

Collectively, the Inns of Court are known as the Bar; its General Council sets standards for the profession. A barrister must accept a case regardless of his personal feelings, but may not do so where a conflict of interest arises. Generally, barristers undertake work only on the introduction of a solicitor, who prepares and delivers the client's instructions to a barrister. In the UK, solicitors outnumber barristers by more than ten to one.

Although he qualified as a barrister, John Collis has a solicitor's mind. He was born on 9 June 1958, not long after his father had joined Conyers Dill & Pearman. John attended Saltus and then Rugby School, in the British Midlands, between the ages of 16 and 18, to study for his A-levels. From there he read for a Bachelor of Commerce degree at McGill University in Montréal, Quebec. Mathematics was his strength, but the career of mathematician held little appeal. He spent his summers working as a computer programmer. When the time came to choose a path, John's father suggested a law degree as an academic discipline, to be approached in a mathematical manner.

John graduated from McGill in 1979 as a Bachelor of Commerce with joint honours in Economics and Finance. The award of a Rhodes Scholarship placed him in his father's footsteps as he went up to Corpus Christi College, Oxford and emerged two years later a Bachelor of Arts in Jurisprudence, to spend a year at Bar School. John met his wife Judy while studying law; she is now a partner in Appleby, Spurling & Kempe. John was called to the Bar at the Middle Temple and served his pupillage at Lincoln's Inn and the Middle Temple.

He was able to obtain permission from the Bar to work for

Linklaters & Paines, a substantial firm of solicitors in the City of London, in their Tax Department. The work, at a busy time for corporate lawyers in London, whetted his appetite for the corporate world. His training was in business and economics; the decision to concentrate on corporate law was "automatic". After two years at Linklaters & Paines, John Collis returned to Bermuda to join the firm of Conyers Dill & Pearman in April 1984 as an associate. He is a licensed pilot and a former skydiver.

Bermuda's international business sector, at the time John came home, was poised for further significant growth. The industry was mature, with a sensible infrastructure and experience going back 50 years. The players were in place: accountants, lawyers, management companies, Government. The hospitality industry boasted several five-star hotels, which those at the top end of the business world regard as a given when they travel.

John worked, initially, under Mutch, who had taken hold of the firm's corporate business, which, was at the time, essentially documentary. The legal work on international transactions would be drafted outside Bermuda and the documents referred to Conyers Dill & Pearman or other Bermuda firms for review as to suitability under Bermuda law. John had been trained differently, to work on originating documents, the 'sharp end' of the transaction.

In the summer of 1984, Sir Bayard retired from the position of Chancellor of the Diocese of Bermuda, a position he had held for 33 years. He had served under five Bishops, including the then incumbent, Anselm Genders. Nicky Dill was appointed to succeed his father by the Most Reverend Gerald Ellison, a former Bishop of London, no relation to John. Nicky Dill has been Chancellor during a difficult period in the Church's history and has helped to rewrite the Constitution of the Anglican Church in Bermuda. During his tenure as Chancellor, the first Bermudian Bishop, Ewen Ratteray, was elected.

Nicky Dill was a trustee of the Cavendish Hall School in Devonshire, built by his grandfather, Sir Harry Watlington. Nicky and businessman Harry Cox became trustees of Saltus Grammar School when the Cavendish trustees first offered to rent the school and later donated it to the Saltus Trustees to serve as a Primary School.

Nicky is Chairman of the Air Transport Licensing Board and director of a number of Bermuda utility companies. He was Commodore of the Royal Bermuda Yacht Club for the two years from 1976, some 40 years after his father held the post. Nicky is also the Honorary Danish Consul in Bermuda. The Consul General of Denmark in New York awarded him the Knight's Cross of the Order of Danneborg, in recognition of his services to Denmark. A section of his office is dedicated to his diplomatic duties; portraits of Queen Margrethe II of Denmark and her consort, Prince Henrik, grace the walls.

1984 was an anniversary year in Bermuda. The Island celebrated its 375th anniversary in more muted fashion than had been the case a quarter of a century earlier. An unsigned editorial contribution to the 12th issue of *Briefcase* summarises the way the firm stood during Bermuda's 375th anniversary year. The unattributed article, entitled *Achievement '84*, reads in part:

> As Bermuda's other media have been filled with tales of heritage and achievements and 375th anniversary goings-on, we too have been delving into our backgrounds and out-of-office activities. We're not just a lot of pretty faces and bulging biceps—there's talent in them thar nine-to-fivers that surfaces far more often than you ever dreamed of.
>
> There's also our reputation of being a good, solid, Bermudian family organisation. Though international in its make-up—some of us come from the United States, Canada, New Zealand,

Australia and the United Kingdom—our staff is, of course, over-whelmingly Bermudian. Collectively, we have clocked up some 900 years of service. One quarter of the staff has worked here for more than ten years and 10 percent can claim over 20 years with us. In some instances, we are seeing second and third generation Bermudians coming into the organisation.

Among the new arrivals welcomed to the firm in the succeeding issue of *Briefcase* was Robin Joan Mayor, who joined Conyers Dill & Pearman in April 1985. *Née* Darling, she was the fourth daughter of Bermudian Peter Darling and his wife, Joan. Robin was born on 5 October 1956 in the town of Tavistock in Devon, deep in England's West Country. Graham was drafting his letter to *The Times* at about the time Mayor was born.

Darling *père* served as an officer in the Royal Marines, saw active service in the War and stayed on as a regular soldier in peacetime. Robin, the lastborn of four sisters, lived in England until she was five years old, when the family moved in a complicated pattern between England and Singapore before settling in Bermuda when she was 14. Robin was educated at the Royal School in Bath and then Hatherop College, near Cirencester, before spending a year at Bermuda College.

At school, she had enjoyed being on stage or backstage at theatrical productions, but without definite career ideas, enrolled at St. Godric's Secretarial School in North London's leafy Hampstead. She worked as a secretary in Bermuda and the UK and in her early 20s returned to the Island to work at the law firm of Julian Hall & Partners.

Hargun was working at Hall's practice at the time, and Mayor and Hargun became friends. When the career of Mayor's fiancé, now her husband, Craig Mayor, took him to England, she decided to complete the education she had denied herself, and enrolled in what is now North

London University, where Hargun had formerly taught. She gained her Bachelor of Arts (Honours) degree and returned once again to Bermuda to marry and spend a year with Appleby, Spurling & Kempe as a Corporate Secretary. A complicated itinerary continued with a return to England for a year at Bar School and a call to the Bar in England and Wales at Lincoln's Inn in July 1984.

Mayor chose for her pupillage the firm of Conyers Dill & Pearman, with Hargun as her Pupil Master. She was thus among the very first to serve pupillage in Bermuda. The process of pupillage, it might be argued, is the first time a newly-qualified lawyer comes to grips with the application of law. Pupils shadow barristers, follow them to court, sit behind them and learn from them, preferably in silence. Although accompanied by no special fanfare, Mayor's pupillage marked a degree of maturity in the development of Conyers Dill & Pearman. No career obligations accrue to a pupil. Most of the members of Conyers Dill & Pearman who completed their pupillage elsewhere did so at a younger age than Mayor, and often saw it as a coda to their lives overseas, prior to returning home. Today, the firm has as many as four pupils a year, but history affords the first an extra emphasis.

On completing her pupillage, Mayor was offered the position of associate in the firm's Litigation Department, which she took up in April 1985. She was called to the Bar in Bermuda and took over Kathy Sharpe's position in the Litigation Department, working alongside Smedley, Dennis Dwyer and Hargun. In due course, Mayor would become a partner in Conyers Dill & Pearman and now, as Head of Liquidations, is named as Liquidator when Conyers Dill & Pearman is handling the matter. In that capacity, she and a staff of four handle mostly solvent liquidations of companies which have ceased to be of benefit to their owners. Assets are marshalled, liabilities discharged, and the balance of the company's assets returned to shareholders. The work is largely documentary.

Insolvencies are usually referred to the Island's accounting firms because of conflicts of interest.

With Conyers Dill & Pearman operating today in six jurisdictions, and other Bermuda service providers in as many as 17 locations off the Island, Bermuda Inc. has exported itself to the world which lies beyond the Island's estimated 150 miles of coastline. In 1985, just as Mayor joined the firm, its impending move to Hong Kong, to establish the first Bermuda professional office in the Far East, anticipated the important role the Island was to play before and after the forthcoming handover of the Territory to the Chinese.

The Royal Gazette ran an article in its *Business* section, headlined "Hong Kong office on cards for leading Bermuda law firm". With inside information, an unnamed reporter crafted a story around an overview of Bermuda's operations in the Far East. The article read, in part:

> Conyers Dill & Pearman, one of Bermuda's largest law firms, is expected to open an office in Hong Kong later this year.
>
> Though the firm last week declined to discuss its Far East expansion, *Business* understands the office will be headed by CD&P partner John Ellison and is to open its doors for business in June. Conyers Dill & Pearman already has some prestigious Far East names on its books.
>
> Conyers Dill & Pearman's plan to set up an office in Hong Kong is only part of a long-running campaign by lawyers, bankers and others to woo business to Bermuda. The Bank of Bermuda, for example, has long had an office in Hong Kong and the Bank of Butterfield is rumoured to be considering a similar exercise.
>
> What they are offering is not so much sophisticated financial and legal expertise, which is highly essential, but which could arguably be matched by suppliers already well-established in Hong

Kong, but the chance to channel business through a respectable and, more importantly, stable jurisdiction.

Hong Kong firms are understandably worried about their long-term future in a UK colony due to become part of China in 1997. That's when Britain's lease expires and that's the time by which many firms there may have drawn up corporate contingency plans possibly including a Bermuda connection.

Such, at least, is the hope of many business professionals in Bermuda.

And their fishing trips to Hong Kong are likely to be using more powerful bait later this year.

Our stamp duty legislation is to get long-awaited changes, aimed at enhancing Bermuda's attractions as an offshore business centre by reducing duties payable on imported trusts and settlements. The changes are considered vitally important because control of much of the business Bermuda wants to lure here is tied up in family trusts in Hong Kong.

The report was largely accurate, although the phrase "corporate contingency plans" considerably underestimated what was to follow.

In June 1985, Ellison did indeed open the firm's Hong Kong office, Smedley succeeding him as Head of Litigation. The idea had been on the partners' table for a number of years. When the time came, Ellison volunteered; he would spend the next seven years based in Hong Kong, building a thriving practice which has extended beyond the handover to allow Conyers Dill & Pearman, perhaps a little incongruously, a foothold in Communist China.

A generalist in a practice on the cusp of specialisation, Ellison's achievement in Hong Kong illustrates one of the strengths of the professional practice. If a hole opens up, someone will step forward or be asked to fill it. If an opportunity arises, matters can usually be arranged in such a way as to free the necessary resources to meet the need.

The handover of Hong Kong to the sovereignty of China lay a dozen years away when Conyers Dill & Pearman put up their shingle at Number Two, Exchange Square. Already a number of companies had pioneered what can be described without hyperbole as a great international movement to relocate to other jurisdictions the holding companies atop the corporate empires quoted on the Hong Kong stock exchange.

Jardine Matheson, among the very largest, was also among the very first to move to Bermuda, in the middle of the 1980s, and is now well-established in the heart of Hamilton. By the time Prince Charles and Governor Chris Patten bade a final farewell to the Fragrant Harbour, more than half the companies listed on the Hong Kong exchange had moved at least part of their corporate architecture to Bermuda. Although some finally settled in other jurisdictions, a good number have chosen to remain in Bermuda.

The official opening of Conyers Dill & Pearman's Hong Kong office on 22 September 1985 was celebrated with a reception at the nearby Mandarin Hotel, with Sir Bayard, Nicky Dill and John Ellison hosting a Chinese banquet for 160 people.

To accommodate its expansion, the firm's Hong Kong office is now in its third Exchange Square incarnation. Its peregrinations have brought the firm back today to Number Two, one of the original twin 50-storey towers which for so long dominated the Hong Kong skyline. Off the perpetually busy six-lane Connaught Road, access to the building is gained through a vast lobby with living trees and a two-story escalator ride between waterfalls, which cascade on either side into beds of sumptuous flowers. The Exchange Square buildings stand close to the harbour's edge, looking across to Kowloon. Other edifices now jostle alongside as the unending job of building and rebuilding Hong Kong continues at a pace

which, to one accustomed to the speed of life in Bermuda, seems little short of frantic.

Conyers Dill & Pearman has a suite of offices on the 34th floor of Number Two, Exchange Square, housing a staff of 12. Beneath the windows of the firm's office in Hong Kong, tugs ply their trade up and down Victoria Harbour, in the busiest sea lanes in the world. Oval Star ferries chug hither and yon, carrying commuters to and from Kowloon. The shipping parade lasts 24 hours a day, with a greater volume of traffic traversing the harbour in a day than Bermuda might see in a year.

Conyers Dill & Pearman exclusively practises Bermuda law in Hong Kong. The firm's clientele is mostly substantial corporate clients, largely Hong Kong Chinese, who have incorporated a Bermuda element into their corporate structures. Many are manufacturers, with plants in Hong Kong or China; of late, the work has predominantly been related to Initial Public Offerings. Clients are referred to Conyers Dill & Pearman by other lawyers, auditors and bankers in what is now the Hong Kong Special Administrative Region of the People's Republic of China, although individual clients also approach the firm directly. Speed is a valued commodity in Hong Kong, and the firm operates, wherever possible, on the principle of an overnight turnaround at the Bermuda end, to enable Hong Kong to start its day armed.

Hong Kong is today populated by half a dozen Bermuda service providers, with The Bank of Bermuda boasting a strong regional headquarters providing, *inter alia*, administrative and custodial services to mutual funds and pension plans. The office Ellison established in June 1985 with two administrative assistants and a constantly-changing rota of messengers is today the firm's largest overseas office, carrying the flags of Bermuda and Conyers Dill & Pearman half way around the world.

CHAPTER THIRTY TWO

Private Clients

The partnership of Conyers Dill & Pearman was built in the service of great enterprises—railways, shipping lines and insurance companies among them. Although these endeavours captured the public attention and will forever be associated with the firm's early days, the practice has never neglected what in modern jargon would be referred to as a 'core business': the needs of individual clients and their families. The Private Client Department of Conyers Dill & Pearman has long assisted primarily individuals in organising their affairs to minimise their exposure to taxation and otherwise to protect and preserve family assets through the use of various forms of trust structures.

Unlike, say, corporate law, where an attorney might never meet his ultimate principals, the essence of legal work for Private Clients resides in the relationship between principal and attorney. An individual—or Board of Directors, since an increasing amount of the firm's trust work is corporate in nature—who appoints professional advisers to construct a safe haven for assets and then administer the resulting fortress, does so only when entirely certain of the probity of those to whom the assets are entrusted.

The word 'trust' derives from the 13th century Norse word *traust*, with an extended meaning related to solace. The modern word applies to arrangements by which property is held in trust and in a more general sense, to the confidence placed in the trustee. Americans once applied the word, capitalised, to a group of enterprises which had combined to monopolise and control the market for a particular commodity, a technique now very much out of favour. The many uses to which trust vehicles are put, by contrast, have never been greater.

The principles underlying the practice of trust, the divorce of ownership and control of assets and the independent capacity of the trustee, are not well understood in parts of the world where the Napoleonic code still operates. The trust industry is based on arrangements whereby an individual or corporate settlor transfers legal ownership of all or a portion of his, her or its estate to another person, the trustee, on the understanding that the trustee will use the entrusted assets only for certain purposes and beneficiaries.

Bermuda trusts are employed to achieve a variety of estate, personal, financial, tax or other business planning objectives. The effective separation of owner and beneficiary makes the trust, in its many variations, a useful tool in the hand of the business planner.

Among the purposes to which clients of Conyers Dill & Pearman put their trusts are to make future provision for spouses and dependents; to protect assets from future personal liability; to minimise estate or inheritance taxes, income tax and capital gains tax; to preserve family wealth and the continuity of family business; to efficiently distribute assets upon death in a timely fashion; to protect against exchange controls; to create charities or make provision for them; to establish pensions or employee stock option plans; and to provide lender protection in corporate financing transactions. A range of trust vehicles is permitted in Bermuda, for all manner of reasons.

In most individual circumstances, the beneficiaries of trusts tend to be members of the settlor's family, or charities. Corporate trusts serve a wide range of similarly-grounded needs, but on a larger scale. Bermuda services, under various trust arrangements, the assets of hundreds of international mutual funds, whose managers onshore and offshore invest, but do not administer, the pooled capital of their customers. The unassuming practice of guardianship is a central service of the Bermudian law firms and banks and another arrow in the quiver of Bermuda's international business industry. Given the privacy inherent in trust arrangements, there is no way to estimate the value of assets in trust in Bermuda or elsewhere, but the figure would likely be measured in billions of dollars.

Since so many other jurisdictions offer trust services, some with less attention to detail, what makes a Bermuda trust so attractive must be Bermuda itself—its legal and regulatory environment, but more importantly, the safety of capital, the permanence of the jurisdiction and the absolute reliability of the trustee.

Drafting trust deeds for individuals, families and corporations conveying assets into trusts is a meaningful part of the work of Conyers Dill & Pearman and Bermuda's other law firms and service providers. Once a trust is established, the firm often supplies accounting, monitoring and administrative services to the trust.

The firm derives new business almost exclusively from referrals; global presence is critically important to the continuing success of a trust service provider. Most of the Private Client work that comes to Bermuda is referred via London, New York, Geneva and Toronto, jurisdictions where the concepts of trust are well understood. The firm's clientele is broadly international and diverse.

Into the world of Private Clients at Conyers Dill & Pearman, in

September 1985, stepped Alec Ross Anderson, who today heads the firm's Private Client Department. Anderson was born in Bermuda on 29 September 1958. His father, Colin Stuart Anderson, was a real estate agent and developer originally from Dundee, Scotland, who was employed in Bermuda for many years before going out on his own. Like a small but consistent number of Bermudians, Anderson *père* married an American, Marilyn McMahan of Pueblo, Colorado.

The couple had three children, two boys and a girl. Alec was the oldest. He attended the charmingly-named Strawberry Hill Nursery School in Paget and then Saltus Grammar School. At ten years of age, he transferred to Dollar Academy in Scotland. Like most Bermudians who grew up in the age of jet travel, Anderson shuttled in and out of Bermuda. From Dollar, via the Island, he transferred to Newark Academy, near Far Hills, New Jersey, an environment more conducive to his dream of becoming a professional tennis player.

Anderson graduated from the University of Virginia at Charlottesville with a four-year Bachelor of Arts degree in foreign affairs. While at the University of Virginia, he decided to study law after he had graduated, and to do so in Europe. Bermuda law is based on English law, and Anderson chose the respected legal programme at the London School of Economics, Hargun's *alma mater*, next door to Lincoln's Inn Fields and the Royal Courts of Justice. In his second year at the LSE, Anderson was awarded the inaugural Conyers Dill & Pearman legal scholarship.

The *Bermuda Sun* reported the story, under the headline: "Alec Nets Big Award". *The Royal Gazette* carried a photograph of Sir Bayard handing Anderson his cheque in the partners' dining room. The award Anderson received was inaugural in name only; the firm had for some years encouraged outstanding Bermudian students monetarily and had contributed to an educational awards programme managed by the Bermuda Chamber of Commerce. The Conyers Dill & Pearman annual

Legal Education Awards, as they are now known, comprise scholarships and bursaries, granted to as many as a dozen worthy candidates. The scholarships are worth $12,500 for each of four years. More than 20 Bermudians have graduated from the programme, many of whom are now employed by the firm.

Anderson graduated from the LSE a Bachelor of Laws and proceeded to Bar School. He started his pupillage at 1, Brick Court, then headed by Robert Alexander, Q.C., who, as Lord Alexander, now heads National Westminster Bank, Frank Mutch's former employer.

Anderson completed his pupillage at Macfarlanes, a medium-sized firm in the City of London, which had built its reputation on its Private Client services to a blend of newly-wealthy British entrepreneurs, beneficiaries of Margaret Thatcher's economic liberalisation, and older, family money being offered new opportunities by reductions in personal taxation and the abolition on 27 November 1984 of British exchange controls. Called to the Bar in England and Wales at Lincoln's Inn, Anderson stayed on with Macfarlanes. On his return to Bermuda in 1985, he joined Conyers Dill & Pearman as an associate.

The process of specialisation was established by the time Anderson joined the firm, but there was as yet no Private Client Department; such business was spread across the partnership. Anderson duly started out as a generalist. He worked on one of the first of a wave of public offerings occasioned by the relocation from Hong Kong, an English company, which had been purchased by a Chinese investor who moved the company from Hong Kong to create a Bermuda holding company, floated on the New York Stock Exchange. Anderson recalls the complicated transaction as a "rigorous educational experience".

In due course, he would take on some of Mutch's trust work and would agree to lend more of his time to the firm's trust business. In the mid-1980s, just as the corporate work was increasingly being drafted by the firm, so fewer clients' trusts were being drafted outside Bermuda. Trust advisers overseas were beginning to understand the wisdom of having trust deeds drafted in Bermuda, involving the firm in trust work *ab initio*.

Anderson joined the firm's Private Client Department, headed by Mutch, in 1986 and was later joined by Nicholas Bayard Botolf Dill, son of Nicky Dill and grandson of Sir Bayard, who has since left the firm to take holy orders. In a memorable contribution to *Briefcase*, the leading edge of the third generation of family members to join Conyers Dill & Pearman described with humorous exaggeration the nature of Private Client work. He wrote, in part:

> Potential clients vary from the Swedish entrepreneur who will fly you, no costs spared, to Stockholm for an abortive meeting; to the local company wanting to set up a pension plan for its two employees; to the person on his death bed who wants to transfer assets before he dies; to a multinational charitable organisation wanting to set up a six-level structure to provide for emergency flight provisions should Bermuda be invaded by a communist power; to the ultra-wealthy client who would rather spend $10,000 on legal bills than pay $5,000 to Uncle Sam. Sorting the genuine from the bogus requires sensitive probing, the ability to say no, and constant scrutiny.

As if to underline the satire, Dill concluded: "Above all is the requirement to obey your secretary in all things!"

CHAPTER THIRTY THREE

Association Captives

Donald Harrigan Malcolm joined Conyers Dill & Pearman in May 1986 as an associate in the Corporate Department. He was born on 6 Jan 1955 in Sierra Leone, then a British Colony. His father, John Mackay Malcolm, was a career Colonial Officer and Provincial Commissioner in the British Foreign Service for Sierra Leone (from *Sierra Lyoa*, 'Lion Mountains', the region's earlier name, ascribed to Portuguese explorer Pedro da Cintra). With Independence from the British looming, John and his wife Marion Malcolm returned with their four boys to Scotland in 1960.

In Ayrshire, a coastal county in the south-west of Scotland, John Malcolm taught Classics. His son Donald, first at Stewarton in Ayrshire, then at Kilmarnock Academy, completed his secondary education with a concentration on languages ancient (Latin and Greek) and modern (French and German), at what must have been breakneck speed. His decision to study law was not an unusual choice for a Classics scholar, but the age at which he made it—16—was. He had been considering the idea of teaching, but decisively rejected it and opted instead for the Law. Donald keeps his languages current these days with a little teaching.

The manner in which he achieved the educational goals he had set himself was extraordinary. As if completing a law degree in two years at Glasgow University were not challenge enough, he accompanied it with a language degree. In what he recalls as "a hard slog", he simultaneously gained Bachelor of Laws and Master of Arts degrees and emerged, barely 20 years old, eminently qualified to address the Law. In what must have felt like a well-deserved reward, he spent a year in France, working in the hospitality industry. Malcolm then served two-year articles with Wright, Johnson & Mackenzie in Glasgow, Scotland and was enrolled as a solicitor at the age of 23. He practised thereafter for four years in Scotland with Kerr Barrie & Duncan, devoting his time to a range of corporate work.

Toward the end of the 1970s, his brother, Robert, was practising as a doctor at the King Edward VII Memorial Hospital in Paget. A short distance from the centre of town, the King Edward is one of a pair of establishments managed by the Bermuda Hospitals Board, and the one at which Bermudians have been born for the better part of 60 years. As a result, most Bermudian passport applications state place of birth as Paget, Bermuda. The Hospital aside, Paget is a mostly residential suburb in which just eight percent of Bermuda's population lives.

Malcolm paid a visit to the doctor in Bermuda one summer and again the following January. He liked what he saw and figured he would enjoy living in Bermuda. On his return to Scotland from the second trip, he wrote to several Bermuda law firms. Woods informed him that Conyers Dill & Pearman did not have a vacancy, but advised him to contact other local firms. Malcolm found a vacancy at the law offices of Peter J.C. Smith, Barrister and Attorney and worked there for a year before joining Charles Vaucrosson at Vaucrosson & Co., a larger Bermuda law firm, where he ran the Corporate Department.

When Conyers Dill & Pearman found in May 1986 that the Corporate Department needed additional capacity, it advertised and Malcolm responded. He was interviewed by Woods. Not prone to exaggeration, Woods dryly told Malcolm he should be prepared to work "around the clock".

A shift of power was occurring, a transition in Bermuda from a community managed by its merchants to a community managed by its professional business managers. The effects of this change are both obvious and not so obvious. Bermuda's decision to pursue the ideas of Tucker, Graham, Sir James, Fred Reiss and others has led, over the years, to inescapable consequences.

The decline in Bermuda's hospitality industry in the face of massive international competition and the rise of the Island's corporate community are not chicken and egg situations, but history on the march. Bermuda's fabled luck paid off spectacularly when it chose as the second leg of its economy a capital-intensive industry which would in time develop into the Island's dominant economic activity. By 1986, the Bermuda insurance industry had attracted capital and surplus of US$12.5 billion, with total assets employed in the sector of US$30 billion. These numbers may seem small by current standards, but in 1986, they meant that Bermuda's insurance industry had become a formidable player on the world market.

The excess of capacity in the insurance industry had been most gravely felt by the largest of insurance companies. Like the ebb and flow of the lives on which it is based, insurance capacity moves in cycles. The cycle which bottomed out in 1986 affected all lines of business. The beginnings of globalisation played a part, as has the use of insurance as a financial tool, beyond its genesis as a means of risk transfer. The traditional response of the industry to an excess of capacity is, naturally, a reduction in capacity. The process takes time, since insurance companies are perforce such conservative endeavours. The growth of the Bermuda captive market in the 1970s and early 1980s had come during hard times for the US commercial market. A sharp cut-back by commercial insurers was the result, particularly in higher-risk areas such as general liability insurance.

In 1986, in response to the cut-backs, Bermuda was selected as the jurisdiction for two large 'association captives'. Such companies, as their title would suggest, are captive insurance companies formed by associations of related companies. Just as the single-parent captive insures, at least initially, the risks of only its parent company, so the association captive is formed to cover the individual and collective liabilities of those companies which are its owners. The association captives formed in 1986 were seeded with hundreds of millions of dollars of capital made available by banks and other large insurers. ACE Ltd. and Exel Ltd. led the way in offering excess liability and professional insurance, notably Directors' and Officers', universally referred to in the industry as 'D&O'. A branch of professional insurance, D&O provides indemnification coverage for corporate officers whose decisions are of great economic magnitude.

ACE came first, looking to redomicile to Bermuda from the Cayman Islands. Bermuda law had no provision to allow such a continuation to take place, so a Private Act was introduced, as another would be when Exel Ltd. was incorporated. The wave of excess liability insurers which ACE and Exel began has subsequently broadened to include only two others, Oil Casualty and Starr Excess, both significant enterprises, though neither begins to approach ACE or Exel in size.

Suddenly, in some quarters where it had been fashionable to downplay Bermuda's insurance industry, the Island was no longer seen as solely a captive jurisdiction. Capital and surplus in the Bermuda sector jumped by 23 percent in 1986; total assets employed increased by 26 percent.

Statistics can be misleading. Measured by dollar volume, the Bermuda insurance market had continued growing between 1983 and

1986. Gross premiums written in the three years all but doubled, and net premiums were ahead by 121 percent in the same period. Following the decision by the stakeholders in ACE and Exel to locate their new ventures on the Island, the volume of the Bermuda market surged forward. More importantly, Bermuda was at the turning point in what had been a long haul towards gaining respect from its peers.

This is not to suggest that Bermuda had ever lost its reputation for the quality of the companies who chose the Island for their operations, but the suspicion had lingered, at Lloyd's and in New York, that Bermuda was an insurer of 'last resort', a jurisdiction of destination rather than origination. Some of the Bermuda underwriting behaviour of the late 1970s and early 1980s might have justified such a view. Although the arrival of the association captives did not change that impression overnight, 1986 can be seen in retrospect as a launching pad for a more broadly-based Bermuda insurance and reinsurance industry.

Today, no one underestimates Bermuda's position as one of the three most important markets in the world. Indeed, a posting to Bermuda from London or New York is now seen as an enviable opportunity to further one's professional experience.

CHAPTER THIRTY FOUR

An Institution Man

In April 1987, Conyers Dill & Pearman expanded its partnership with the admission of four new partners: John Collis, Hargun, Sharpe, and Trollope, who had reinvented himself since first joining the firm as a Chartered Secretary a dozen years earlier. After working for several years in North Rock, in close contact with the legal work of Conyers Dill & Pearman, Trollope had decided to pursue a professional legal career. Studying for the most part in the evenings and on weekends, he had attended Holborn Law College, part of London University, on a full-time basis for six months in his final year.

After he had graduated as a Bachelor of Laws, the firm granted Trollope sabbatical leave to sit his Bar exams and serve his pupillage in London, with several company Chambers in Lincoln's Inn. He was called to the Bar at the Inner Temple. Trollope's hard work and decisive career change were rewarded when, in April 1987, he was named a senior associate in the firm of Conyers Dill & Pearman. He and Hargun were the first senior associates. As non-Bermudians, they lacked the legal capacity to enter into partnership with Bermudians, but upon becoming Bermudian, both later became full partners.

Just two months later, in May 1987, Sir James Pearman retired from the firm he had co-founded, after a period of service lasting 58 years and seven months. His photograph on the cover of *Briefcase Number 18* shows a contented man, holding a fishing rod. Sir James was much more than that, but at 82 years of age, he wanted to concentrate on his fishing and his bridge. His professional partnership with Sir Bayard had endured for 60 years; each had been the other's perfect foil. Their friendship, and all that sprang from it, can be said to have changed the world of international finance.

Barely six months later, in its issue of Monday, 9 November 1987, *The Royal Gazette* was the bearer of unexpected and sad news, carried at the very top of the front page. Chet Butterfield had died. In part, the *Gazette's* story read:

Long-time Conyers Dill & Pearman partner Mr. H. Chester (Chet) Butterfield died suddenly on Saturday night. He was 60.

Friends and business associates eulogised Mr. Butterfield as an energetic, bright and compassionate man who worked tirelessly both in the office and for his varied private interests.

"The very sad thing is that he had recently been talking about taking a little more time off work," said Senator Charles Collis, a partner of Mr. Butterfield's at Conyers Dill & Pearman. "He was thinking about semi-retirement."

Mr. Butterfield was the son of the late Sir Harry and Lady Butterfield and followed in his father's footsteps by joining the Bank of N.T. Butterfield from Oxford in 1953, where he had studied as a Rhodes Scholar.

"Even though he went into banking, the law was always his first love," said Sen. Collis. "He started at the bottom when he went to the Bank of Butterfield and worked his way up the ladder there, before leaving in 1969 to join Conyers Dill & Pearman."

Mr. Butterfield specialised in commercial law and international company law during his tenure with Conyers Dill & Pearman and was president of the Bermuda Bar Association at the time of his death.

"Chet was a man with a great capacity for concern about other people," said Sen. Collis. "If you were his friend, you were his great friend. He was a very good friend of mine, and I shall miss him."

Sen. Collis said Mr. Butterfield was a lover of classical music and had avidly pursued this interest over the years.

"At one time, he even had a little singing group in Bermuda, called the Grate Sounders," Sen. Collis said. "He was a member of the Philharmonic here for many, many years and I believe only earlier this year he and his wife attended a music camp in the US."

But Mr. Butterfield's major interest was education and for many years he was both secretary of the Rhodes Scholarship selection committee and chairman of the Saltus Grammar School board of trustees.

"You could not find a man more dedicated to the school and its principles than Chet Butterfield," said Mr. David Anfossi, who succeeded Mr. Butterfield as chairman of the Saltus trustees. "He had an astute mind and was very, very fair in all of his dealings.

"His death certainly came as a shock and we at Saltus will miss the leadership and guidance which he provided the school."

Mr. Anfossi said that four years ago he and Mr. Butterfield launched the school's centenary fund to raise money for improvements at Saltus in time for its 100th anniversary in 1988.

"We raised close to $1.5 million and I must say Chet deserved the bulk of the credit," Mr. Anfossi said. "Chet stepped down both as chairman and as trustee at the time, so that he could supervise these fund-raising activities."

When Saltus opened its new administration building two years ago, the school's trustees voted unanimously to name it in honour of Mr. Butterfield.

"This was done in recognition of Chet's numerous contributions to the school," said Mr. Anfossi. "His dedication to Saltus was all the more impressive because although he studied there for a short time, he did not go all the way through the school and he didn't have any sons to go there."

Mr. Butterfield is survived by his wife, Laura and three daughters, Laura, Katherine and Margaret, as well as his brothers, Richard and Nathaniel.

The December 1987 edition of *Briefcase* went to press shortly after Butterfield died. It contained the following report:

Just a few weeks ago, on Tuesday 13 October, news of the firm's dear friend and partner Harry Chester (Chet) Butterfield's indisposition through heart failure sent a chill and anxiety through the office, particularly those who had for so long known and respected him.

His relentless devotion to work and his responsibilities as a dedicated husband, father and barrister had earned him the esteem he so justly deserved from all sides.

It was therefore most heartening when a delightful letter to "everyone" made the rounds of the office a week later, written in his inimitable style, acknowledging and thanking all those who had boosted his morale when he needed it most. His familiar, humorous approach to things came through so very clearly in what, he apologised, was a 'word processed' rather than a 'long hand' effort. He was always so intent on things being done right!

And though he was then facing numerous tests and a prognosis unknown, his determination to recover and get back with what he described in his letter as "a great team" never faltered. It was his personal concern for everyone in time of his own adversity that set Chet apart from many.

But it was not to be, and the weekend of 7 November saw his family and his friends Island-wide devastated by the news of his untimely passing.

As our publication makes its seasonal appearance, we take this opportunity to express the heartfelt love and admiration one and all in the firm had for Chet and convey to his wife, Laura, and their three daughters our deepest sympathy. May he rest in peace.

On 17 November 1987, a group of more than 30 lawyers gathered at Supreme Court Number One to remember and pay tribute to Mr. Butterfield's "achievements and commitments within the legal profession and in his personal life". *The Royal Gazette* reported on the gathering:

The solemn ceremony was presented much as a courtroom proceeding would be, with the High Court Judges presiding from the Bench and remembrance speeches, in the form of submissions, from representatives of the legal community and the Government.

The High Court bench consisted of Chief Justice the Hon. James Astwood, Puisne Judge the Hon. Mr. Justice Martyn Ward, Puisne Judge the Hon. Mrs. Justice Norma Wade and Puisne Judge the Hon. Mr. Justice Gerald Collett.

Remembering Mr. Butterfield from the lawyer's bench were

Attorney General Mr. Saul Froomkin, partners Sir Bayard Dill and Mr. Nicholas Dill of the law firm Conyers Dill & Pearman, Mr. Arnold Francis, Q.C. and lawyer Mrs. Dianna Kempe, the new president of the Bermuda Bar Association, who succeeds Mr. Butterfield in that position.

Also present was Mr. Michael Crystal, Q.C. of the London Bar Association.

Amid the gowns and wigs of those present, Mr. Butterfield's memory was highly spoken of.

"He was a devoted father and husband, a devoted member of the community and a compassionate man," said Mr. Froomkin. "Chet was, above all else, a gentleman. He was a patriot in the sense that he was motivated in his social attitude and behaviour by what he considered to be the good of the country," said Mr. Francis. "Chet was an institution man. He had a devout loyalty to the institutions with which he became associated."

One of Mr. Butterfield's greatest achievements, said Mr. Dill, was creating a bursary and scholarship programme at the Saltus Grammar School, where he sat as chairman of the board of trustees.

"He had a deep sense that Bermuda must have an integrated boys' school. He was instrumental in raising funds and contributions for the Rhodes Scholarship programme," said Mr. Dill, who also reminisced about Mr. Butterfield's love of music.

"Music was very important to him," Mr. Dill said. "He learned to play the piano, he sang with the London Philharmonic, and when he came to Bermuda, he sang with the Bermuda Philharmonic. His memory will linger for anyone who wants to learn about him," said Mr. Dill.

"Most of all, he will be remembered for his humanity," said the

Chief Justice in summation. "He was always concerned first and foremost about the community. Not just certain segments, but all of the community.

"For his family, they can rest assured that his contributions and his name will go down as one of the giants in Bermuda's history."

The loss was a profound shock to the firm, one which took years to overcome.

Butterfield was a man who straightened out paperclips. A great story-teller and a more than adequate pianist, he was the most outgoing of men, the kind of social creature entirely at home with all his clients. By every account a hard worker, he was a natural genealogist, with Bermuda as his chosen area of application. He knew the histories of Bermuda's families from the moment of their arrival. Sir James Astwood was right: Butterfield is remembered today with uniform warmth, for his humanity and for his sense of humour.

To him is attributed the famous remark on the making of decisions by the partners of Conyers Dill & and Pearman in the days before a Management Committee was instituted. "The rule was: we would never make a decision," Butterfield would say, adding, after the tiniest of pauses: "And if, by some fluke or accident we did make a decision, we would reverse it the next day." A propos, Cooper recalls Butterfield discussing their becoming partners in the firm. At one point in the conversation Butterfield said that they had come awfully close to making a decision, and they had better think twice before they did.

Butterfield also left his mark on the firm in the way he chose to serve the Bermudian community, a duty which was, and remains, very much recognised policy at the firm. Butterfield had served on the Public Transportation Board and the Race Relations Advisory Council in addition to his efforts on behalf of the Rhodes Scholarship Selection

Committee, the Saltus' trustees and the Bar Association.

In crossing the borders of public and private service, Butterfield was the link between his predecessors in the firm, who had mostly sought public office, and those who came after him, who have not. Instead, like Butterfield, they devote their efforts to causes of personal or family interest and, in certain areas, act together in the name of the firm to promote individuals and events consensually considered of importance to the community.

The end result, it might be argued, is much the same, but the change in the way Conyers Dill & Pearman serves Bermuda has altered the way in which the Bermudian community sees the firm, which is today perceived as a friendlier, more community-oriented organisation, thanks in good measure to the example of Chet Butterfield.

CHAPTER THIRTY FIVE

New Spirit

At the start of 1988, McCabe returned to Bermuda from Guernsey. He recalls coming back to a Conyers Dill & Pearman with a different feel from the firm six years earlier. The office in Hong Kong had been opened while he was away, the firm's professional work was taking on a sharper profile, the international client base had expanded and a slew of new staff had been added. The firm's philosophy remained much the same as it had since its foundation, but a new spirit was in the air.

Regardless of the degree of sophistication an international enterprise may achieve, its headquarters will always be the epicentre, satellite offices just that. It says a lot for the way that Conyers Dill & Pearman operates that McCabe and Ellison could venture overseas for a period of years and, on their return to the firm in Bermuda, slot back in almost as if nothing had happened in the interim. McCabe returned to the firm's Property Department, which he once again heads.

Shortly after his return, in February 1988, Lisa Joanne Marshall joined Conyers Dill & Pearman as an associate in the Corporate Department.

Born on 18 November 1959, Marshall is a fifth generation Bermudian of Portuguese heritage who grew up wanting to be a history teacher. Her parents, Herbert and Sylvia Marshall, were both involved in the business world. Sylvia was a pioneer, one of the first Portuguese-Bermudians to be hired by The Bank of Bermuda, an achievement capped when she was appointed Company Secretary of the bank, the first woman to be appointed to that level in its history. Her daughter, Lisa, was destined to become the first female partner in Conyers Dill & Pearman, as well as the first Portuguese-Bermudian partner.

Marshall attended Warwick Academy, Sharpe's old school, and then Atlantic College in Wales, one of the United World Colleges. A number of Bermudians have been sponsored by the United World College Bermuda committee, the parent committee of which was headed by Lord Mountbatten when Marshall was at Atlantic. Set up in the mid-1970s by Bermuda Governor Sir Edwin Leather and Mountbatten, the United World College organisation has subsequently been chaired by Prince Charles, Queen Noor and Nelson Mandela.

In Wales, the course allowed Marshall to mingle with others of her age from around the world. She discovered a taste for debating, a practice which developed in the 15th century and was then known as mooting. Marshall left Wales two years later with her International Baccalaureate, a pre-University qualification and a head start on the Bachelor's degree to follow. Despite her earlier aspirations, the degree she chose was not History, but the Law, her appetite whetted by the taste of debating, her intellect challenged by the radical manner in which law was taught at Hull University. Hull, officially Kingston-upon-Hull, is a major national seaport in the north-eastern corner of England and is, today, the last bastion of Old Labour party attitudes.

Traditional legal education teaches individual subjects over dedicated periods of time: torts for, say, two months, or six consecutive weeks of contract law. The professors at Hull argued that life does not happen like that, and that the best way to learn law is the way in which it is practised—as a response to problems and opportunities. Hull was abuzz with radical thought at the time, and Marshall was drawn to the atmosphere of inquiry and change which its University campus had created. She earned her Bachelor of Laws (Honours) and opted for the profession of solicitor, intent on pursuing corporate law. She had been guided in that decision by Ernest Vesey, a long-time partner in Appleby, Spurling & Kempe. Marshall had the opportunity to meet Vesey when she worked during one summer at his law firm. Everyone else to whom Marshall spoke concurred with his advice.

An intense year ensued at the School of Law in Chester, where, again, she followed in Sharpe's footsteps. The year's tuition at the School has a heavy practical bias. The object is to learn not only a solicitor's practice and its ethical canons, but also how to manage a business which receives, holds, manages and disburses clients' funds.

Following an introduction by Sharpe, Marshall completed two years of articles with Wedlake Bell, Solicitors, in Bedford Street, off Covent Garden in London. The practice was not dissimilar to that of a Bermudian firm, small enough to allow an articled clerk to know the Managing Partner and modern enough to allow that articled clerk to have her own files and deal, with guidance, on a number of active matters.

In due course, Marshall was enrolled as a solicitor in England and Wales, adding another first to her family's roll: the first female Bermudian solicitor. Later the same year, she returned to Bermuda and would spend four years as an associate at Appleby, Spurling & Kempe, becoming in the process a corporate specialist with a particular emphasis on insurance. In February 1988, in search of greater personal scope and professional achievement, she joined the law firm of Conyers Dill & Pearman, although she retained an association with her former employers when she married

Peter Bubenzer, now a partner at Appleby, Spurling & Kempe. A formal interview at Conyers Dill & Pearman was not necessary; she and Sharpe had ironed out the details. Marshall took on a number of corporate insurance clients which had once been served by Chet Butterfield.

The firm she joined had reached 135 people and registered its second Olympian athlete when Anderson represented Bermuda at tennis in the Seoul Olympiad of 1988. If life had not allowed him to make tennis his professional career, he at least had the great honour of representing Bermuda at the ultimate amateur event. He played well, but was not among the medal winners.

By this time, capital and surplus in the Bermuda insurance industry had reached US$15 billion. Total assets employed exceeded US$40 billion. The total number of international companies on the Bermuda Register had reached 5,689 at the previous year's end. The number of Bermuda exempted partnerships, allowed to trade from but not within the Island, stood at 82, and 525 non-resident (or 'permit') companies were also listed. With 1,328 local companies, the Register had swollen, in total, to 7,624. Bermuda had not added an inch of land since the mid-1930s—it was, in fact about 12 percent smaller, allowing for the areas then in use as Armed Forces bases—but its international business sector had become an international force to be reckoned with.

In December 1988, the Taxation Convention signed by representatives of the Governments of Bermuda and the United States two years earlier was brought into force. The Taxation Convention, known colloquially in Bermuda at least as the 'tax treaty', was perhaps the greatest achievement of Premier John Swan's 13 years in office, if one excludes the continuing prosperity. The Convention allowed American companies holding business meetings or conventions in Bermuda to write off the cost of the trip in computing their US taxation. Failure to achieve this concession might have crippled Bermuda's growing convention business.

In return, the Bermuda Government agreed to co-operate with the American authorities when they presented *prima facie* evidence of financial wrong-doing by a Bermuda-registered company. Under the agreement, so-called 'fishing expeditions' would not be tolerated by the Government of Bermuda. A fishing expedition occurs when authorities in one country believe that an individual or company might bear closer scrutiny, although necessary evidence of malfeasance has not yet presented itself. The Bermuda Government was, and is, willing to look into an allegation of wrong-doing when suitable evidence is presented.

The 1988 Convention also designated Bermuda as a country qualifying, under the 1986 United States Internal Revenue Code, as an FSC jurisdiction. An FSC is a Foreign Sales Corporation, a corporate vehicle designed to encourage the export of products manufactured in the United States. Exclusions from income tax, combined with allowable deductions for depreciation of assets and interest payments, enable an FSC to accumulate its earnings free of US taxation.

Broadly, FSCs fall into two practical categories, non-leasing and equipment, and two principal types: the 'Buy-Sell', or 'Ownership' FSC and the 'Commission' FSC. Equipment ownership FSCs have proven especially beneficial to US airlines and other carriers and allowed Bermuda to develop yet another avenue of service.

By the time of Marshall's arrival at Conyers Dill & Pearman, its Corporate Division had earned a reputation as a busy place to work. Since the passage of the 1988 Convention, the practice of aviation law, a specialty of Malcolm's, has become another thread in the firm's continuing involvement with transportation.

If Conyers Dill & Pearman had become a busy place to work, the atmosphere was neither as frantic nor remotely as greedy as that conveyed at the time by the actor, Michael Douglas, Sir Bayard's nephew and Nicky Dill's first cousin, in his portrayal of financier Gordon Gecko in the movie

Wall Street. One long-serving member of the firm does however recall that the first power suspenders—braces, in British English—were spotted at Conyers Dill & Pearman at about this time.

PLATES II

xl. *Nicky Dill*

xli. *Richard Pearman*

xlii. Alex Cooper

xliii. *From left: Graham Collis, Charles Collis*
and John Collis

xliv. *Narinder Hargun (left) and Robin Mayor*

xlv. Alec Anderson (left) and Nicolas Trollope

xlvi. From left: David Cooke, Anthony Whaley
and Lisa Marshall

xlvii. *James Macdonald (left) and Nicholas Johnson*

xlviii. *Donald Malcolm (left) and Michael McCabe*

xlix. From left: Stephen De Silva, Roger Younie
and John Buckley

l. From left: John Sharpe, Frank Mutch
and James Pearman

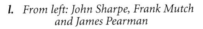

li. *From left: Robert Briant, David Astwood, Alex O'Neill
and David Alderson*

lii. *From left: Andrew Greenstreet, Helen Cooper
and Stephen Rossiter*

liii. *From left: Dawn Griffiths, David Lamb*
and Christopher Garrod

liv. *From left: Julie McLean, Christian Luthi*
and Patrick O'Hagan

lv. Peter Pearman (left) and Craig MacIntyre

*lvi. From left: Roger Burgess, Kevin Butler
and Felicity Cole*

lvii. From left: John Thompson, May Coye
and Leon Nearon

lviii. From left: Ian Fung, Laurence Stott
and Marion Scaife

lix. Brenda McLean (left) and Daniel Bordage

lx. From left: Barry Bailey, Sandra Cann, Ken Siggins
and Liz Quarterly

lxi. Tucker Hall (left) and Memsie Weakley

*lxii. From left: Chips Outerbridge, André Dill
and Wayne Morgan*

lxiii. From left: Grant Hall, Michael Ashford, Catharine Lymbery
and Malcolm Mitchell

lxiv. From left: Andrea Sullivan, Stan Chetkowski
and Randy Trott

lxv. From left: Keith Rossiter, David Lunn, Jim Spence
and Edwin Mortimer

lxvi. From left: Kathy Sharpe, David Stockman
and Donna Pilgrim

lxvii. *Louise Payne (left) and Naomi Pickard*

lxviii. *St. Peter Port, Guernsey. From left, front row: Debbie Du Feu, Colin Pickard, Kirsty Bromley; second row: Marilyn Dunn and Norma Gillespie*

lxix. Hong Kong. Lilian Woo (left) and Rosemarie Chen

lxx. Exchange Square, Hong Kong. From left, front row: Margaret Wong, Lavina Gangaramani, Bernadette Chen, Christopher Bickley, Kemmy Cheng, Rowan Wu; second row: Mina Jinn, Jennifer Wan, Lun Ping Yeung, Reena Khua.

lxxi. *Beef Island, British Virgin Islands. From left: Roselyn Francis, Malcolm Becker, Enid Gordon, Guy Eldridge, Shaunda Scatliffe*

lxxii. *Grand Cayman Island, the Cayman Islands. From left: Keisha Powery, Neil Cox, Theresa Pearson*

lxxiii. The Royal Exchange, London. John Ellison (left)
and Martin Lane

lxxiv. From left: Beverley Minors, Darlene Tavares, Vicki Johnston,
Darlene McGinnis, Che Burgess and Robin Tucker

lxxv. Clockwise, from bottom left: Denise Whitter, Michele Bisson, Robin Trott, Sylvia Simpson, Marlene Flynn-Simons, Deidre Shakir and Eddrena Zuill

lxxvi. From left: Kirsty Johnson, Randell Woolridge, Karen O'Connor, Paul Lambert, Shella Udoh, Debra Lindsey and Sharmaine Butterfield

CHAPTER THIRTY SIX

Half A World Away

Rosemarie Chen Peck Yee joined Conyers Dill & Pearman as an associate in its Hong Kong office in November 1988. She was born on 12 August 1960 in Malaysia. Her father, Brigadier General *Dato* Raymond Chen Kwee Fong, was a career military man, trained at Sandhurst, who married *Datin* Sylvia Kwok Chee Hor. *Dato* and *Datin* are honorary titles bestowed by any of the nine hereditary monarchs of Malaysia, or its Federal Government. The Chens' titles were granted by the Sultan Idris Iskandar Shah of Perak, a Malaysian state bordering Thailand.

Although she grew up half a world away from most of the other principals in Conyers Dill & Pearman, Chen's schooling followed the firm's now-familiar pattern: basic education locally and secondary training in Britain. Chen was educated at Convent Bukit Nanas in Kuala Lumpur until she was ready to study for her A-levels in English Literature, History and Mathematics, at which time she attended Farlington School in Horsham, Sussex, a residential town south of London in the area designated by planners as that city's green belt.

Chen had grown up speaking English. Although she learned Bahasa Malaysian in school, it was not spoken at home. She also speaks a little Cantonese. Before attending Farlington, Chen had laid no particular career plans; she knew only that she wanted to pursue a professional career. By the time she had completed her A-levels, she was decided on the Law; a first in her immediate family. From Farlington, she proceeded to the University of Bristol in the west of England for three years, to earn her Bachelor of Laws. Then on to London and a year at Bar School.

In her second year at Bristol, Chen had accepted a scholarship from the Malaysian Armed Forces. Upon completing her legal education and being called to the Bar at Gray's Inn, she was commissioned as an Officer, with the rank of Captain, under a service obligation arising out of the scholarship. Chen was granted special leave from the Directorate of Manpower to serve her pupillage, which she completed in nine months with the firm of Abdul Aziz, Ong & Co. in Kuala Lumpur. She returned to her military service, but within a year had concluded that her father's career would not be hers; private practice was exerting its siren call. By coincidence, father and daughter completed their service careers at the same time, his retirement from the Engineers Corps after 32 years coinciding with her resignation.

Chen's legal career resumed against a changing international background. First stop: Singapore, a move which required her to requalify by means of a second pupillage, which she completed with the firm of Arthur Loke & Partners, then the local correspondent of the international law firm of Baker & McKenzie. Having been called to the Bar in Singapore, Chen spent two years with Arthur Loke before returning to Kuala Lumpur to join the firm of Rashid & Lee, where she spent a year in the practice of general corporate and commercial law.

Chen had hoped to make Malaysia her permanent home, but family circumstances late in 1988 took her instead to Hong Kong. Newly arrived, she saw an advertisement in the *South China Morning Post*, placed by a Bermuda law firm looking to expand its Hong Kong office. Ellison interviewed her, and within a few weeks of arriving in Hong Kong, Chen joined Conyers Dill & Pearman's small but growing Hong Kong office in November 1988 as an associate in general practice.

She arrived not long after the firm's Hong Kong office had celebrated the marriage of John Sharpe, who had been seconded for some months to Hong Kong the year before, to Fong Leong, a Malaysian. The couple had met in Bermuda, but Leong had been posted to the Fragrant Harbour to act as Ellison's secretary. Following their marriage, the Sharpes returned to Bermuda. The office Chen joined was staffed by Ellison, by now thoroughly *au fait* with his new life in Hong Kong, and two secretaries and an office assistant. Within a few months, the great exodus of Hong Kong companies had begun and, as a consequence, Chen's nomadic existence had ended. She has been with Conyers Dill & Pearman ever since.

Ellison did not plan to stay in Hong Kong for the rest of his days. He would be 60 in a year or two; the call of home could be heard faintly over his shoulder. He had begun the search for someone to take over the running of the practice. Chen's employment as a second lawyer in the firm's Hong Kong office was more than mere anticipation of the work which lay ahead. With the efficiency of a firm doing the right things at the right times, Ellison made the right choice first time. Chen, who has spent time in Bermuda and has been called to the Bermuda Bar, is today a senior associate in the firm and Resident Partner in Hong Kong, a responsibility she shares with Lilian Woo.

Her arrival at Conyers Dill & Pearman was not the only sign that the firm was becoming an increasingly international venture as the end of the 1980s drew nigh. Late in May 1989, a handful of the world's most prestigious law practices banded together to form Lex Mundi, Latin for 'Law of the World'. The organisation's Bermuda representative was

Conyers Dill & Pearman.

The global association adopted a Statement of Purpose:

> Lex Mundi is an organisation of independent law firms providing for the exchange of professional information about the local and global practice and development of law, facilitating and disseminating communications among its members and improving the members' abilities to serve the needs of their respective clients.
>
> The members of Lex Mundi shall maintain complete autonomy; shall render professional services to their respective clients on an individual and separate basis; shall not be restricted in referring, handling or accepting cases or in joining other professional organisations; and are not affiliated for the joint practice of law.

A formally informal association, Lex Mundi, like Multinational Fiscal Associates 20 years before, extended the reach of its members beyond their own countries to the world at large. Meetings of the Board of Lex Mundi, and of its full membership, are held annually. The 90 original member firms have grown to 129, representing more than 7,000 attorneys in 72 countries. The 1997 North American Regional meeting was held in Bermuda and hosted by Conyers Dill & Pearman.

Taken as a whole, the laws of the world must change, somewhere on the face of the planet, daily. The laws of Bermuda change less frequently, although towards the end of the 1980s, Bermuda's Legislature began reviewing its legislation more often than it had previously.

Government has made its products more user-friendly while applying greater scrutiny through the strengthening of the regulatory powers, notably, of the Bermuda Monetary Authority and the Registrar of Companies. Legislative change is discussed, and ideas batted back and forth, between Government and the representative committees of both local and international business communities. Lawyers at Conyers Dill & Pearman serve on the legislative change committees of the Bermuda International Business Association, as often proposing change as considering changes suggested by others.

CHAPTER THIRTY SEVEN

Changing The Guard

In 1990, Younie was preparing to retire. He had been with Conyers Dill & Pearman for 28 years and had become an institution within the firm. GRY—principals are referred to internally by their initials—had installed and operated accounting systems which carried the firm from less than 30 people to more than 150. Younie worked for many years in tandem with Alan Brown. Brown was in his early 50s at this point. Woods was 56, and he too was thinking about the pros and cons of an early retirement and a return to his native Oxford.

Regardless of Woods' intentions, a changing of the guard in the administrative Departments was in the offing. The firm's formal plan would have revealed the need to pass its business management forward into the hands of as yet unidentified successors. Into that breach in February 1990 stepped John Buckley, today the General Manager and Partnership Secretary of Conyers Dill & Pearman.

Many firms operate with a Managing Partner, whose responsibilities, as the title suggests, encompass the firm's administration. Conyers Dill

& Pearman has taken a different approach. The work of the Partnership Secretary, broadly, is to manage the partnership's activities so as to enable the partners to concentrate on conducting the firm's legal business. Buckley, the man selected to eventually take over the Partnership Secretariat from Woods and some of Younie's responsibilities, had already performed in a broad capacity at another local institution which had shared in and driven the Island's growth over the past two decades: The Bank of Bermuda.

Younie knew Buckley. Woods knew Buckley. Buckley met the partners, many of whom he knew, and in 1990 Conyers Dill & Pearman had a new Controller. Younie set about handing over the reins; he would retire a couple of years later.

John Buckley was born on 31 August 1946, in Liverpool, England, as were Mutch and McCabe, although none of them has a Liverpudlian accent. Buckley's father, Arthur, had served in the Merchant Navy and became a marine engineer by profession. He was recruited in 1950 by the Hong Kong Government as a Marine & Ship Surveyor. Buckley *père*, with his wife Mary and their three boys, sailed on the P&O line to Hong Kong, where he would work for a number of years. John recalls his younger brother, Richard, learning to walk during the voyage.

John spent four years in Hong Kong before following his older brother, Roger, to Repton, a private boarding school in Derbyshire attended by, among others, C.B. Fry, the cricketer, Harold Abrahams, the Olympic gold medallist portrayed in the film *Chariots of Fire*, and three consecutive Archbishops of Canterbury. John's summer holidays began and ended with flights to and from Hong Kong, and later the British Protectorate of Aden, where he picked up what has proven to be a lifelong love of travel and exotic places.

After Repton, Buckley attended business school at what is now part of Manchester University on a programme known in the educational jargon of the day as an 'open-top sandwich', a combination of practical work experience and theoretical learning which would be referred to today as an integrated work/study programme. The training led to Buckley gaining a Diploma in Business Studies, a degree-equivalent professional qualification, and Fellowship in the Institute of Management Services.

At the age of 20, he joined English Electric, then one of Britain's three major electrical companies, now a component of General Electric, at the company's headquarters in Stafford, a market town in England's Midlands. Stafford lies in a green belt separating the industrial areas in the north and south of the county of Staffordshire, famous for its pottery. As part of an in-house management programme, Buckley was posted to Clayton-le-Moors, an old Lancashire cotton-spinning town, where an English Electric subsidiary made parts for railway engines and fighter planes. Buckley's three years with the company were spent in management services work, which is Organisation and Methods appraisal aimed at improving corporate efficiency. From English Electric, he transferred to the Civil Service, at Cheshire County Council, where he carried out work of a similar nature.

An advertisement in the London *Sunday Times* for The Bank of Bermuda's newly-created Computer Department caught Buckley's attention near the end of the 1960s. The Bank of Bermuda and the Bank of Butterfield had purchased similar computers, so that one might back the other up in the event of a problem. Mainframes in those pioneering days of large commercial computing crashed with a frequency which we would today find completely unacceptable in our enormously more sophisticated desktop equipment.

Buckley's childhood hobby, stamp collecting, and his love of travel—all those flights to and from Hong Kong and Aden—combined to produce in him a fascination with the glamour of the far-flung, which lasts to this day. Among a dozen marathon overland treks he has undertaken, in the spring of 1997, he walked 140 miles across the Sahara Desert solo, stepping out on his adventure dressed in a Conyers Dill & Pearman T-shirt.

He had joined The Bank of Bermuda as the 1970s got underway, thinking to stay a couple of years before returning to the United Kingdom, and instead became a 20-year man at the bank. He worked throughout the organisation, which changed beyond all recognition between 1970 and 1990, the period in its history which resulted in the bank being referred to in local shorthand, not without some accuracy, as "the house that Donald (Lines) built".

After two decades, Buckley was looking for a different house to build, and one which he himself could manage. His express goal in pursuing a career in business had always been to run an organisation. The prospect of the Partnership Secretariat at Conyers Dill & Pearman would exactly fill his career bill, in an atmosphere he thought he might enjoy.

The firm which Buckley joined in February 1990 had roughly the same staff complement as had the bank he had joined 20 years earlier. That meant he had already experienced in no small measure what the firm would expect of him in the years ahead.

A few months after Buckley joined, the firm announced its intentions to open a third overseas office—this one in the British Virgin Islands. An unattributed article in *The Royal Gazette* read, in part:

> One of Bermuda's two big law firms is opening an office in the British Virgin Islands.
>
> Mr. James Pearman of Conyers Dill & Pearman said the new office, which will operate under the name of Codan Trust (B.V.I.) Ltd., will help international businesses and companies which, for whatever reason, believe the British Virgin Islands are a better home than Bermuda.
>
> "We have a number of clients for whom the formation of a

Bermuda company is unnecessary and expensive," Mr. Pearman said. Over the past two decades, he said, his firm has helped international businesses set up in such places as the Turks & Caicos Islands, the Cayman Islands, the Bahamas and Panama.

As international businesses increasingly used the British Virgin Islands, Mr. Pearman said, Conyers Dill & Pearman did legal work for them in Bermuda and also used lawyers in the islands' capital of Road Town. "As business developed, we decided that it would be a good idea to open our own office there," he said.

Mr. Pearman, who is heading south this week to set up the office with David Astwood, said its doors should be open in mid-February.

Initially, it will be a one-person operation staffed by a Virgin Islander, who is now undergoing training at the law firm in Bermuda.

Conyers Dill & Pearman already has a four-person office in Guernsey in the Channel Islands and a five-person office in Hong Kong.

The firm had established companies in the British Virgins two years earlier. Alongside Codan Trust (B.V.I.) Ltd., another company, Codan Trustees (B.V.I.) Ltd., was set up to act as a trustee of international trusts under British Virgin Islands' law. Within six months of Pearman's announcement, the firm's newest office was well-established under Astwood's guidance. Two other service companies were established: Codan Services (B.V.I.) Ltd., which operates as a Corporate Director, and Codan Managements (B.V.I.) Ltd., which provides Corporate Secretarial services. The firm's new office was located in the heart of Road Town, the main centre of the principal island of Tortola. Astwood was one of four members of staff.

The British Virgin Islands are a water-sports paradise. Fairly con-stant easterly trade winds keep boats in motion and make an otherwise hot, tropical island bearable for residents. Essentially rural, Tortola reminds visitors in some ways of a Bermuda now lost to progress.

Astwood, an arachnophobe, was impressed by the enormous quantity and size of the spiders in the islands, among whose number are counted several species of tarantula. "But don't worry about the spiders," he told his colleagues in the Autumn 1990 issue of *Briefcase*, "because I do enough worrying for all of us."

CHAPTER THIRTY EIGHT

Commitment & Focus

Reinsurance is probably nearly as old as commerce itself. Its uniquely international outlook, for some the source of its glamour and mystique, began in the late 1600s at the London coffee house of Edward Lloyd. Before the coffee house became Lloyd's of London, the world's premier insurance market, brokers toted their policies around London, asking wealthy merchants to subscribe to a share of the risk—and a share of the profit—by signing their names under the appropriate details. These early 'underwriters' quickly made reinsurance the main business at Lloyd's insurance exchange. To ensure a steady flow of business, Lloyd's required the members of its syndicates to reinsure at least 35 percent of the risk with their fellow members.

In time, Lloyd's became a powerhouse in reinsurance, which almost brought about its collapse in the early 1990s when the oil rig *Piper Alpha* blew up in the North Sea. The catastrophe was largely a Lloyd's risk; its famous names were liable down to the groceries in their refrigerators. Hurricane Andrew in 1992 cost $16 billion in insured losses. Had Andrew touched down a few miles north, in Miami, rather than in Homestead, Florida, insured losses might have amounted to $50 billion.

The asbestos experience had shown that the general liability side of reinsurance could be even more frightening. The highest claims arising from this dangerous material came 20 years after some policies were first written. In the United States, environmental loss claims arising from pollution legislation, which was retroactive, stopped only when Congress legislated the problem out of existence.

Reinsurance was one of the first businesses to become truly global. Early reinsurance deals covered marine risk, international transactions expressed in several currencies. In the early days, reinsurance was an exclusive club, whose members were men who knew and trusted each other. It has become a business of partnerships in which, given the unpredictable nature of catastrophes, reinsurers choose their partners carefully. Reinsurance is a big business conducted in small circles, ideally suited to a small island like Bermuda.

Into that world in October 1990 stepped Charles Grant Ross Collis, who joined Conyers Dill & Pearman as an associate some 34 years after his father had joined the firm. Charles Collis *fils* was born on 18 February 1962 and, like his father and older brothers, attended Saltus Grammar School, where he sat his O-levels. He then attended Rugby School in Warwickshire, England, to take his A-levels in Chemistry, Economics and Mathematics. Charles then followed his brother Graham to Toronto, Canada where he attended Trinity College at the University of Toronto, and earned a Bachelor of Arts degree with a double major in Economics and Commerce.

A sabbatical year followed, a chance to travel the world. Beginning with a four-month stint working for a large multi-national corporation in Johannesburg, South Africa, Charles saw the world with a friend from his college days. He felt fortunate to take a year off after earning his undergraduate degree and would recommend every college graduate to do the same. The experience left him with fond memories, and enabled him to start Law School with a greater sense of commitment and focus than might otherwise have been the case.

Having circumnavigated the globe, Charles enrolled in the Law School at University College at the University of London, a liberal college established by the founder of utilitarianism, Jeremy Bentham. Utilitarianism is the doctrine that we ought to seek the greatest happiness of the greatest number of people; an action is 'right' if it is likely to produce greater happiness than any other action. One of Britain's better non-boarding public schools, University College School, was established in Hampstead to act as a feeder for the College. Charles graduated from University College as a Bachelor of Laws.

Having completed his Bar exams, he chose to serve his pupillage in London, serving six months in the Chambers of Michael Crystal, Q.C. at South Square, Gray's Inn and a second six months in the Chambers of Robert Wright, Q.C. in Lincoln's Inn. Charles was called to the Bar in England and Wales at the Middle Temple. He returned almost immediately to Bermuda with his wife, Jane, who had also just qualified as a barrister in London. Without looking elsewhere, he joined his father and oldest brother John at Conyers Dill & Pearman as an associate in October 1990.

Charles was assigned to the firm's insurance and reinsurance practice to assist Cooper and Marshall. Although ACE, Exel and Centre Re (now Centre Solutions) were established prior to Charles joining the firm, the principal focus of the firm's insurance practice continued to be the captive industry.

One may only imagine the pride Charles Collis *père* must have felt to have all three sons qualified as lawyers. He spoke on the subject to reporter Heather Ratteray of the *Mid-Ocean News* a month after Charles joined the firm. The article read, in part:

He's a senior partner in a successful law firm and a distinguished Senator, but Charles Collis says his family is probably his greatest source of pride.

"It's been a great pleasure for me seeing my children—John, Graham and Charles—grow up and make their own marks," he said. "Although I did not push them into their ultimate pursuits, all three are qualified lawyers and received their Bachelor's degrees in Commerce, as I did."

Senator Collis spoke of the restructuring of Bermudian education, a 15-year undertaking which entered its middle phase with the 1997 opening of CedarBridge Academy, a Government Senior Secondary School for 1,100 students in Prospect. The Senator then turned his attention to community service:

Sen. Collis said he has always felt it incumbent upon anyone with ability or talent to make a contribution to the community. He was for many years involved with a number of local organisations before entering politics.

He served on the Treatment of Offenders Commission, the Development Applications Board and the Bermuda Monetary Authority Board prior to becoming a Senator, and was also an active member of both the Public Accounts Investment Committee and the Bermuda Chamber of Commerce.

"I had known John Swan for years," Sen. Collis said. "When he became Premier, he asked me out of the blue if I would join his team and act as Government leader in the Senate."

Sen. Collis said he enjoys being a member of Government, but sometimes finds it difficult balancing his political role with his career at Conyers Dill & Pearman. "The schedule is very demanding and requires an enormous amount of time," he explained.

The Senator said he has no desire to advance any higher up the political ladder and admitted that his days in the Senate may in fact be numbered. "After nine years, I believe I've made my contribution. I mustn't stand in the way of competent younger people now coming on to the political scene," he said.

Bermuda retained the bicameral legislative system which had worked for so long as the House of Assembly and the Legislative Council. The Senate, which meets in the Cabinet Building, has limited powers to delay legislation. A total of 11 Senators are selected by the Premier, the Leader of the Opposition and the Governor, and one among their number is chosen President. The party appointees tend to obey a notional whip, but the activities and independence of the Senate are often enhanced by its unaffiliated members, appointed from outside the world of politics.

CHAPTER THIRTY NINE

Learning A New Language

In April 1991, Conyers Dill & Pearman admitted Anderson and Marshall to the partnership, made McCabe a senior associate and appointed Buckley to the Executive. Now a total of 18 were eligible for lunch in the partners' dining room. Four months later, in August 1991, Anthony Devon Whaley joined Conyers Dill & Pearman. He, too, would be taking lunch in the dining room in due course.

His father, Anthony Reed Whaley, was a US Marine, posted to the Naval Annex in Southampton, Bermuda in the late 1950s. Until the American, British and Canadian Bases closed, almost simultaneously, in the middle of the 1990s, the Bermuda population routinely included as many as 1,500 foreign servicemen posted to the Island. Whaley *père* met and married Sandra Guerlain DeSilva and worked for many years thereafter in security at the Bermuda Electric Light Company Ltd.

The second of three sons, Anthony attended Warwick Academy and Bermuda College, which was undergoing a spurt of growth following its consolidation into a unified campus at Stonington on the South Shore.

The College was founded by Act of Parliament in 1974, amalgamating the Bermuda Hotel and Catering College, the Bermuda Technical Institute and the Academic Sixth Form Centre. Marshall currently sits on the Board of Governors, under whose first Chief Executive, Mansfield H. Brock, Jr., the College made great strides in developing the curriculum and establishing its identity. Brock was for some time Chairman of the National Drug Commission, and oversaw its high-profile campaign to reduce the incidence of substance abuse in Bermuda. He also heads the Bermuda Monetary Authority, on whose Board Whaley now sits.

The Board of Governors of Bermuda College is now led by Bermudian businessman Brian Hall, the first non-US resident director in the 150-year history of Johnson & Higgins, insurance brokers and managers, before the company merged with Marsh & McLennan. Bermuda College, under Dr. George L. Cook, its President, is entering the 21st century in an aggressive and expansive mode. Hall had previously established the Bermuda Foundation for Insurance Studies, which has Bermudians and New Yorkers learning in both locations to graduate as Commercial Property and Casualty Underwriters from the College of Insurance in New York. On campus at Bermuda College is a fine hotel, Stonington Beach, at which students gain first-hand experience. Bermuda College's three academic faculties offer 11 Associate degree programmes recognised for advanced standing in universities and colleges overseas, as well as more than a dozen Certificate programmes.

Whaley, a few months shy of his 18th birthday on graduating from the College, had no strong sense which direction his career should take. Accountancy seemed as good an idea as any, but a meeting with the Vice Chancellor of the University of Kent at Canterbury, followed by a chance encounter with Richard De Friend, a law professor there who has since risen to become the distinguished Pro Vice Chancellor of the University, led Whaley to opt for Kent and the Law.

His application for a scholarship to Conyers Dill & Pearman resulted in him meeting several members of the firm, among them Woods and Cooper. Woods asked Whaley what plans he had for the summer. Whaley had thought of working in construction, a provider of solid casual earnings for young men with strong backs and the know-how in the busy summer months in Bermuda. If nothing is fixed, asked Woods, why not join us as a summer student next year?

The pool of summer students at Conyers Dill & Pearman into which Whaley dove in the mid-1980s is no longer a tradition. The arrival of specialisation affected the way every aspect of the firm was structured. Today's interns are assigned to individual lawyers and given a hands-on dousing in the legal experience, as Whaley himself would be later in his pupillage. But his summer's experience, like that of Cooper a quarter of a century earlier, was significant. Whaley and half a dozen others in the pool lent a hand, networked, watched and listened. He recalls coming to the Law as "learning a new language".

He graduated from Kent as a Bachelor of Arts with Honours in the Law. A year at Bar School followed. Success in the final examinations and a call to the Bar at Lincoln's Inn bestowed upon Whaley the honourable and ancient title of barrister.

In short order, he also won the Rhodes Scholarship. Whaley would become the fifth Rhodes Scholar to join the firm, following Charles Collis *père* and Richard Pearman, in succeeding years, Chet Butterfield and John Collis. At Brasenose College, Whaley earned a Master's degree in law, which made him, under the Oxford system, a Bachelor of Civil Law. Once again, the Master became the student when Whaley spent six months in pupillage at 24, Old Buildings, the specialist company law chambers where several members of Conyers Dill & Pearman studied.

Having seen a law firm at close range during his summers as an intern at Conyers Dill & Pearman, Whaley was decided by now for corporate law. He joined the prestigious London firm of Slaughter and May, spending two years—the time limit imposed by the British Government on such work permits given to Bermudians and other citizens of the Overseas Territories—in their Corporate Department. He was employed at Slaughter and May as a *stagière*. The term applies to those who have qualified in one branch of the Law, but whose opinion and abilities are nonetheless valued in another. Whaley was a barrister but was employed in a capacity which allowed him to bring his talents to the table without confounding the Bar regulations.

On several occasions, he advised clients who were establishing mutual funds based in Bermuda and found himself in touch with his friends at Conyers Dill & Pearman. But just one month before his permit expired, staff changes in Slaughter and May's Hong Kong office created an opening for him there. With slight trepidation, Whaley set off for the Far East. The assignment was for a year, to help steady the ship. Eighteen months later, at 27 years of age, he returned to Bermuda. Following a meeting with Woods and John Collis, by then heading the firm's Corporate Department, Whaley joined Conyers Dill & Pearman as an associate in the Corporate Department in August 1991.

He did so after talking to other law firms. The award of a scholarship or bursary is not intended to tie the recipient to a career with the donor, but, like the International Companies' Education Awards organised by the Bermuda Chamber of Commerce, the banks' various scholarships and the annual handbook's worth of other education awards in Bermuda, the idea of the Conyers Dill & Pearman scheme is to identify talented Bermudians and encourage them in the name of the community.

The millions of dollars Bermuda-resident organisations annually volunteer towards the education of Bermudians is an important ingredient in Bermuda's recipe for success. The international companies which maintain a physical presence in Bermuda are consistently generous. If

Government collected taxes to fund further education in this fashion, a percentage would be lost to Civil Service overhead. One job in every seven in Bermuda is already in the public sector.

Bermuda, in 1991, was still ingesting the excess liability companies which had landed on its shores. With capital and surplus in the insurance sector approaching US$20 billion, total assets passed the US$50 billion mark for the first time. The captive industry continued to show strength. Captives come and go, but today the Island retains better than 40 percent of the world's total captive companies, roughly the same percentage which it held when Whaley joined the firm. The consensus is that the lead Bermuda has established in the area of captive insurance will probably never be eclipsed.

CHAPTER FORTY

Trust

Nicholas Paul Johnson joined Conyers Dill & Pearman as an associate in the Trust Department in September 1991, a month after Whaley. Johnson was once that comparative rarity, a young boy who knew he wanted to be a lawyer. He was born on 19 July 1962 in Epsom, Surrey, and grew up in Great Bookham, three miles from Leatherhead, a residential town south of London in the green belt. Johnson's father, James Eric (Johnny) Johnson, was a career civil servant at the British Home Office, the Government Department under whose administrative remit the Court system falls. Johnson *père* met and married Joan Chinery, who also worked at the Home Office for several years before becoming a homemaker.

Johnson *fils* attended St. John's School in Leatherhead, where the idea of pursuing the Law was displaced, temporarily, by the desire to read Economics, for which he was accepted at York University. The course at York had a strong reputation and was considerably over-subscribed. Johnson's older sister Susan, a court reporter who became Features Editor of *The Daily Express*, a British national newspaper, was engaged at the time to a barrister, Jonathan Crystal, who offered some guidance. Johnson reinstated his original career ideas and went to Queen Mary College at the University of London to read law. Three years later, he completed his studies as a Bachelor of Laws and headed to Bar School.

Johnson served his pupillage at 3, Gray's Inn Place and was called to the Bar in England and Wales in what was to be a significant summer for him. In Bermuda, he married Karin Dill, the daughter of Nicky and Bitten Dill. Johnson had been introduced to Karin when she was in London attending a post-graduate course at Sotheby's Fine Arts. The couple had decided to return to and stay in London for a while. Johnson joined Steamship Mutual, a Bermuda P&I insurance club with managers in the City of London, as in-house counsel. His choice, which echoed his father-in-law's great specialisation, the P&I clubs, was purely coincidental; his genial manner, so like that of all the Dills, perhaps less so.

Johnson spent two years with Steamship Mutual, dealing with shipping disputes between companies around the globe. For a lawyer starting out, the international experience was invaluable. He then joined another Bermuda company in London: The Bank of Bermuda, at its offices in the Shearson Lehman building in Broadgate. The bank was considering a range of possibilities for its London office at the time, under the active guidance of John Hawkins, who now manages the bank's Private Client operations worldwide and stands second only to President and Chief Executive Officer Henry Smith.

Smith ran the bank's office in London for some years himself before being brought back to Bermuda to take the helm in 1997. Driven by his own vision of a global presence, Smith is consolidating the expansive legacy of predecessors Donald Lines and Charles Vaughan-Johnson. Under Smith's guidance, the bank has sought to expand its capital base to allow it to compete in the international arena. The bank must increase both its equity capital and its lines of credit if it is to take on the necessary heft to rub shoulders with the giants. A half-billion dollar standby facility was arranged in the spring of 1998, which was oversubscribed by 70 percent, a vote of confidence from the international banks, showing their willingness to make money available to fund Smith's ambitions. There is only one way the bank can hope to increase its equity capital, but its application to be exempted from the 60/40 ownership regulations initially received a mixed reception.

Bermuda has considerably liberalised many of its laws, but has doggedly retained the ratio of 60 percent Bermudian ownership thought up in Conyers' day. Exchange controls on Bermuda residents have all but vanished in the 1990s, although the Bermuda Monetary Authority's review process has been considerably strengthened under its experienced General Manager, Malcolm Williams. A fourth local bank is in the wind; the Island's investment management houses blossom with the continuing increase in stock market values around the world; and the Bermuda Stock Exchange (symbol: BSX) is rapidly becoming the world's first truly electronic offshore exchange.

Former investment banker Arthur Sculley is the hands-on Chairman of The BSX. His mother is Bermudian; he grew up on the Island and fondly recalls fishing off Flatts Bridge at the age of five. Sculley is a former head of private banking at J.P. Morgan & Co. Inc. and President of Sculley Brothers LLC, an investment and advisory firm he manages with his brothers John, the former President of Pepsi-Cola and Apple Computers, and David, formerly in charge of product development at H.J. Heinz.

The BSX has established a multi-billion dollar market in crossings, trades which occur outside New York Stock Exchange hours, and has ambitious plans to add a range of products to its armoury. The BSX has undergone significant international growth, with further developments planned for the local market, although 60,000 people will never accumulate sufficient capital to make the local board a huge venture. A few of the larger insurers based in Bermuda have sought secondary listings on The BSX, but the majority remain quoted on the NYSE.

Investors recall that before the recent stock market boom, the international markets turned unexpectedly at the end of the 1980s. The Bank of Bermuda decided against establishing itself in London in quite the depth it had originally envisaged—a good decision, in hindsight, since it allowed the bank to develop instead its international network of 17 locations around the world, in which its London operations are a vital, but not dominant, link.

The turn of events at the bank allowed the Johnsons to take stock, and they decided that, having lived in London, it was time to live somewhere else. The bank's move presented them, essentially, with a choice: move to the country or out of the country. Johnson was, by now, familiar with Bermuda. The bank did not want to lose him, and transferred him to the Island to act as Legal Counsel to its Private Banking division. He would work there with Vaughan-Johnson before the latter went on to head the bank.

Nicky Dill had mentioned to Johnson the constant search for lawyers which Conyers Dill & Pearman was experiencing, but Johnson knew he "had to do something else first". He was not certain exactly what, but as is so often the case, the answer presented itself: the trust business, a core service of the bank's Private Banking division. After two years there, Johnson concluded that the truly interesting legal opportunities presented themselves to outside law firms, particularly now that Bermuda was originating a much higher percentage of documents than had previously been the case. He duly applied for a position with Conyers Dill & Pearman. Mutch and Woods interviewed him and Johnson joined the firm in September 1991.

The Trust Department was relatively newly established as a separate function. Johnson joined Anderson, and began to take over some of

Mutch's work, as well as developing his own. Mutch, 55 when Johnson came on board, was anticipating an early retirement.

When a lawyer is considering retirement, great thought is given to the choice of a successor for each client, matching personalities and skills with clients and their needs. The nature of Private Client work, particularly, requires good choices. Mutch, it must be said, had a spread of clients probably second only to that of Sir James Pearman. Mutch had been introduced to most of his clients at their birthplace, North Rock Enterprises, and had been with them every step of the way since.

Johnson joined an industry in change. A further policy liberalisation in Bermuda in 1991 allowed foreign trust companies to open offices on the Island for the first time. The move came in the face of concern from the local banks that the liberalisation might damage Bermudian interests, which, ironically is the same fear now depriving The Bank of Bermuda of its ability to obtain a secondary listing overseas.

Since the passage of the 1991 Trust Companies Act, a dozen international trust companies have opened offices in Bermuda. Financial institutions of the calibre of Barclays, Coutts & Co., Lombard Odier, Rothschilds and Schroders have broadened the Bermudian market rather than weakening it, and are in the process of becoming an integrated division of Bermuda Inc. The trust companies brought work to the Bermuda service providers, including Conyers Dill & Pearman; Collis *père*, for example, served for many years as a Director of one of the best-known trust companies.

The Private Client Departments of the Island's professional firms have traditionally specialised in personal trust for individuals and families with high net worth, often now dealing with the children and grandchildren of clients who first came to the firm years ago. Lately, the Trust Department of Conyers Dill & Pearman deals with as many trusts established for commercial uses as for personal. Codan Trust Company

Limited, the firm's affiliated trust company, grew out of the Private Client Department and now administers most of the firm's clients' trusts.

Today, Johnson is one of six lawyers in the Trust Department of Conyers Dill & Pearman, whose client list would read like an international Who's Who were it not for the fact that in the rarified and cautious world of trust, even the existence of a relationship, let alone a client's identity, is never discussed publicly.

CHAPTER FORTY ONE

Rite Of Passage

The events of the first four months of 1992 formed an extraordinary chapter in the life of Conyers Dill & Pearman. It began when Graham Brenton Ross Collis returned to Bermuda in January and joined his father and brothers at the firm.

Graham was born on 5 April 1960 and, like his father and brothers, was educated at Saltus Grammar School, from which he graduated at the age of 16, top of his class. Graham had, from an early age, admired his father's enthusiasm for his work and the enjoyment and satisfaction he derived from it. His father's example led him to assume that he, too, would be a lawyer one day. Over the years, no other influence was strong enough to divert Graham from this course.

He recalls, as a 15-year-old, being less immediately interested in his future than in the bike he would be able to ride on his next birthday. With so few roads, Bermuda limits car ownership to one vehicle per household—and imposes an Island-wide speed limit of 20 m.p.h. Bermudian teenagers do not therefore anticipate, as do their American and British cousins, their first car. Riding one's first moped, however, is a central rite of passage. For many Bermuda residents, the bike remains the vehicle of choice even into their dotage. More than half the staff of Conyers Dill & Pearman ride their bikes to work, many of the men wearing below their shirts, ties and jackets the knee-length shorts and long socks which are part of Bermuda business dress. Sir Bayard rode his bike well into his 80s, as did Parliamentarian and banker Sir John Cox, a familiar sight for many years puttering along on his bike, his helmet a tartan deerstalker.

Attending boarding school in England at the age of 16 meant Graham would lose his new-found mobility. He therefore had mixed emotions on attending Rugby School to complete his A-level examinations. He proceeded from Rugby, old enough now to drive a car, to Trinity College at the University of Toronto, where he earned a Bachelor of Commerce degree. He then attended his father's *alma mater*, Corpus Christi, Oxford. Graham played a little rugby, rowed for the College and studied hard, graduating after two years as a Bachelor of Arts in Jurisprudence.

A year at Bar School followed and then pupillage, in two parts. First, at 11, New Square, in the Chambers of Barry Pinson, Q.C., with a focus on revenue law, and later at 24, Old Buildings, in the Chambers of Richard Sykes, Q.C., where the emphasis was on corporate law. Graham preceded Whaley at 24, Old Buildings and had the opportunity to work there with John Gardiner, Q.C., now an eminent UK tax barrister. Gardiner worked for Conyers Dill & Pearman in Bermuda for six months in the early 1960s and is now, to complete the circle, at 11, New Square.

Called to the Bar in England and Wales at the Middle Temple, Graham felt that at 26, he was too young and inexperienced to return to Bermuda; besides, he was enjoying life in London. He joined Macfarlanes, the City of London solicitors where Anderson had completed his pupillage. Graham spent four years learning corporate work with his sleeves rolled up. He was seconded for six months to the Luxembourg branch of

Webber, Wenzel, one of the largest South African firms. In Luxembourg, he met Caroline Hamus, who would become his wife.

In January 1992, then, Graham Collis joined Conyers Dill & Pearman as an associate in the Corporate Department. His brother, John, had by now spent almost ten years with the firm, five as partner. His father, Charles, within a couple of months of Graham's arrival, became Senior Partner upon the retirement from the practice on 31 March 1992 of Sir Bayard Dill.

Sir Bayard worked at Conyers Dill & Pearman for 63 years and five months. The cover story in the 24-page *Briefcase* for March 1992 carried a photograph of Bermuda's most recognisable citizen with Clarendon House behind him and the Cathedral of the Most Holy Trinity behind Clarendon House, a fitting image indeed.

Sir Bayard's departure was attended by three developments. Robin Mayor was admitted to the partnership on 1 April 1992. At the same time, Ellison returned to Bermuda and the firm's headquarters, after seven years in Hong Kong. And on the day after Sir Bayard retired, entirely by coincidence, the firm introduced a 686-page Operating Manual, outlining policies and procedures with firm-wide application. Today, that manual has more than 1,000 pages and is a closely-guarded repository of the wisdom of 70 years.

Sir Bayard's retirement and Mayor's admission to partnership were marked by a party. Sir Bayard had for many years crafted his speeches within the firm around a basic model which changed little. "It became comforting after a while, to hear him address much the same turf in these speeches, a sign that everything was all right with the world," one partner recalled, noting that Sir Bayard's departure left all concerned with the feeling that nothing at Conyers Dill & Pearman would ever be quite the same again.

Sir Bayard made relatively few references to the firm in his

Reminiscences of an Islander, preferring instead to concentrate on matters political and familial. He concluded the book, however, with two paragraphs on Conyers Dill & Pearman, evidently written just a few months before he retired. The final paragraph reads, in part:

> Sir Reginald Conyers died in 1948; Sir James Pearman retired in 1987; the writer proposes to retire in March 1992. The name of the Firm will continue, since Sir Reginald Conyers was such a spectacular person in furthering Bermuda's economy and both Sir Bayard and Sir James have progeny who are continuing with the Firm. (Having) started in 1928 with five persons, in 1991 the firm has 35 lawyers and 170 managers, accountants, secretaries and other personnel, the majority of whom are in Bermuda, but some are spread in offices overseas in Hong Kong, Guernsey and the British Virgin Islands, with the help and blessings of the main office.

Sir Bayard took his well-earned retirement, leaving behind a firm with more than 2,500 active clients and a body of experience unmatched in the offshore business community.

Sir James also made news in the spring of 1992, in a different field. *The Royal Gazette* of 10 April carried a rather endearing report, entitled: "Sesame Street Reprieve", which read, in part:

> Fears that *Sesame Street*, the widely-acclaimed children's show, would be axed at the end of this month were ended yesterday after a generous offer by a retired lawyer.
>
> Sir James Pearman has pledged to provide the funds necessary to keep the educational programme on the air for another year.
>
> "I did it for the children," Sir James said. He made the decision

after reading an article which appeared in *The Royal Gazette* yesterday.

He said he felt it was important the show remain on the air because of the learning experience it offers pre-schoolers.

The show appeared on public television for 21 years at an annual cost of $111,701.20 to Government, a spokesperson said.

This figure was reduced by $44,000 last year after the Bermuda Broadcasting Company agreed to subsidise the programme for two days of the week.

However, budgetary constraints in the Department of Community and Public Affairs led to a withdrawal of sponsorship.

In the *Gazette* article, a group of mothers said they were planning to circulate a petition to try and keep the show on the air.

Having failed a dozen years earlier to divulge anything to a reporter, Sir James was now willing to bare his soul in a public act of tender kindness for the good of the Island's children.

Jamais deux sans trois. Just six days later, in what was becoming 'Conyers Dill & Pearman' month in the local media, the third of the firm's founders made front page news, this time in the *Bermuda Sun*, under the headline "School Lands Trust Legacy"—Exclusive by Tony McWilliam. The sub-head read: "$70,000-a-year boost". The article referred to the will which Conyers had summoned Dill to his deathbed to amend.

McWilliam's article read, in part:

Port Royal Primary School is set to benefit from funds bequeathed in a will nearly 45 years ago.

The money will represent the annual income from the trust estate of lawyer Sir Reginald Conyers, who died in 1948.

A clause in the will which made provision for Port Royal was activated by the death last year of Sir Reginald's wife, Lady Florence Conyers.

There is no official word on the total value of the estate, but reliable sources have told the Sun that the annual yield will be in the region of $70,000.

Today, on-going talks about the trust estate were scheduled to resume between the school, the Bank of Butterfield as trustee of the Conyers estate, the Ministry of Education and Port Royal's Parent Teacher Association.

It has been a delicate matter, chiefly because of changes in the school's circumstances. Port Royal was a private school when Sir Reginald made his will, but is now Government-funded.

The Bank of Butterfield has been anxious to stymie any moves to funnel money away from the school and into Government's general coffers.

A bank spokesman told us that legal advice had been taken, and expressed confidence that Sir Reginald's original wishes would be fulfilled.

The spokesman added: "A very good working relationship has been established with all interested parties."

Because of the delicate nature of the issue, the school, the PTA and the Education Department would not comment.

It is known, however, that the PTA plans to give parents information about the trust estate at its annual general meeting in June.

There is no clear indication about what the extra money would be used for, but it is known that the school wants a 'Reading to Write' room.

The final say on how funds are spent will be at the discretion of estate trustees at the Bank of Butterfield.

McWilliam had the bones of the story. Conyers' will left in trust the income from his million-dollar estate to his wife, for the duration of her life. Out of gratitude to the people of Southampton, who had elected him in 1933 when he had forgotten to pay his deposit in Pembroke, his traditional electoral fastness, the income from the trust was to go towards the education of the children of the West End upon his wife's death.

Conyers' legacy was fulfilled by the Conyers Trust. A procedure was put in place by the Bank of Butterfield Trust Company for the benefit of the school. Port Royal School already had a 'Reading to Write' room, but wanted a library. Heron Bay School, nearby, wanted a 'Reading to Write' room, and with co-operation all around, now has one. Fulfilling the spirit of Sir Reginald's wishes, Port Royal School gained a library in the horse-trade.

Over Easter 1992, Hamilton's newest building, Richmond House on Par-la-Ville Road, was opened. Barely 200 yards to the north of Clarendon House, the new edifice is a handsome and functional six-storey building with a good deal of marble. Richmond House was jointly owned by three entities, allowing each to occupy or let two floors of the building. One of the joint owners is Conyers Dill & Pearman.

Bermuda, perhaps uniquely, takes a two-day public holiday each year on the Thursday (Cup Match Day) and the Friday (Somers Day) before the first Monday in August, when the summer's heat and humidity are at their fiercest. The Island celebrates the occasion with a two-day cricket match between teams representing either end of the Island. The venue for the occasion alternates between St. George's Cricket club at the East End and the Somerset Cricket Club at the West.

Bermudians, whether or not they have ties to either end of the Island, support one team or the other with devotion. Although for many years the two-day match almost always ended in a draw, enthusiasm for the event has never waned. A stroll around the ground at some stage is well-nigh mandatory. Cup Match permits Bermudians a rare chance to gamble legally, on a dice game called Crown and Anchor. A great deal of high spirits attends the weekend, and an impromptu, moving party lasts for days.

Those less interested in the cricket or the accompanying social scene make Cup Match one of the Island's great sailing occasions. The harbours and marinas empty, as they do at the start of the season, on 24 May, which is Bermuda Day and was formerly celebrated as Queen Victoria's birthday. The occasion is also marked by a massive and lively festive parade which winds through Hamilton en route to celebrations at Bernard Park.

For the business community, Cup Match provides an annual mid-year break. It was during the holiday in 1992 that Conyers Dill & Pearman moved its accounting and computer functions, and the activities of Westbroke Limited, into the third and fourth floors of Richmond House, retaining half a floor for future expansion by letting it out on a relatively short lease. Today, that extra space is occupied by Codan Trust, accessed and managed separately from the other elements of the firm in the building.

The Managing Director of Westbroke Limited, Stanley Chetkowski, is a Certified Public Accountant and a former Executive Officer of The Bank of Bermuda. Having taken over the management of Westbroke from Alan Brown, Chetkowski has become an eight-year Westbroke man. He has for many years been one of the driving forces behind the Bermuda Festival, an annual celebration of the arts which for 23 years has attracted performers of the highest rank from around the world to Bermuda for three weeks in February. Ellison was pressed into service by then-Governor Sir Edwin Leather when the Festival was first being contemplated, along with Richard Butterfield, Richard Gorham, Dutch resident Ferdinand Kranenberg, Dr. Stanley Ratteray and others. Ellison served as the first chairman of the Festival.

Festival posters, greatly valued by collectors, adorn the Westbroke offices. Westbroke provides accounting and administrative services to clients who, in the main, do not have offices of their own in Bermuda. It acts as Registrar and transfer agent for mutual funds and provides general management services to larger companies.

Presumably, the Bermuda-based partners of Conyers Dill & Pearman would enjoy working from a single, unified location in Bermuda, but the firm's history of unending development has rarely permitted that eventuality to occur for very long. The casual visitor to Richmond House takes away an impression of efficiency and calm. The outstanding design feature of an otherwise admirably functional building is red plastic trim, which seems oddly transitory in so stable an environment.

CHAPTER FORTY TWO

Property & Catastrophe

Estimates place at 70 or 80 the number of Bermudians studying law in the United Kingdom and other overseas countries at any given moment. Given the preponderance of Bermudian pupils in the UK, and the long period between the beginning of the academic year and the advent of the summer holidays, Conyers Dill & Pearman has for many years hosted a dinner in London in November to which all those students with whom the firm is in contact are invited.

Bermudians studying law in the UK face a long and arduous task. They may spend as many as six winters in England—a peculiar hardship for those who grow up in the sub-tropics. Considerable effort is expended to find interesting locations for the annual dinners with some relevance to the corporate and legal institutions of the United Kingdom. Dinners have been held, for example, at the Institute of Directors, the House of Commons, the Law Society, the Inner Temple, the International Bankers Association and the Old Hall of Lincoln's Inn. It would be misleading to suggest that the only business conducted at these affairs is legal; much networking takes place, as does a great deal of updating on matters personal, Bermudian and otherwise. As is so often the case when groups of 'Onions' are gathered overseas, a party often ensues once the dinner is at an end, usually in less formal surroundings.

James Morrison Macdonald joined Conyers Dill & Pearman in March 1993, without having attended one of the firm's London dinners as a student. Macdonald was born in Twickenham, in the west of Greater London, on 6 March 1954 but did not pursue his legal qualification in Britain. Twickenham—'Twickers' to generations of English schoolboys of whatever age—is renowned as the home of English rugby football.

Macdonald's parents were both islanders: Ian Macdonald was from the Islands of Uist in the Outer Hebrides, a small chain in the county of Inverness in Scotland. Macdonald *père* saw Army service in World War II and met his wife, Ellen Pearman Eve, in her native Bermuda, where they were married. Macdonald's regiment posted him to England after the War.

At the age of seven, James and his older brother Alastair moved back to Bermuda with their mother. James attended Dellwood School for four years and at 13, entered Saltus Grammar School. A year later, on a scholarship, he transferred to Appleby College in Ontario, Cooper's *alma mater*. Cooper was in fact instrumental in the direction Macdonald's schooling was to take. Cooper's family thought Appleby College would suit Alastair, and in due course James followed. From there he moved on, as had Cooper, to Trinity College at the University of Toronto. Macdonald studied zoology, a four-year science degree. In his final year, the reality of the need to make a living caused him to rethink his plans. He had tried research and rejected it. He had entertained notions of becoming a doctor or a vet, but finally decided on the Law.

The Canadian route to qualification began with a Bachelor's degree in law, which Macdonald earned at Osgoode Hall, for many years run by the Law Society of Upper Canada and lately transferred to York

University at the northern end of Toronto. Macdonald then served his articles at the commercial practice of Smith, Lyons, Torrance, Stevenson & Mayer in Toronto, exposing him to all facets of business law. Called to the Ontario Bar, he stayed with the firm for a further three years before returning to Bermuda to spend nine years in the capacity of Legal Counsel for The Bank of Bermuda. These were the years of the bank's greatest expansion and, like Buckley, Macdonald was exposed to a broad spectrum of activities as the bank expanded across the world.

As his 40th birthday and tenth year with the bank approached, Macdonald reevaluated his career objectives, and decided that he wanted to be closer to the Law. At Conyers Dill & Pearman, Cooper had for some time filled the role of Staff Partner, responsible for the firm's personnel management. Macdonald met Cooper and Woods and an offer was forthcoming for Macdonald to join the firm as an associate in the Corporate Department, which he did in March 1993. By then, Mutch had decided to retire in a year's time. Macdonald began to take over some of the positions Mutch held in the firm's insurance and reinsurance portfolio.

At about the time Macdonald joined the firm, the Bermuda Government decided in principle to adopt into its own laws international commercial arbitration law based on the model adopted by the United Nations Commission on International Trade Law. Legislation was subsequently passed to incorporate the UNCITRAL Model Law into Bermuda law. A total of 23 countries had previously adopted the Model Law, making it as well understood in the United States as it is in, say, Germany.

The initiative reflected a commitment on the part of Government to promote Bermuda as a desirable jurisdiction for international arbitration, adopting one of the main recommendations of the London Court of International Arbitration at a major conference held in Bermuda a year earlier. Corollary changes accepted by the Bermuda Government included the enactment of legislation necessary to ensure free accessibility to the jurisdiction by the parties, their legal advisers and the arbitrators. As a result, participants in Bermuda arbitration are exempted from the usual work permit requirements applicable to foreign lawyers practising in Bermuda.

The adoption of the Model Law was a big step towards Bermuda's establishment as an international arbitration centre. The Model Law provides a modern and flexible legal framework for the conduct of international arbitration, with Bermuda ideally suited as a neutral jurisdiction for arbitration between transatlantic and trans-American parties. The necessary infrastructure existed in Bermuda for the conduct of such arbitration, and the addition of a dedicated centre at the Bermuda College embodied the newest division of Bermuda Inc.

Arbitration was to add a new dimension to Bermuda's standing as an international business centre, but the establishment of the property/catastrophe insurance market in Bermuda, over an 18-month period which culminated in December 1993, changed the nature of Bermuda's insurance and reinsurance industry much more dramatically.

The new reinsurance market in property/catastrophe coverage developed as a result of an enormous imbalance between supply and demand for such coverage. The imbalance was a consequence of a number of severe natural disasters, among them Hurricanes Hugo in 1989 and Andrew in 1992. Unprecedented insured losses caused many of the primary insurance carriers who survived the disasters to purchase additional catastrophe coverage. Simultaneously, many reinsurers decided, or were forced, to reduce the level of coverage they could offer. The problem was further exacerbated by the general contraction of capacity at Lloyd's of London in the wake of potentially ruinous claims made on the centuries-old insurance body. With demand for quality, high-level insurance far outstripping supply, the price of catastrophe reinsurance coverage soared. Many of the largest insurance companies and brokers saw opportunity in the catastrophe reinsurance market and began the process of establishing reinsurance companies.

Marsh & McLennan started the ball rolling late in 1992. In conjunction with J.P. Morgan and X.L. Insurance, they promoted the incorporation of Mid-Ocean Reinsurance Co. Ltd., which raised in excess of $700 million in a private placement followed by an initial public offering. A wave of similar incorporations of new Bermuda reinsurance companies followed, almost all funded by huge amounts of capital raised through private placements.

U.S.F.&G. led a small group of investors in the incorporation of Renaissance Reinsurance Ltd., initially capitalised at US$141 million. The American International Group promoted International Property Catastrophe Reinsurance Co. Ltd., with capital in excess of US$300 million. During the summer of 1993, General Reinsurance Corporation promoted Tempest Reinsurance Company Ltd. and seeded it with US$500 million. Johnson & Higgins, in partnership with Goldman Sachs, promoted Global Capital Reinsurance Ltd., raising US$450 million. Morgan Stanley and Centre Re raised more than US$300 million to establish Centre Cat Ltd. Later in 1993, Swiss Re teamed up with investor John Head to promote Partner Re, raising more than a billion dollars through a public offering on the New York Stock Exchange. Finally, near the end of the year, Aon Corporation led a small group of investors in raising more than US$300 million to capitalise LaSalle Re Ltd.

When the dust had settled, the new property/catastrophe reinsurers had added more than US$4 billion in capital to the Bermuda market. Each of the new companies established Bermuda offices and staffed them with a mix of local and international employees. In one form or another— consolidation has reduced their number, if not their capacity—the individual companies which make up the market have thrived.

The arrival of the 'prop cats' brought to an end any lingering debate over whether Bermuda was a 'real' insurance jurisdiction. Capital and surplus in the Bermuda insurance sector reached US$30 billion by the end of 1993, with assets topping US$70 billion. In terms of size, in 1998 Bermuda's insurance and reinsurance sector stands third only to New York and London. With New York having failed to innovate and the distressing developments at Lloyd's, Bermuda can be said to be second to none in terms of market vibrancy, prospects and excitement.

CHAPTER FORTY THREE

A Fair-Minded Man

On 13 September 1993, an obituary filled four columns at the foot of the front page of The Royal Gazette. A couple of months shy of his 88th birthday, Sir Bayard Dill had passed on. The article read, in part:

Sir Nicholas Bayard Dill will be remembered for his fairness, said friends and colleagues yesterday. Sir Bayard, who with Sir James Pearman founded the law firm now known as Conyers Dill & Pearman, died on Friday night from a heart attack. He was 87.

A longtime Member of the Colonial Parliament, who played a key role in negotiating arrangements for the American bases, Sir Bayard was also an avid yachtsman who sailed many Newport to Bermuda races.

"He would have made a great Judge," said Mr. Richard Pearman, a partner in Conyers Dill & Pearman and son of Sir James. "His fairness was one of his major characteristics.

"He was always able to see a problem and analyse both sides of it. He was always able to look for a compromise. He was a real gentleman."

Mr. Doug Fetigan, who was with Sir Bayard in seven Newport-Bermuda races, said he was "a wonderful person to sail with.

"He would rarely raise his voice if one of the crew wasn't doing exactly what he wanted. He would be very calm about it. It was an infectious thing, and everybody else stayed fairly calm."

In London, *The Times* carried its obituary on 20 October 1993. Relentless in its use of lower-case capitals—"the governor's cabinet"—in John Major's new 'classless' Britain, the obituary read, in part:

Sir Bayard Dill, CBE, leading Bermuda politician and lawyer, has died in Bermuda aged 87. He was born on December 28, 1905.

Bayard Dill secured his place in Bermuda history through his role in the Second World War negotiations over the building of American bases in the colony. He was largely responsible for overseeing the relocation of families on St. David's Island (where the air base was established) and fought successfully to ensure that the local people were paid a fair price for their land. In the early summer of 1944 he travelled to Whitehall in the company of the then governor, Lord Burghley, for consultations during the run-up to D-Day—and the implications for Bermuda as a US basing area.

It was Dill who personally persuaded Winston Churchill to intercede with the authorities in Washington over the bases. The Americans had originally planned one gigantic complex in the middle of the main island, ironing out the hills and re-writing the local geography. They agreed under pressure, however, to site their air base on St. David's and the navy on the Great Sound.

Dill was at the time a new member of the executive council

(the governor's cabinet) as well as being chairman of the Board of Works and the Public Works Planning Committee, two of the administrative posts he held under the colonial government.

The Dills were one of Bermuda's oldest families and had a large investment in the colony. The third son of the attorney-general, Colonel T. Melville Dill, Nicholas Bayard Dill was educated locally at Saltus Grammar School, then at Trinity Hall, Cambridge, where he read law.

Called to the Bar by the Middle Temple in 1927, he immediately returned to the islands where his forebears had first settled in the 1720s and founded a new legal firm with another young barrister, James (later Sir James) Pearman. They linked up with a third, more established lawyer, Sir Reginald Conyers, to form Conyers Dill & Pearman—from which Dill retired as senior partner only last year.

In 1938 he was elected to the colonial parliament for his own parish of Devonshire and held the seat for more than 30 years. He went on to serve in the Legislative Council, the government's upper house, for five more years, leaving politics in 1974.

During the War, in addition to his government responsibilities, Dill served as a captain with the Bermuda Volunteer Engineer Force, helping to man an artillery battery protecting the main coastal approaches to Bermuda.

In the last two decades, Dill concentrated on the law, his business interests and, in his spare time, on his passion for ocean sailing. In 1960 he skippered the yacht *Doncherry* in the first Newport-Bermuda race with the then Governor, the late Sir Julian Gascoigne, on board—only to lose his mast when lying in first place. He went on to skipper his own boat, *The Duchess of Devonshire,* in 11 subsequent races. He also sailed for Bermuda against the United States on a number of occasions and belonged to a wide variety of yacht clubs including the Royal Thames.

A calm, reassuring, fair-minded man who rarely raised his voice, Bayard Dill had an instinct for sensible compromise which was one of his strengths. The Anglican Church was among those who benefited from his shrewdness during his many years as chancellor for the Bermuda diocese. He is survived by his wife Clare whom he married in 1930 and by two sons.

In *Briefcase,* Charles Collis wrote a short tribute, which read, in part:

Nicholas Bayard Dill, Kt. was, for me, the ideal mentor, being one of the handful of men who ran the Government and the business life of Bermuda. Never once in 35 years of working together did I hear Bayard raise his voice and we certainly never exchanged a cross word. He was always available and willing to discuss problems large and small.

Bayard had a remarkable and fulfilling life, as witnessed by his political and community involvement, his professional and military careers and his sporting activities. As a result, he developed such a wide range of friends and clients, political supporters and sporting opponents, that he was known, not only throughout Bermuda, but in the boardrooms of London and New York and to senior politicians in the United Kingdom and America.

Outside of his family, the helping of others was one of Bayard's principal interests in life. Indeed, it may be said that his work for the Church, the Parish Councils, our schools and the public at large through Government, constituted a life of service to others. He had a generosity of heart that allowed him to forgive others their transgressions and to empty his pocket to those in need. No one who knew him did not respect and like him.

About Bayard it can truly be said that he could walk with the Kings but that he never lost the common touch. He was a wonderful and loving man, who is already missed by all of us in the firm, by his numerous clients and by Bermuda at large. He was, however, first and foremost a family man, the patriarch of the Clan Dill, and it is they, particularly his wife Clare and sons Nicholas and David, who will miss him the most.

There was no 'side' to Sir Bayard. He was a straight shooter who saw only people, whether rich men or paupers. A collection of individuals nearer the latter end of that spectrum made a visit to Conyers Dill & Pearman a weekly part of their routine. They did not bring legal work to the practice, they came to see Sir Bayard, whom history must record, in this context, as a soft touch.

Bermuda's cast of characters has always included the colourful, and has always found room for everyone, even, until recently, those eccentric characters unable to hold down regular employment. Sir Bayard supported more than his share of these individuals. His largesse was legendary, and would have ruined a lesser man and his entire family. Sir Bayard's administrative staff knew the men, and in one case, a woman, and received them with the same grace as they would, half an hour later, greet a client who owned an international business empire.

In the final stages of his relationship with the firm, Sir Bayard would go in because he had always gone in. He was on hand when notarial services were needed and many a younger partner sought out his opinion. Sir Bayard was an animal lover, a dog man, who had his own boats built in the yards of *recherché* builders of great reputation. As with most aspects of his life, his sailing exploits have taken on a legendary air.

But underneath the man the public knew burned a sense of what was right. Long-established families refine the code for living down to a few simple rules. Always the most important of these to Sir Bayard Dill was to bring fairness to all his dealings.

CHAPTER FORTY FOUR

Authority & Calm

Six months later, *The Royal Gazette*, at the foot of the front page of its 14 April 1994 edition, carried the news of Sir James Pearman's passing. The report read, in part:

Sir James Pearman, a former top Government politician and one of the Island's most respected lawyers, has died aged 89.

His son, Mr. James Pearman, said Sir James suffered a cardiac arrest on Sunday night and died at about midnight on Tuesday.

Sir James, of Point Shares, Pembroke, had a political career lasting more than 30 years. He was the only surviving founder of legal firm Conyers Dill & Pearman.

Born in Bermuda, Sir James attended Saltus Grammar School, Bromsgrove School, Merton College, Oxford and the Middle Temple, London.

He was admitted to the Bermuda Bar in 1927, the year he began a law partnership with Sir Bayard Dill. The partners later joined up with Sir Reginald Conyers.

Sir James Pearman was a member of the Executive Council from 1955 to 1963 and from 1968 until 1972, when he held the portfolio for marine and aviation services. In 1972, he became a Cabinet Minister.

Sir James served from 1934 to 1936 on the Board of Trade, and then on the Board of Agriculture, of which he was deputy chairman from 1939 to 1942. He was also on the Board of Public Works and the Board of Public Health. He headed the Transport Control Board and the Public Transportation Board.

He played an important part in the eradication of mosquitoes from Bermuda during the building of the US Naval Air Station. He was also a prime mover in the establishment of international business in the Island.

Sir James received a CBE in 1960 and a knighthood in 1973. He was chairman of the Bermuda Bakery from about 1945 to about 18 months ago, when he became honorary chairman.

He also served as deputy chairman of The Bank of Bermuda and as a prominent director of Masters, Bermuda General Theatres, Bermuda Broadcasting, Bermuda Fire and Marine Insurance, Bermuda Radio and Television, Bermuda Properties, Mid Ocean Club and Holmes Stevedoring.

From 1967 until recently, Sir James was Honorary Consul for Bolivia.

A keen golf player, angler, bridge enthusiast and sailor, he belonged at various times to the Royal Bermuda Yacht Club, Mid Ocean Club, Royal Hamilton Amateur Dinghy Club, Bermuda Bridge Club, Rod and Reel Club (Florida), Bermuda Anglers Club and the Royal and Ancient Golf Club (Scotland).

Sir James collected art, which he exhibited in the National

Gallery.

One of his last public acts was in 1992, when he donated about $100,000 to make sure the educational children's TV show *Sesame Street* stayed on the air.

Sir James' first wife, Prudence, died in 1975. His second wife, Antoinette, survives him.

Also surviving are sons Mr. James Pearman and Mr. Richard Pearman. Mr. James Pearman followed his father as a Pembroke MP, and both sons are senior partners at the law firm.

After Sir James received his CBE, *The Royal Gazette* noted his "authority and calm" in the House, and recalled Sir Henry Tucker's tribute to his "fine mind".

In *Briefcase*, Charles Collis wrote of the man who had hired him almost 40 years earlier. The tribute read, in part:

Whilst many of the staff of Conyers Dill & Pearman may not have known Sir James Pearman, he was a somewhat authoritative but kindly person with whom I enjoyed a long and enduring friendship from the time when he invited me to join the partnership until his death.

Jim was the sort of person to whom anyone could turn for help, as I often did, but he was never critical, except in a constructive way. It was, however, noticeable that when we occupied adjoining offices in the new bank building, he arranged for the installation of sound-proofing in his office.

From the time when I first knew him until 1972, Jim was a Member of Parliament and held various of the highest offices in Government. In those days, there was a group of about a dozen men who ran the public affairs of Bermuda, and both Bayard and

Jim were numbered among them. Their involvement gave me a marvellous understanding of Government.

Throughout his life, Jim was an active sportsman and, in the years before I knew him, one of Bermuda's better golfers and a keenly competitive sailor. By 1956, he had switched his interest to fishing, which occupied his weekends when our weather was good enough and his vacations abroad for salmon fishing in some of the more remote parts of the world.

All of this was made possible by the good health that he enjoyed until his declining years. I believe that he was never absent from the office because of sickness and, in consequence, he had difficulty in understanding such frailties in others.

Jim had the good fortune to have two sons, James and Dick, who followed in his footsteps and joined the firm in the late 1950s. He was, of course, supported throughout his career by his wife, Prudy, who pre-deceased him, and subsequently by his wife Ann, who comforted him in his later years.

In sum, James Eugene Pearman was one of the most fortunate of men, who enjoyed a long, healthy, prosperous and happy life. We miss him and I, for one, thank him for his friendship and kindliness.

The man whom a coin toss had dictated would be named last in the firm's title had survived the longest. Conyers was a national figure when he first proposed partnership to two young lawyers. Sir Bayard's star shone most brightly when the pressures of war dimmed Bermuda's prospects. Graham, fairly buzzing with electricity, seized a moment in history when opportunity met possibility. Sir James was, throughout, a confederate and supporter. Without his often unseen hand, how much of what came to pass would have proved possible?

Sir James is recalled as direct, insightful and driven. He was among the last of the old school. His life and many of his achievements were private, in a way that others' were not. His family businesses were privately held. The firm's business was, by its very nature, entirely private. Some of his most momentous political accomplishments were achieved behind the scenes.

In Bermuda, it's not who you know—since everyone in any particular layer of society more or less knows everyone in it and a range of others besides—it's what you know about them that counts. What Sir James knew could have made him the most sought-after man in Bermuda, but he was not much interested in that. Traces of his shyness remained with him all his life. He rarely acknowledged people in the street, for example, which was interpreted by those who knew him only slightly as standoffishness; it was, however, more closely related to his fear that he might not be recognised.

His was a mind which could grasp in an instant what others needed time to ingest. Those who knew him speak of his concision. Sir James was a man who could summarise a problem from all its angles and suggest alternative ways forward, quickly and precisely. He knew the odds, as do so many, and could accurately weight them, as do so few. His debating talents enabled him to assess situations from both sides before forming a conclusion. He played bridge extremely well throughout his adult life, and as any good bridge player will confirm, the game has less to do with the cards dealt and a great deal more to do with the cards played.

It might be argued that of all the players in the history of Conyers Dill & Pearman, it was Sir James who travelled the greatest distance. One imagines Sir Reginald, old before his years, simply hardening the original model into an more mature version. Similarly, the young Sir Bayard and the old Sir Bayard were essentially the same man.

Sir James, by contrast, rose from the shy young fellow marked by enthusiasm and promise to become an acknowledged master of his field. With his guidance and almost flawless business sense, the Pearman family consolidated its past and grew more comfortable. His law firm has endured for 70 years, growing in textbook fashion; it was his management style, and his willingness to listen to the advice of others, that tamed the demands of continual growth. His greatest political contributions, his work in Transport aside, required the art of facilitation. Sir James made it possible for the public sector to join the private in the partnership which lies at the heart of Bermuda's forward motion.

Once convinced of the value of a proposition, he became its greatest advocate. His delivery honed in the courts, Sir James had the better of those who came to him ill-prepared. Directness, often the reserve of those with the sharpest minds, can be misinterpreted as impatience or arrogance by those who favour a more circuitous approach. Sir James could be devastatingly direct.

Above all, he was a product of his time, more so even than of his place. Sir James was a man who observed more of you than you knew, a characteristic vividly recalled by Sir Ian Percival, Britain's Solicitor General in Prime Minister Margaret Thatcher's first administration. A long-standing friend of Bermuda and Sir James, Sir Ian, who died in April 1998, was an unabashed admirer of Sir James.

An undated and slightly torn photograph, now mostly brown and white, found among Sir James' effects, shows him and his wife and parents, in a carriage, leaving a social event of some magnitude. The men sport top hat and tails. The likely date of the image is 1929 or shortly thereafter, putting young Pearman in his mid-20s. His father wears an imperious air.

Pearman himself is caught looking at the camera. His gaze reveals two conflicting traits. There is timidity, but also present is inquisitiveness. By contrast, the portrait which hangs in the reception area at Clarendon House, painted half a lifetime later, shows a man who has spent his time accumulating knowledge, because in the 20th century, as Sir James Pearman knew, knowledge is power.

CHAPTER FORTY FIVE

An Era Ends

In March 1994, Frank Mutch retired from the partnership of Conyers Dill & Pearman at 58 years of age and became a Consultant. He had passed on many of his clients to others at the firm, but a man of his talents does not escape that easily. Today, he is in evidence at Clarendon House much of the time, as if he had never retired at all. In what spare time he has, he is a trustee of the Centre on Philanthropy, a coordinating facility for Bermuda's many charitable ventures, taking an active role in many of the charities themselves.

Six months after Mutch changed categories on the firm's letterhead, David William Peter Cooke joined Conyers Dill & Pearman. Cooke was born at the King Edward Hospital on 17 February 1962. His father, Colin Cooke, is a Bermudian antiquarian, a well-known figure in Flatts Village, where his Lazy Corner Antiques was based. When his parents separated, Cooke *fils* moved at the age of seven to the Virgin Islands with his mother, Victoria Prince, who later married Frenchman Roland Jimenez. Cooke attended St. Croix Country Day School for five years, before attending high school in the United States.

Having been told often enough that he would make a good lawyer, Cooke had thoughts of becoming an attorney for much of his early life. At the age of 17, he attended Bates College in Maine to pursue a Liberal Arts degree, choosing only in his senior year to major in Politics. One year of the four-year programme was spent at the University of Bath in England. Cooke graduated from Bates a Bachelor of Arts.

Returning to Bermuda, he thought he might first try his hand at one of the investigative professions and was hired as a news reporter by *The Royal Gazette*. He lasted four months, long enough to reconfirm his desire to be a lawyer. While preparing for his chosen career, he furthered his knowledge of antique restoration by working with his father. Cooke *père* had remarried Lucelle Pierre-Louis, who would later serve as General Manager of the Bermuda Monetary Authority.

Cooke's research into English law schools yielded the University of Kent at Canterbury, Sharpe and Whaley's *alma mater*. Cooke enrolled for the three-year law programme, which he completed in two years. Conyers Dill & Pearman awarded him a scholarship prior to his first year at Kent, and Appleby, Spurling & Kempe did the same prior to his second year. By the time he graduated from Kent, Cooke had already decided that his future lay in Bermuda. So Bar School it was: a year at the Inns of Court School of Law. Then a call to the Bar of England and Wales at Lincoln's Inn and on to Queens' College, Cambridge for a year, to emerge, one June day, a Master of Laws. The very next day, he married Sarah Jameson, whom he had met at Bates College.

Once again with his eye to the future, Cooke joined the respected firm of Allen & Overy, based at St. Paul's, in the heart of the City of London. He knew that corporate practice in Bermuda would be international in nature and would entail fairly constant dealings with the large firms in North America and Europe. He thought he might pick up useful experience of what would, in time, be the other end of his life's work.

After he had been with Allen & Overy for a year, the travel bug hit the Cookes. They roamed extensively around South East Asia before returning to Bermuda. Sarah joined Conyers Dill & Pearman as a Corporate Manager, while Cooke joined Hollis & Co., a four-lawyer practice, rather than one of the Island's larger firms, in the belief that the range of work to which he would be exposed would be more interesting in a smaller practice. After five years, and due consideration, he opted to move on.

Cooke played rugby for the Bermuda national team. Woods, also a rugby man, had stayed in touch. Following a series of professional discussions between the two, Cooke joined Conyers Dill & Pearman in September 1994, at the age of 32, as an associate in the Corporate Department and was named a partner in April, 1998.

Not long after Cooke's arrival at the firm, another new overseas office was added to the growing web. Situated away from the necklace of islands in the Eastern Caribbean, the Cayman Islands are a group of three islands, not closely gathered. Cuba lies 150 miles to the north, and Jamaica 180 miles to the east-south-east. Little Cayman sits 60 miles east-north-east of Grand Cayman; four miles further away is Cayman Brac. The tropical climate is tempered largely by the north-east trade winds which predominate for most of the year, assuring a mild climate. Although the islands lie in the hurricane belt, serious hurricane activity has not been experienced in the Cayman Islands since 1932. More than 500 banks are registered there, of which about 80 maintain a physical presence.

While Cooke was establishing himself at Conyers Dill & Pearman, the firm was establishing itself in the Cayman Islands through a local trust company. The offices of Codan Trust Company (Cayman) Limited in Zephyr House in George Town, Grand Cayman, look out over the warm waters of the Western Caribbean Sea. The view, for many months of the year, includes the numerous cruise ships which anchor just off George Town, an echo of the view which some members of the firm once enjoyed from the western side of the Bank of Bermuda building on Hamilton Harbour.

In George Town, modern office buildings share boundaries with city lots that sprout ackee, mango, avocado and banana trees, among others. An abundance of coconut palms is manifested by the many mature nuts that are left untouched where they fall. Parking a car thus becomes something of an exercise in forethought.

Like Bermuda, the Cayman Islands are a British Overseas Territory. The Governor is the Queen's official representative, and an Executive Council and Legislative Assembly oversee an economy based, like Bermuda's, on tourism and international business. As New York, Atlanta and London serve as Bermuda's air access hubs, so flights to and from Miami and London keep Cayman connected with the outside world. The Cayman dollar trades at a premium on the US dollar and both currencies are accepted in shops and hotels.

More than 10,000 work permit holders augment Cayman's 30,000 population, a far higher percentage than is the case in Bermuda, where only about 5,000 permit holders work alongside 60,000 Bermudians. In the Cayman Islands, the various arms of Conyers Dill & Pearman provide service in all aspects of corporate and commercial law, specialising in mutual funds, insurance and reinsurance companies and trusts. The firm's presence in Cayman remains developmental.

Bermudian Neil Cox, a Fellow of the Institute of Chartered Secretaries and Administrators, was seconded to the Cayman Islands in 1996 from Codan Services Ltd. to manage the firm's operations there. Like Mutch, Cox is a former Bermuda Police Officer, who attained the rank of Inspector during his career in the Service. After retiring from the Police, he worked at a Bermuda conglomerate as the manager in charge of corporate administration and personnel prior to joining Conyers Dill & Pearman.

An era ended at the firm with the retirements on 1 April 1995 of Woods and James Pearman. At a party to mark the occasion and the admission to the partnership of Graham Collis and Whaley, Mutch's departure was consolidated into what must have been a bittersweet event. The firm had never been stronger, but a generational shift was taking place. Three key players in the firm's development were moving on; James Pearman, with 35 years of service in the firm his father founded, although he remains to this day a consultant with the firm; Mutch with 22 years' experience with the firm; and Woods, Partnership Secretary for 17 years, following a decade as an adviser and consultant.

James Pearman was presented on the occasion of his retirement from the practice with a line drawing by artist Peter Woolcock, whose often caustic editorial cartoons enliven the pages of *The Royal Gazette*. Pearman is shown standing in a small boat, smoking a cigarette and reeling in a fish, on a lake in some North American wilderness. His thoughts are encapsulated in a bubble: "This is one place I can smoke."

Pearman had combined a distinguished public life with his legal career. A United Bermuda Party Member of the House of Assembly for eight years between 1962 and 1970, he was the first Secretary of the Bermuda International Business Association and an early Chairman. Pearman followed in his father's footsteps when appointed Minister of Transport, following years of service on the Transport Control Board. Pearman *fils* also served on the Transport Advisory Council, the Board of Works & Agriculture, the Ports Authority and the Fisheries Advisory Committee. He represented Bermuda in the Eisenhower Trophy golf competition in 1962 and 1964; a representation of the Cup was included in Woolcock's cartoon. Pearman continues to manage his family's wide business interests from an office in the centre of Hamilton.

Woods also received a Woolcock original on his retirement, showing him on the links, in a flutter of sheet music, representing his love of choral music. In the background are a small sailboat and tombstones, a reference to his years on the Military Cemeteries Committee of the Bermuda National Trust, for which he received the Trust's Silver Palmetto Award in the year he retired from the firm and returned to Oxford. Woods visits Bermuda from time to time to renew acquaintances and to look in on the firm he helped to build.

Mutch, of course, continues to work his way towards the nominal idea of doing less.

Following Woods' departure, the firm's administration was streamlined. Cooper remained Staff Partner, responsible for all aspects of the firm's personnel administration. Buckley became General Manager and Partnership Secretary and has organised his troops into four administrative Departments.

Edwin Mortimer, a respected Bermuda historian who had worked at North Rock for many years before it became Codan Services, was appointed Manager of Administration, overseeing the firm's administrative procedures, documentary systems and plant.

Sandra Cann continued as Manager of Human Resources, the position she took over from Joan Hebberd. Cann joined the firm after spending several years with International Risk Management Ltd., the company Fred Reiss founded, where she had responsibility for a portfolio of captive insurance accounts in addition to her responsibilities as Personnel Manager. Cann, who earned degrees in Geography and Education from Queen's and York Universities, respectively, had represented Bermuda as part of the United Kingdom delegation to the International Model United Nations, held at the U.N. headquarters building in New York.

Stephen De Silva, for many years Treasurer of Fidelity International Limited, is responsible for financial information and controls. Ken Siggins, who has more than 20 years' experience in information systems in Bermuda and Canada, and Barry Bailey, a Chartered

Accountant with extensive experience in computer-based accounting and administrative systems, manage the firm's Information Technology.

A law firm marches on its administrative system. The work Isabelle Lusher once carried out by hand is now the bailiwick of a team of dedicated professionals, none of whom were born when Lusher first underlined her cash book totals in red ink.

CHAPTER FORTY SIX

A No Vote

Bermuda experienced an extraordinarily dramatic two days in August 1995, when the Independence referendum was held. The idea of Independence may have great appeal in the hearts of many Bermudians, but those that voted on the matter did so with their heads. The idea of a referendum had been proposed by Premier Swan, but his United Bermuda Party proved hopelessly split on the subject. The Opposition Progressive Labour Party urged its members to abstain from voting at the referendum, since the Party views Constitutional amendments as necessary precursors to Independence.

The night before the referendum was to be held, a *deus ex machina* threatened to intervene in the democratic process, in the shape of Hurricane Felix. Bermuda lies in the path of hurricanes coming up from the south and south-west, mostly. That night, the skies to the north-east of the Island turned a sour gray, and the sun took on a baleful, lemon-coloured hue.

Early on the morning of the referendum, Felix struck the South

Shore a glancing blow. The referendum was postponed for 24 hours. The damage from Felix was mostly minor. Some of the Island's beaches, notably John Smith's, were smaller that morning than they had been the night before, but Ariel Sands, the charming hotel and club owned and managed by the Dill family on the South Shore in Devonshire, was a net receiver of sand.

The referendum was held on the following day, when the motion to seek Independence from Great Britain was rejected by a three-to-one vote. Premier Swan, who had tied his colours to the mast, conceded defeat and, true to his word, resigned the following day. Finance Minister David Saul was voted into office as Bermuda's sixth Premier, quite by surprise, before the end of the week. His tenure was brief, about 18 months, during which time the man who coined the phrase 'Bermuda Inc.' set about doing what he could to bring continued prosperity to the Island. Chief among the achievements of his administration was the re-classification of Bermuda's 1,400 insurance companies, an idea Finance Minister Saul had instigated but was unable to fully implement before becoming Premier. Registrar of Companies Kymn Astwood completed the project in the fall of 1995.

The passage of the Insurance Amendment Act 1995 changed and significantly strengthened Bermuda's insurance regulations. Previously, every company licensed to write general insurance business in Bermuda was subject to the same regulatory framework, regardless of whether the company was a single-parent captive, writing only its parent's risks, or a billion dollar property/catastrophe company writing multi-million dollar layers of coverage for commercial insurance companies worldwide.

The 1995 Act made radical changes to the Insurance Act 1978 in order to meet the requirements of a true third party insurance market and created four classes of insurance licence. Class 1 is for single-parent captives, writing only related business. Minimum capital, and minimum capital and surplus, is $120,000. Class 2 companies are multi-owner captives and those single-parent and multi-owner captives writing up to 20 percent of net premiums from non-related business. The minimum capital requirement for a Class 2 insurer is $120,000, and minimum capital and surplus is $250,000.

Class 3 insurers are all those not in any other category, more than 20 percent of whose net written premiums derive from unrelated business. Class 3 includes finite reinsurers. Minimum capital is $120,000; minimum capital and surplus is $1 million. Class 4 companies are the highly-capitalised giants with minimum capital of $1 million and capital and surplus of at least $100 million. A range of requirements for solvency margins, audits and actuarial reviews added teeth to the new law.

The 1995 Act, welcomed by the insurance companies, who had been consulted during the drafting of the legislation, underlined how important Bermuda had become in the overall shape of the insurance world. Not a single Bermuda insurer failed to meet the requirements of the new law, although the owners of half a dozen of the more than 1,400 Bermuda insurance companies found during the review process that they did not wish to continue to operate their dormant businesses.

In September 1995, Peter Pearman began his pupillage at the firm. The son of James Pearman *fils*, Peter now works in the firm's Corporate Department. Also that month, the firm "dipped its collective toe in the murky waters of the so-called information superhighway," in the words of associate Guy Eldridge in *Briefcase*, by establishing a Website on the Internet.

A dedicated cable linked the firm's site (www.cdp.bm) to the server just a few hundred yards down the road from Clarendon House. The advent of e-mail broadened the firm's capabilities, but the Conyers Dill & Pearman web pages enable the firm to spread the word about itself and Bermuda to the entire world. Many of the firm's detailed brochures on various business activities in the jurisdictions in which it is represented are now available on the Net.

Today, we take the World Wide Web for granted, and the firm conducts much of its non-confidential business across the electronic information ocean. The late 20th century may forever be recorded as the dawning of the Information Age, a time of revolutionary developments in the transmission and availability of information.

At about the time Conyers Dill & Pearman was placing itself squarely at the forefront of electronic developments, it began a new programme providing career education and encouraging interest in the firm and Bermuda's international business sector among high school students. The Corporate Office Apprenticeship Programme also aims to support the efforts of Bermuda's education system for the personal and career development of students and to instill the attributes expected of good employees through mentoring.

The COAP programme initially targetted four schools for a pilot programme. Each evinced an interest, and three incorporated the programme into their regular curriculum. The initial intake saw five students from Mount St. Agnes Academy, Warwick Academy and the Berkeley Institute—Keisha Bassett, Faith Bridges, Crystal Cassidy, Anna Lopes and Kammy Smith—visit the firm monthly during the school year for training in the basics of corporate administration and to spend time with assigned mentors. Bassett and Smith went on to summer employment in the firm.

Students are offered summer employment or the opportunity to enter Bermuda College. On graduation, suitable candidates may then be offered scholarships to pursue relevant certification and, assuming satisfactory progress, entry level employment within the firm, leading to an administrative portfolio of their own. COAP is the corporate equivalent of the 'farm' system used by professional sporting teams to identify youngsters with talent who merit further coaching.

The common belief in certain Bermudian quarters is that international organisations such as Conyers Dill & Pearman would rather import talent than develop it locally. The reality could hardly be more different. Hiring an employee from overseas is an expensive and time-consuming business, often requiring overseas travel and a consequent loss of income. Immigration approval and acclimatisation take time. Suitable accommodation is limited and can be hugely expensive. A Bermudian, by contrast, is already housed, with children, if any, already in school. A Bermudian can start work immediately at the conclusion of the period of notice given to his or her former employer.

Nowhere is that better evidenced than in the case of North Rock Enterprises, which was renamed Codan Services early in the 1990s and is probably the largest management company in Bermuda. Conyers Dill & Pearman set out to recruit and train Bermudians to manage its ever-increasing portfolio of companies under management, fees from which represent a significant part of the firm's revenue. Managers were created from Police officers, teachers, accountants, engineers and others. All were encouraged to qualify as Chartered Secretaries; existing managers from department stores and conglomerates were similarly recruited and retrained. Members of this group were instrumental in setting up and leading the Bermuda branch of the Institute of Chartered Secretaries and Administrators. The development of this layer of Bermudian management must count as one of the firm's most significant achievements within the Bermuda economy.

The fact is that Bermuda, a community of just 60,000, will never be able to produce the range of talents its main industries—tourism and international business—require. Non-Bermudians have made a significant contribution over the years to the Island's development, bringing needed skills and perspective. Bermuda's cosmopolitan atmosphere, so central to its modern personality, would have been impossible to develop without the input and efforts of its expatriate community.

On 1 April 1996, Conyers Dill & Pearman admitted Johnson to the partnership as a senior associate—he has since become a full partner—but his admission to the partnership did not alter the number of principals, as Sharpe simultaneously retired, to continue with the firm in the capacity of consultant. He had just turned 42 at the time, so this was by no means the end of his career. He felt, in simple terms, that he would like to try something else. He now devotes only his mornings to the firm and is a wine importer and wholesaler in the afternoons.

By the autumn of 1996, the offices of Conyers Dill & Pearman in the British Virgin Islands had matured to the point where the firm applied for a licence to operate a law practice in the islands. With the increasing range and sophistication of international business vehicles being established in the B.V.I., it was felt that the practice should expand the scope of its operations, and a Trade Licence was sought to allow the firm to give a full range of advice on B.V.I. law. A new suite of offices was obtained in Romasco House in Road Town, to which the Codan companies and staff were transferred. The firm's legal practice advises on a full range of B.V.I. legal matters, including the establishment of companies, partnerships, trusts, mutual funds and insurance companies, of which the British Virgin Islands has more than 200, mostly credit life reinsurers and captives.

The new offices are managed by Eldridge, another Conyers Dill & Pearman associate with legal qualifications from the University of Kent at Canterbury and Malcolm Becker, a career accountant.

Eldridge was born in Bermuda on 6 April 1963 and attended Mount Allison University prior to earning his Bachelor of Law degree from Kent. Becker, who was born in Bristol, England on 31 March 1959, came to Bermuda in 1987 and earned his Bermuda Insurance Diploma before joining the firm. The two men's postings to the British Virgin Islands is a further example of Bermudian expertise being exported to the world, a sub-text of the Bermudian success story in the 1990s.

CHAPTER FORTY SEVEN

A Vibrant Life

On 1 April 1997, the firm changed its style by retiring the comma which had nominally separated Conyers from his cohorts for 68 years, Macdonald was admitted to partnership and Ellison retired after 32 years with the firm in Bermuda and Hong Kong. 'Retired' may not be the correct term for a man as active as Ellison. Over the years, he had served Bermuda in a number of capacities, firstly as the second President of the National Trust and later on the Development Applications Board. He and Michael Darling, Robin Mayor's uncle, persuaded Government to lease to the Trust the land and buildings that are now the Bermuda Maritime Museum at Dockyard. Ellison was also instrumental in bringing the Bermuda Musical and Dramatic Society to its present home at Daylesford.

In *Briefcase*, which he had edited for many years, Ellison formally took his leave on a characteristically humorous note:

A few weeks ago, lunching at a Chinese restaurant in Road Town in the British Virgin Islands, we were all given fortune cookies. Mine read: "You are next in line for promotion at the office." How right it was: right out of the door. Seldom can a fortune cookie have predicted the future with such unerring accuracy.

The cookie may have been more accurate than Ellison realised. In retirement, he appears to be playing a more active role than was the case in his last year or two with the firm. Most recently, he has been instrumental in setting up the latest overseas addition to the practice, in London. A former President of the Bermuda Autocycle Union at a time when the club was able to secure Coney Island as a circuit for motor cycle scrambling, Ellison is relaxed these days, as have been the Regulations of the Bermuda Bar Association on advertising. Under the Association's new rules, it became permissible for the firm to take the lead in publicly sponsoring a different kind of cycle scramble: the Conyers Dill & Pearman Grand Prix of cycling, a four-day event held during the first week of May.

The Grand Prix has become something of a *Tour Des Bermudes*. A series of races is held over the four days, with stages at Southside on St. David's Island, the site of the former US Base, and in Hamilton. The firm also sponsors the intense Conyers Dill & Pearman Classic, a criterium. Race participants enjoy a freedom few on the Island share, to travel as fast as they possibly can. In the criterium event, held over a short, looped course no more than a mile and a half long, cyclists can reach up to 50 m.p.h. The Island-wide speed limit of 20 m.p.h. is officially suspended on the course for the duration of the race. The event starts at an astonishing pace which never seems to slacken, except when the riders climb Burnaby Hill. Professional riders from all over the world fly in clusters past excited crowds of race fans.

The firm has separately sponsored a Bermudian cyclist, Elliot Hubbard, who now rides for Team Navigators. Hubbard is a rising star, with the potential to beat the very best, which he proved during the third year of the Grand Prix, in May 1998. Unfancied against a field of top international riders, but "determined to show his home crowd what he was made of", as one fellow rider put it, Hubbard produced a peak performance to win the Classic.

In the autumn of 1997, Colin Pickard took over the management of the firm's Guernsey office from Alisdair Scott. Pickard is a qualified accountant who, prior to establishing his own practice, was external Audit Manager for the firm's Guernsey operations and formed a solid working relationship with the firm. When he started his own practice, he shared office space with the firm and is now Resident Manager of the firm's operations in Guernsey, based on the second floor of Tower Hill House, a five-minute walk from the centre of town of St. Peter Port and its harbourfront. At 31 December 1997, a total of 15,046 companies were registered in Guernsey, almost 1,600 of them added in the preceding 12 months.

The headline in *The Royal Gazette* of 28 January 1998 came as an enormous shock: "Bermuda mourns Charles Collis". He had been unwell, but appeared to be holding his own until that day, just a couple of months before he would have reached the firm's official retirement age of 65. It had been agreed that he would not retire from the firm at that time, but would continue his work for a year or two longer.

The *Gazette's* report, written by Raymond Hainey, is in a style entirely different from that of an earlier, unnamed journalist on the occasion of Conyers' passing. Hainey's report read, in part:

The political, legal and international business worlds were plunged into mourning yesterday after the death of ex-Government Senate leader and top lawyer Charles Collis.

Premier Pamela Gordon first entered politics as a Senator

under Mr. Collis, who was then the Government's Senate leader. She said: "It's very shocking news—Charles Collis made a significant contribution to Bermuda and the political scene, as he did outside politics by being part of our society."

Former Premier Sir John Sharpe said he first met Charles Collis 40 years ago, when the rugby-playing lawyer was on the BAA management committee. Sir John said: "He was perhaps the most 'can do' person I have known. Whether it was sports administration, business or Government, where others saw a problem, Charles would apply his clear thinking and fertile imagination to the solution. Everything he did—which was a lot—he did well."

Sir John credited Mr. Collis with being "a driving force, if not *the* driving force," behind Bermuda's successful foray into the international business sector.

Sir John also paid tribute to Mr. Collis' political savvy, both in Senate and in Cabinet, where he served as Minister Without Portfolio, Minister of Legislative Affairs and Minister of Telecommunications.

Mr. Collis was appointed Government Senate Leader in 1982, resigning his post a decade later. He also served on a number of Government Boards, including the Bermuda Monetary Authority, the Treatment of Offenders Board and the Development Applications Board.

Mr. Collis was also president of the Bermuda Chamber of Commerce from 1980 to 1982. Most recently, he took over the chairmanship of the Telecommunications Board, following the death of Dr. John Stubbs in 1994.

Mr. Collis, who was 65, was the senior partner in the law firm of Conyers Dill & Pearman. He received an OBE in the 1994 Queen's Birthday Honours List.

Sir John said: "Charles Collis was outstanding in every respect—educated, intelligent, aggressive in pursuit of solutions and socially, he was the most amiable of men."

"But the essence of Charles Collis was, I think, his enthusiasm. He has served the legal fraternity, Bermuda, international business and the country very well. A vibrant life has been snuffed out prematurely."

Legal colleague and friend Nicholas Dill, a senior partner in the same firm, knew Mr. Collis from their schooldays at Saltus Grammar School. Mr. Dill said: "He is a very considerable loss to the firm. He was involved with a lot of development over the latter years, and also during the whole period of the firm.

"Charles was involved in international company business and known all over the world. He was a people person, a very bright person and always willing to help others."

Mr. Collis, who lived in Devonshire, was the winner of a coveted Rhodes Scholarship and graduate of Oxford University. He qualified as a barrister in 1956 and became a Queen's Counsel in 1992.

He is survived by his wife Margaret and three sons, John, Graham and Charles, all of whom followed him into the law and Conyers Dill & Pearman.

Education Minister and Deputy Premier Jerome Dill, himself a lawyer, said he knew Mr. Collis as a politician who gave sound advice when Mr. Dill became a Senator in 1992 and as a barrister.

Mr. Dill, speaking from Frankfurt, where he is conducting a Bermuda International Business Association briefing for German business people, said: "I knew him as a senior member of the Bar, and I met him as a student. I came to respect him a great deal. He was able to provide inspiration and leadership to a lot of

Bermudians, both younger and older, in the Bermuda legal profession.

"He had the opportunity to serve the UBP Government and the people of Bermuda, all of which he did very well."

Nicky Dill, who would also have qualified for retirement at the end of March 1998, took on the mantle of Senior Partner and, as had been agreed, will remain with the firm as it approaches its 70th Anniversary.

A few days later, at an extraordinary meeting of the Bermuda Bar, Collis was remembered by his colleagues. John Burchall, now Senior Writer for *RG Magazine*, attended on behalf of *The Royal Gazette*, and filed for that newspaper, under the headline "Collis fondly remembered", a report which read, in part:

Charles Collis exemplified leadership, self discipline and dedication during the more than 40 years that he practised law in Bermuda.

And as a consequence of his life and his unstinting and unselfish work, Bermuda's prosperity was built on a solid foundation.

This was the consensus of the Bar after an hour-long tribute to Mr. Collis' life in Supreme Court yesterday.

Mr. Collis' classmate and colleague at Conyers Dill & Pearman, Nicholas Dill, was the first barrister to address the Court. He described his relationship with Mr. Collis, whom Mr. Dill knew before he met and married his wife Margaret.

Mr. Dill said that Mr. Collis was an organised and focussed lawyer who worked in legal aid, estate work and international company law. He was a good advocate who had a keen grasp of facts and figures, Mr. Dill said, adding that Mr. Collis was a sportsman who served as President of the Bermuda Athletic Association.

He was also past president of the Bermuda Chamber of Commerce and a trustee of Saltus Grammar School.

Managing Partner at Appleby, Spurling & Kempe, Dianna Kempe, said that many members of Bermuda's present legal fraternity were the beneficiaries of Mr. Collis' efforts. "He worked hard to make Bermuda a pre-eminent offshore jurisdiction," said Mrs. Kempe.

Senior barrister Peter Smith described Mr. Collis as a "careful and very dedicated lawyer," who exuded self discipline. "If a job came in that he loved, he did it," Mr. Smith said. "If a job came in that he did not like, he also did it, and did not put it off."

Mr. Smith said that Mr. Collis was the driving force behind the Companies Act 1981, which has been an important plank in Bermuda's edifice of prosperity.

Bermuda Bar Council President Narinder Hargun said that Mr. Collis had a very rounded view of the law and did not look at it as an obstacle for business; rather, he viewed it as a means of assisting business.

The tributes also included words of condolence from barristers Arnold Francis, Deputy Premier Jerome Dill, Alan Dunch and Julian Hall and Chief Justice Austin Ward.

Collis had served the firm well in the role of *paterfamilias*. Possessed of a sharp legal mind, the speed with which he grasped the meaning of figures often astonished those with whom he dealt. He remained throughout as interested in the firm's housekeeping as he was in its grand strategy. He was particularly ardent on all aspects of the firm's buildings.

With his partners' consent, it was Collis who set about internationalising the firm's physical presence to match the nature of its business. In this regard, he picked up the mantle of architect from Pearman in a slightly more literal sense. Already Minister of Legislative Affairs, Collis was appointed Minister of Telecommunications in 1986. Although his tenure in the Department was short, it began a lasting association in the field. As Chairman of the Telecommunications Board, he produced two reports which persuaded the Government to introduce competition in the telecommunications industry, putting Bermuda on the leading edge of technological development. Collis, in his time, had also served as Deputy Chairman of the Law Reform Committee.

Just five weeks after Collis was buried at St. John's Church, more bad news was received. Alan Brown, that good and faithful servant, had also passed on.

The report in *The Royal Gazette*, read in part:

Alan Leslie Brown, MBE, FCA and former chairman of the Duke of Edinburgh Award Scheme, died last week at the age of 60.

Long-time friend and associate Roger Younie spoke of Mr. Brown as a very intelligent and liberal man who was very much involved in his family and community. "In effect, he was the creator of the Duke of Edinburgh Award Scheme in Bermuda," Mr. Younie said, a sentiment echoed by the current Chairman of the Duke of Edinburgh Award programme Lawrence Trimingham. (In 1998, Nicky Dill is Chairman of the programme.)

"Alan was very active with the Junior Chamber of Commerce," Mr. Trimingham said. "In 1965, they had several committees going with the purpose of developing young peoples' organisations.

"Alan was the head of the Award Scheme committee ... over the years he built it up to be a very successful programme."

With approximately 350 young persons involved in the local

chapter, Bermuda's Duke of Edinburgh group has one of the highest per capita involvements in the world, Mr. Trimingham explained.

"That's due in many ways to Alan's tenure as chairman," stressed Mr. Trimingham.

It was for his contribution to the success of the youth programme that Mr. Brown received his MBE, Mr. Younie said.

"That's very unusual," he added. "Alan was one of the exceptions."

Former colleague John Buckley of Conyers Dill & Pearman spoke very fondly of the late Mr. Brown and described him as "an exceptionally charming man.

"He was devoted to every case he ever fought for, especially the Duke of Edinburgh's Award Scheme, and his work, clients, friends and family," said Mr. Buckley.

Mr. Brown retired from the law firm approximately five years ago and is survived by his wife, Nan, sons Nicholas and Martin, four grand-children, three step-children and their families in Toronto.

Conyers Dill & Pearman has soldiered on. On 1 April 1998, Cooke and Charles Collis *fils* were admitted to the partnership. The firm has continued with the international development plans Collis *père* laid in place, which may in time be considered his greatest professional achievement. *The Royal Gazette* reported in February 1998 that the firm would open a London office, which it duly did on 20 April 1998, at 34 Threadneedle Street, not far from the Bank of England.

The *Gazette* report, written by David Fox, read in part:

The trend towards business globalisation has led to a decision by the partners of Conyers Dill & Pearman to open a London office.

A nearly four year-old idea, the international expansion now comes after nine months of detailed consideration and is designed to improve the flow of new business directly to Bermuda.

Retired partner John Ellison, who established the firm's Hong Kong office and is now living in England, has been involved in the legwork for the firm in advance of the establishment of new offices on Threadneedle Street. Conyers Dill & Pearman London will complement the firm's other satellite offices in the British Virgin Islands, Cayman Islands, Guernsey and Hong Kong.

Yet partner John Collis concedes that Conyers Dill & and Pearman's London office has the potential to become as significant, or more, in attracting new business than the highly successful Hong Kong office, saying: "The business we expect to get from London is easier to predict."

The London office will be headed by Englishman Martin Lane, who was with Conyers Dill & Pearman as an associate in Bermuda for nearly four years until 1994.

Mr. Collis said the London office is a significant step and is expected to enhance his firm's service to European clients, allowing real-time advice to those considering using Bermuda as a base for their offshore structures.

Conyers Dill & Pearman in London will advise on a full range of Bermuda legal matters, including the establishment of companies, partnerships, trusts, mutual funds and insurance companies and all aspects of corporate and commercial activities that may arise from their ongoing operations.

Mr. Collis said: "The availability of Bermuda legal advice in London can only enhance Bermuda's attractiveness to Europeans as the jurisdiction of choice for their offshore deals.

"The combination of Martin Lane's experience and knowledge of the United Kingdom marketplace makes him an ideal choice to lead our London operation."

Mr. Lane, who is in Bermuda planning the London office launch, said: "Because of its clear strengths, the Island remains a popular choice for European businesses, but Bermuda is facing fierce competition from European offshore jurisdictions.

"If Bermuda is to compete on a level playing field, then real-time legal advice needs to be available in London."

Mr. Collis said that the firm would be staffed modestly at first, but he could foresee four lawyers being on staff in the not too distant future.

The establishment of a London office by Conyers Dill & Pearman comes after US firms in particular have moved into Europe, and especially London, in a big way, as borders in the European Union are being torn down.

Mr. Collis conceded that Conyers Dill & Pearman's objectives were slightly different from those of other firms going into the leading financial centre, where European and financial interests have been converging for years.

He said: "This puts us on the ground right where they will be doing international bond issues and other significant transactions. Like our Hong Kong office, this move provides us with a base in London.

"But our *raison d'être* is Bermuda business. We hope to attract to Bermuda business from London or Europe that may have gone elsewhere. Also, we have a number of clients in Bermuda with London and Bermuda bases."

In the first 28 years of its existence, Conyers Dill & Pearman employed just four lawyers. Now, here was the son of its fifth, forecasting four lawyers in the London office alone "in the not too distant future". Perhaps no other comparison quite so succinctly shows the tremendous distance what had once been a small country practice had travelled in its first 70 years.

EPILOGUE

Threescore Years & Ten

MISCELLANEOUS
IS YOUR BICYCLE INSURED? 10/- will
cover yours against loss or damage for one
year to a maximum of £11. Wadson's,
Burnaby Cycles, Astwood's, Parris, Bda.
Bicycle Garage or Conyers Dill & Pearman
will sell you a policy.

FOR SALE
1 VICTORIA CARRIAGE and 1 English
Dog Cart in good condition. Apply
Conyers Dill & Pearman.

—*The Royal Gazette,* classified
advertisements, 20 June 1942

Oliver Wendell Holmes wrote: "To be 70 years young is sometimes
far more cheerful and hopeful than to be 40 years old."

As the 70th Anniversary of the founding of Conyers Dill &
Pearman approaches, its practice is as substantial and diverse as any has

ever been in Bermuda. Conyers Dill & Pearman is a full-service law firm, with an emphasis on corporate and commercial law, and the provision of property, trust and management services to companies and individuals.

The firm of three Knights and five Rhodes Scholars competes internationally with firms of like size and larger. It may not have dog carts for sale, whether in good condition or not, partly because other vehicles are in greater demand and partly because the Bermuda in which the dog cart was so common an accessory has largely vanished.

When change is the only constant in an organisation, its development unavoidably mirrors the times in which it lives. If Conyers Dill & Pearman is never again likely to count just five staff members, Bermuda seems unlikely ever to regain its former relative lack of momentum— although time changes everything, as the 'Bay Street Boys' in the Bahamas learned when the lead in the international business industry passed out of their hands to Bermuda.

The tripartite enterprise agreed upon in Conyers' office in 1928 has yielded an organisation 272 strong at 31 May 1998, with offices in two buildings in Bermuda and five other jurisdictions. Twenty-nine individuals have been partners or senior associates in the firm. Five have died and four have officially retired, although John Ellison continues to be of service. Three remain with the firm in the capacity of consultant. Three men have managed the firm's administration on a full-time basis.

Seventy years young, indeed. The baton of the firm has been passed from one generation to another, while a third waits patiently in the wings, working 12-hour days. Sir James and Sir Bayard's longevity with the firm—125 years of service between them—prolonged their control. The leadership of the firm they and Sir Reginald Conyers created, and David Graham empowered, passed first to Charles Collis and now to Nicky Dill and is today the preserve of hundreds of people, none of them Conyers' descendants and relatively few of them Dills or Pearmans.

The new breed of lawyers which has inherited the practice is less flamboyant and less controversial than its forbears. Charles Collis was the last great political figure to work at Conyers Dill & Pearman; the new breed carries out its social commitments to and across the community without a great deal of fuss, although its scholarships, awards and cycle racing sponsorships represent a more visible contribution.

Many of the younger partners come from military families. These Young Turks are among the first generations in a long time to reach middle age without fighting a war. World War II was their parents' war. Being largely Bermudian and British, they were exempt from the Vietnam conflict. This generation of Bermudians has never known a time, except for an occasional downturn and the lingering effects of the odd recession, when economic cold winds blew over the Island. They have grown up, more or less, as comfortably as any generation, anywhere, in the history of the world, thanks in good measure to the foresight of the men and women who, seeing the need to diversify Bermuda's single-industry dependency, laid the foundations on which Bermuda's international business industry would be built.

As a direct result of their predecessors' forethought, this generation of Bermudians grew up with the reasonable certainty that a man or woman capable of earning a professional qualification would find meaningful work in 'the House that Jack built'. The members of this generation grew up when Bermuda had in place a fully functional international business industry, the unquestioned leader in the world of offshore business.

Every one of the partners in Conyers Dill & Pearman worked or studied overseas and gained international experience before dispensing international law. Theirs is an open-door culture, literally. Unless the occasion calls for it—a meeting, a confidential telephone call—office doors at Conyers Dill & Pearman are left open all day long. This is not Madison Avenue; partners and associates have their own offices. The visitor to

Clarendon House or Richmond House, or any of the firm's overseas operations for that matter, finds people working very hard. A firm in perpetual growth develops perforce an air of urgency about its dealings, slightly incongruous in a Bermuda which has not yet, perhaps, seen its very last dog cart.

Two technological developments lie at the heart of the firm's growth and that of the 20th century: the aeroplane and the computer. Without the first, members of the firm due at international meetings would be, like the young Bayard Dill in desperate need of transportation to the United States, down at the Yacht Club cadging a ride. Without the second, the volume of work would be impossible to service.

Conyers Dill & Pearman practises mostly 20th century Law. Among its main specialties are the laws of the mutual fund (invented in 1924), commercial aviation (the early 1930s) and the offshore company (1935). The spread of personal wealth to a clientele beyond a comparatively tiny élite has taken place largely in the past three decades. With growth has come complexity. Where the firm's founders could agree upon a course of action over a drink at the Yacht Club, today's principals must operate by committee and an extended consensus.

At the hub of the firm's activities is a Management Committee comprised of three partners and the Partnership Secretary, which meets at least weekly. Other partnership committees, as few as possible but numerous nevertheless, address individual aspects of the practice. Each overseas office is nominally the responsibility of named Bermuda partners: Donald Malcolm for the British Virgin Islands, Alex Cooper for the Cayman Islands, Nicolas Trollope for Guernsey and John Collis, through Rosemarie Chen, for Hong Kong. The establishment of the London office has also been the responsibility of John Collis, but it will pass to another once the office is fully established.

Managing a legal practice is all in the planning. The firm that once joked about being incapable of making a decision now makes them virtually 24 hours a day, right around the world. An annual three-day meeting of the partners, senior associates and overseas managers, a convocation of sorts, is held annually at the end of October in Bermuda. Its focus is mainly forward-looking. Its purpose is to set a strategic course for the year ahead and beyond.

The real business of the day-to-day practice, the nuts and bolts, is conducted informally at lunch around the table in the partners' dining room on the fifth floor of Clarendon House every Wednesday. The view of Hamilton Harbour dominates the room, even though Clarendon House is nowhere near Hamilton Harbour.

The view is a mural, painted by Clarence Wilson, commissioned by the practice when Clarendon House was renovated in the early 1980s and the firm moved to its new headquarters from the Bank of Bermuda building, overlooking Hamilton Harbour. Wilson has lovingly recreated the outlook from the firm's old fifth-floor aerie. The partners who moved to Clarendon House were too attached to their view to leave it entirely behind—a rare display of sentimentality in the otherwise formally functional confines of Clarendon House.

At the Wednesday lunches, the agenda is partnership matters and the mutual enjoyment of lunch with friends, for a legal partnership is nothing if not a formalised working arrangement among friends. Here is the partnership made flesh, in the casual but crucial network at its heart. Although other firm's events are attended by greater circumstance—annual meetings, Christmas and summer parties—consensus is forged over an entrée prepared in the *en suite* kitchen and finalised over coffee. Prosaically, no one retires to a smoke-filled drawing room after lunch. For one thing, Clarendon House is a smoke-free zone.

Consensus is by no means too strong a term. Every partnership agreement since 1928 has a provision worded more or less along these lines:

In the event of any difference of opinion arising in respect of these Heads of Agreement or of any decision to be taken by the Partnership, then the matter shall be decided by a majority vote of the Partners voting their respective interests therein and such decision shall be final and binding on all Partners.

Yet, in all the firm's long years, the partners of Conyers Dill & Pearman have never once taken a vote. The partners act *ad idem*, with one mind.

Those not on the Management Committee introduce topics of importance either in advance through the Partnership Secretary, or in person at the table. The lunches are less frequently attended by the firm's senior partners, whose job specification includes frequent travel, its purpose a mix of networking and indirect marketing. Conyers Dill & Pearman does not knock on doors looking for business. For one thing, Bermuda's nearest prospects lie about 700 miles west or more than 3,000 miles to the east.

The winter 1996 issue of *Briefcase* included "The Philosophy of the Firm":

Conyers Dill & Pearman is very probably the premier offshore law firm in the world. We intend to maintain our pre-eminent position by providing our clients with high quality responsive service conducted in the warm and friendly manner that is uniquely Bermudian. Ours is a people business and we must always remember to treat clients and colleagues in the way we wish to be treated. As such, we shall strive to maintain an environment that is professionally and financially rewarding for our staff. Whilst we expect demand for our legal, corporate and trust services to grow, we shall not compromise our standards for the sake of growth.

With exceptions, the firm's story to date is largely that of Bermudians, mostly schooled at Saltus Grammar School, heading into their teenage years without much of an idea of what career path to follow, bright young men and women with a range of choices and the luxury of deferring the decision, often, until their University days. Most came to the Law and private practice under the influence of older and wiser minds.

In exactly the same spirit that Conyers invited Dill and Pearman to join him—if not, perhaps, in quite such plain English—lawyers are invited to join the partnership because, their skills undoubted, the necessary chemistry exists. Much the same applies at every level of staffing.

Professional partnerships do not enjoy the corporate luxury of limited liability. Their members have only a few written Heads of Agreement, which address such mundane matters as furniture, postage stamps and votes they will never take. But they share a much more complicated, unwritten professional relationship on which each has staked his or her all. That relationship is embodied, beyond the computer networks and buildings, in the professional reputation of a partnership, as Charles Collis was fond of observing, of unequals.

Acknowledgements

A work of this nature can only be the product of a team effort.

The role of Hamish Shorto went well beyond the provision of photographs; he was a critical sounding-board and a constant source of ideas.

John Buckley marshalled the project on behalf of the firm, which appointed an editorial committee comprised of Charles T.M. Collis, Nicky Dill, John Ellison and Richard Pearman. Michael Woods also reviewed the text and proved an inspiration. David Cooke, Rosemarie Chen and Frank Mutch were of great individual assistance. Edwin Mortimer provided a good deal of essential material, including the principal interviews with David Graham and others. The knowledgeable Keith Rossiter helped with the firm's collection of maps and watercolours. Debra Lindsey, Gloria Dill and Beverly Minors made a real contribution through their administrative efforts. Many of the firm's past employees recalled or confirmed important details. Thanks are in order to the principals and staff of Conyers Dill & Pearman, who somehow found in their busy days all the time asked of them.

Melissa Pearman very kindly allowed access to her grandfather's papers and photographs. Neville Conyers and the Dill family were more than generous with their time and resources, as were more than 150 Bermudians and others whose input, freely given, was crucial. Would that there were space to name and thank them individually.

Ellen Hollis of the Bermuda National Library carried out much of the research. Nan Godet of the Bermuda Archives provided material photographic help. To Doris Goodman and Susan Johnston fell the task of transcribing many of the interviews. The Ministry of Youth Development, Parks, Sports & Recreation of the Bermuda Government and its Curator of Forts Lance Furbert; Government Information Services; the Corporation of Hamilton and the Bermuda Maritime Museum made possible the principal photography. James Cooper and Antoine Hunt were of invaluable assistance in the photographic process. Assistant Cabinet Secretaries Robert Horton and James Smith and historian Brendan Hollis provided background and information. Malcolm Williams, the General Manager of the Bermuda Monetary Authority, was kind enough to clear the use of the 1928 shilling with the Bank of England and the Press Office of the British Royal Mint. Elvyn Pitcher and his colleagues kept the project rolling along.

In London, Sir Ian Percival found the time to recall his long acquaintance with Bermuda and Walter Crombie advised on a range of matters. In Canterbury, Richard De Friend provided valuable insight. In New York, Prakash Mehta and Mohamed Abdelnali helped move the project forward. In Bermuda, David Zuill provided valuable design services at short notice.

Friends and family members too numerous to mention helped out as the project unfolded. Liz Jones, Lynne and Peter Matcham, Gavin Shorto and Elizabeth Virgo, in particular, went beyond the call of duty.

Grateful acknowledgment is made to the following: The Bank of

Bermuda Limited, for material from its own published history, *First, 1,000 Miles* ..., Copyright © 1992 The Bank of Bermuda Limited; The Bermuda Press Ltd., for material from the *Bermuda Sun;* David Graham, for the text of his letter to *The Times;* The Royal Gazette Ltd., for material from several of its publications; and Suzannah Lessard, for an excerpt from "A Close Gathering", Copyright © 1979 Suzannah Lessard, first published in *The New Yorker,* reprinted with the permission of The Wylie Agency, Inc.

St Catherins forte
F

Pembroks forte
K

Kings Castell
M

St George Towne
D

Warwicks forte
E

The tribes
1. Sands
2. Southampton
3. Warwick
4. Padget

State house

Smiths forte
I

Thes Letters
A.B.C. shew
the sittuation of
the 3 bridges P
the Mount.D.E.
F.G.H.I.K.L.M.
N.O. ÿ forts how
and by whom they
wer made the histo:
ry will shew you.
The discription of ÿ land
by Mr Norwood
All contracted into this order
by Captaine Iohn Smith.